THE CHARACTER GAP

PHILOSOPHY IN ACTION
Small Books about Big Ideas

Walter Sinnott-Armstrong, Series Editor

THE CHARACTER GAP

How Good Are We?

Christian B. Miller

OXFORD
UNIVERSITY PRESS

Oxford University Press is a department of the University of Oxford. It furthers
the University's objective of excellence in research, scholarship, and education
by publishing worldwide. Oxford is a registered trade mark of Oxford University
Press in the UK and certain other countries.

Published in the United States of America by Oxford University Press
198 Madison Avenue, New York, NY 10016, United States of America.

© Oxford University Press 2018

CIP data is on file at the Library of Congress
ISBN 978–0–19–026422–2

9 8 7 6 5 4 3

Printed by Sheridan Books, Inc., United States of America

To William Christian Miller, my joyful son

CONTENTS

PREFACE

The day after Thanksgiving, Black Friday, can bring out the worst in our characters, and the year 2012 was no exception. The scene was a local Target store in South Charleston, West Virginia, just after midnight. One of the shoppers was Walter Vance, sixty-one, a pharmacist who had lived his entire life in the area and was admired by his friends as a generous and kind person. He was busy looking for some new Christmas decorations. As a coworker said, "He was so excited about Christmas this year, he wanted everyone to enjoy the holiday he loved so much."[1]

But Vance had struggled with heart problems for many years, and suddenly he collapsed to the floor.

Imagine you are shopping at Target and happen to turn down a crowded aisle where you encounter a man in distress. What would you do? Help him in some way, of course. Wouldn't everyone?

Well, it turns out that many of the shoppers did nothing at all. They walked around his body. Some even *stepped over* his body! It was only later that several nurses administered CPR. But it was too late. Walter Vance died that night in the hospital.

We might immediately think—surely those were awful, cruel, and heartless people, the dregs of society, the worst of the worst. Unlike ourselves and the people we know, the shoppers were the exceptions, the "bad people."

However, we need to be cautious. For as we will see in this book, there is good reason to think that *many of us* would have done the same thing if we had been in a similar situation. We have characters that can lead us to neglect a person's obvious and immediate needs.

"Where is the good Samaritan side of people?" said Vance's coworker. "How could you not notice someone was in trouble?"[2]

These are important questions. This book will begin to answer them.

The Purpose of This Book

Most of us, I suspect, tend to think of ourselves, our friends, and our families as good people. We may not be saints, but we are not morally corrupt either. We are honest, kind, trustworthy, and reasonably virtuous people.

One of the central themes of this book is that such a picture of our character is badly mistaken. Indeed, the results of hundreds of studies in psychology call into question this way of thinking about ourselves and others. Like those particular shoppers in Target on Black Friday, we have serious character flaws that prevent us from being good people. In fact, we do not even recognize that many of these flaws exist, as they often fly below our conscious radar screen.

Does this mean that, instead, we are simply wretched people who are cruel or hateful? Granted, maybe a few of us are like that, and hopefully the most dangerous are locked away. At the same time I also want to suggest in this book that most of us are *not* morally wretched either.

What is going on here—most of us are not good people, but we are also not bad either?

Exactly.

The more our character is put to the test, the more we find that it is decidedly a mixed bag.

On one hand, most of us have the capacity to do tremendous good in the world, and sometimes we actually pull it off. There are also times when we have an opportunity to do something morally bad that would benefit us (steal money, fake our resume, cheat on our spouse). But we do not do it, even if there is no chance of getting caught. That is to our credit.

On the other hand, most of us also have the capacity to do tremendous evil in the world, and unfortunately on occasion we do just that. Even when we have a chance to help someone else, sometimes we just walk away (or walk over a collapsed body, as the case may be). That is to our discredit.

Our hearts are not morally pure, but they are not morally corrupt either. Rather, they are a messy blend of good and evil.

These are the central themes at the heart of this book. They are explored at length in Part II under the heading of "What Does Our Character Actually Look Like Today?" There I summarize many findings from psychology on when and why we help, hurt, lie, and cheat. This discussion culminates in chapter 7, "Putting the Pieces Together," where we will be in a position to see what the overall picture of character looks like for most of us.

But so what? Why is it important to get a better understanding of what our character is like? And what does "good character" even mean in the first place? How can we know whether we have a good or bad character without first defining our terms?

Part I—"What Is Character and Why Is It Important?"— addresses these questions. The first chapter discusses what it would take to have a good or virtuous character. The second chapter then makes a case for why it is so important to care about developing one.

So Part I suggests that developing a good character is really important. Part II suggests that most of us do not have a good character (or a bad one either). Hence by the end of Part II, we can appreciate the serious *character gap* between (1) how we really are, and (2) the people of good character we should become. The pressing question thus emerges—how can we become better people? What can we do so that gradually over time our children, our friends, and we ourselves are closer to being virtuous than we are now? How, in other words, can we *bridge* the character gap?

At this point a final theme emerges. It is incredibly hard to develop a good character, and the obstacles in our way are significant. There are no easy solutions, quick fixes, or magical pills to take. But all is not hopeless, and we should not give up trying. In fact, Part III—"What Can We Do to Improve Our Character?"—offers a few strategies which seem to show promise in doing just that. I do not want to mislead you, though—this book will not offer any detailed, step-by-step procedures to follow. It is not a self-help book for character education.

Most of the strategies presented in Part III will be secular strategies. I end the book by claiming that religious approaches should be considered as well. A promising path to developing a good character, at least for some people, involves not just human effort but divine assistance.

My Background and the Character Project

I do not have all the answers on these topics. I just have some ideas that I hope will be interesting and important to discuss.

I have been thinking about character for the past ten years as part of my research as a philosophy professor at Wake Forest University.

During that time I became convinced that a highly interdisciplinary approach was needed if we wanted to make real progress in this area. We need philosophy and religion to help us understand what a good or virtuous character looks like. We need psychology, sociology, and economics to help us see how people actually think and act today in their moral lives. We need to draw on literature, history, anthropology, and many other disciplines for their own insights into character as well.

With this interdisciplinary focus in mind, I put together a team of psychologists, theologians, and philosophers to investigate the subject of character. Thanks to a generous grant from the John Templeton Foundation, we were able to launch the Character Project in 2009 at Wake Forest University (www.thecharacterproject.com). This exciting project had two main focuses. One was to fund researchers from all over the world as they worked on state-of-the-art projects of their own on character. For instance, we helped a psychologist in Barcelona test character using virtual-reality simulations. We also funded a project at the University of Michigan that used technology to increase our empathy for the suffering of others. Throughout this book I will draw on some of the discoveries made by these projects, presenting them to a wider audience, often for the first time.

The Character Project also had an internal focus at Wake Forest University. We did a lot of the things that academics normally spend their time doing—organizing major conferences, writing papers, discussing our work with one another, speaking at professional meetings, and publishing our findings. We launched two major websites—one for scholars on the academic study of character (www.thestudyofcharacter.com), and the other for a general audience with resources for learning more about character (www. thecharacterportal.com). There you can find an array of links, videos, and other materials for further exploring this fascinating area.

Along the way I was able to write two academic studies of character titled *Moral Character: An Empirical Theory* (2013) and *Character and Moral Psychology* (2014). These books offer a more detailed treatment of some of the ideas presented in the pages to come. In particular, chapters 3 through 7 here summarize a much longer and more complicated discussion that takes place in those books.

I didn't want that discussion to get buried in academic books of philosophy. The conclusions about character that I had arrived at struck me as extremely important. If I am right, then we are wrong much of the time about other people's character (and our own too). This can lead us to make all kinds of misguided judgments and predictions, that can have devastating effects. Or really inspiring ones too, as we will see. So I decided to write this book to try to share what I found, and also to think about ways in which we can work at getting better.

Yet despite what researchers at Wake Forest and elsewhere are doing, much of our character still remains a mystery. In the following pages, let me share with you where this journey has taken me so far.

Notes

1. http://usnews.msnbc.msn.com/_news/2011/11/26/9035999-report-shoppers-unfazed-as-man-dies-at-target. Accessed on February 15, 2012.
2. Ibid.

ACKNOWLEDGMENTS

I am very grateful to various publishers for permission to make use of the following materials:

In chapter 1, permission to use the image of Dante's Purgatory from *The Dante Encyclopedia*, Ed. Richard Lansing, New York: Routledge, page xxv, was granted by the Copyright Clearance Center.

In chapter 1, the image of the hand is from https://pixabay.com/en/checkbook-coupon-fill-check-688352/. The image of the thought bubble is from http://www.clker.com/clipart-cartoon-thought-bubble.html. Accessed on January 28, 2017. Free public domain images.

The opening section and concluding paragraph of chapter 2 are adapted from my article "Answering 'Why Be Good?' for a Three Year Old." Slate.com. http://www.slate.com/bigideas/why-be-good/essays-and-opinions. Copyright retained by author.

In chapter 4, permission to use the image of the virtual reality learner has been granted by David Gallardo-Pujol at the University of Barcelona.

In chapters 3 through 5 and chapter 7, permission to use some revised material from my 2013 book *Moral Character: An Empirical Theory* (Oxford: Oxford University Press) has been granted by Oxford University Press.

In chapter 6, permission to use some revised material from my 2014 book *Character and Moral Psychology* has been granted by Oxford University Press.

In chapters 8 and 9, permission to use some revised material from my paper "Virtue Cultivation in Light of Situationism," *Developing the Virtues*, eds. Julia Annas, Darcia Narvaez, and Nancy Snow (Oxford: Oxford University Press), has been granted by Oxford University Press.

In chapter 10, permission to use some revised material from my paper "Atheism and Theistic Belief," *Oxford Studies in Philosophy of Religion*, ed. Jonathan Kvanvig (Oxford: Oxford University Press), has been granted by Oxford University Press.

I am very grateful to Peter Ohlin and Walter Sinnott-Armstrong for believing in this project in the first place, and for all of their support. My research that informs this book was funded by a grant for the Character Project at Wake Forest University. Subsequent grants for the Developing Character Project and the Beacon Project by the Templeton World Charity Foundation and the Templeton Religion Trust provided me with additional time to work on this book. I am very grateful for all the support from these foundations, and especially to Michael Murray, John Churchill, Alex Arnold, and Chris Stewart. The opinions expressed here are my own and do not necessarily reflect the views of the Templeton Foundation.

For extremely helpful comments on the entire manuscript which improved it a great deal, I am very grateful to Peter Ohlin, Walter Sinnott-Armstrong, Jessie Lee Miller, Edwin Poindexter, and especially Joyous Miller. For extremely helpful comments on particular chapters, I am very grateful to Alan Wilson, Brandon Warmke, Ryan West, Nate King, Jonathan Deaton, and Giorgio Hiatt. Thanks to Jason Baldwin for excellent work on the index.

On a more personal note, I could not have done this without all the support of my parents, Charles and Joyous Miller, and my mother-in-law, Eileen Smith. Most of all, I want to thank my wife, Jessie Lee Miller, who has made so many sacrifices for our family. During the writing of this book, our third child, Lillian Joyous Miller, was born. Having three children under the age of five has been an incredible experience. Not to mention a real test of our characters. It has helped to confirm that what I say in this book about the character gap is true first and foremost about me.

What Is Character and Why Is It Important?

WHAT ARE WE
TALKING ABOUT?

A few years ago I was talking to someone at a reception:

"What do you research as a professor?" she asked.
"I study character."

She responded by asking if I went to a lot of drama productions to gather data. I hesitated, bewildered by her response . . . and then it clicked. We were talking completely past each other. She was wondering if my research had to do with studying theater and learning more about characters like Hamlet and the Phantom of the Opera.

"Well, not quite," I told her.

What Is This Thing Called "Character"?

Think about your best friend in the entire world. Do you have him or her clearly in view? Now ask yourself—what do you admire most about your friend? I bet a lot of us would say something like

He is always there for me.
I can trust her.

He never lets me down.
She is just so kind.

We can see from these answers that what we often care most about in our friends is their character. In these examples, it is their dependability, trustworthiness, loyalty, and kindness that spring to mind. And not just for our close friends—whether it is a politician or our children, a Hollywood celebrity or our parents, we tend to put a great deal of emphasis on people's *moral characteristics* or *moral traits of character*.[1]

Character traits are different from people's hair color. Or their sense of humor. Or their intelligence. Or their wealth. Or their popularity. They are what someone's moral fiber really is all about.

This moral fiber matters. Joseph Stalin was cruel, heartless, insensitive, brutal, and ruthless. These character traits were part of his moral fiber, and led him to behave in ways that were horrendous as the leader of the Soviet Union. By some estimates, he was responsible for twenty million or more deaths.[2]

Mother Teresa, on the other hand, served thousands of the desperately poor, sick, and orphaned in India for forty-five years. She was loving, compassionate, kind, selfless, and forgiving. Those character traits were part of her moral fiber and led her to behave in ways that were saintly.

Where do the rest of us fall? Are we closer on the spectrum to someone like Stalin or to someone like Mother Teresa (now Saint Teresa of Calcutta)? Well, that is the topic of the second part of this book. For now the point is that each of us has a variety of moral character traits that make up our character, and those traits are important. Some of those traits have to do with telling the truth, others with helping people in need, others with keeping promises, others with not cheating, and so forth.

It turns out, though, that the category of "character" is broader than just the moral traits someone might have. Consider *curiosity*. Someone might be a very curious person, but also morally wicked too. The same goes for other examples of character traits, like being *clever* or *open-minded* or *persistent* or *competitive*. If you think that personality characteristics like being *talkative* or *introverted* or *warm* are part of someone's character, then add them to the list too.

To illustrate the idea, see figure 1.1. In this book, I want to be clear that we are only focusing on the moral character traits. That will be more than enough to keep us busy.[3]

For many centuries, going all the way back to the earliest philosophers in ancient Greece, like Plato and Aristotle, the moral character traits have been organized into two groups: the *moral virtues* and the *moral vices*. In order to have a perfect moral character, the thought has been that we have to have all the moral virtues and none of the vices. Easier said than done, of course.

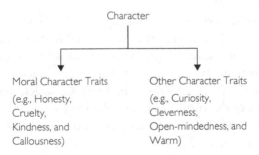

Figure 1.1 Moral Character Traits and All the Rest

While scholars can't agree on one comprehensive list of moral virtues and vices, we do have some famous lists to use as examples. Aristotle's list includes courage, temperance, liberality, magnificence, and justice.[4] In his letter to the Galatians, Paul writes that "the fruit of the Spirit is love, joy, peace, patience, kindness, goodness, faithfulness, gentleness, and self-control."[5] The cardinal virtues, going all the way back to Plato, are justice, courage, wisdom, and temperance.

In the fourteenth century, Dante Alighieri wrote what I regard as the greatest work of Western literature, the *Divine Comedy*. In the second volume, the *Purgatorio*, Dante vividly portrayed his list of the vices in the form of a mountain with seven different levels, each corresponding to a different vice. We can see what Dante had in mind in figure 1.2.

For Dante the vices represented here are pride, envy, wrath, sloth, avarice, gluttony, and lust. To ascend to heaven, a person first needs to climb Mount Purgatory. This involves suffering an appropriate amount of punishment on each level to atone for her past wrongdoing and to improve her character. As she climbs the mountain, her vices fall away and she develops the opposing virtues of humility, kindness, patience, diligence, charity, temperance, and chastity.[6]

Many other writers have come up with their own unique lists of virtues and vices, both in the Western and Eastern traditions of thinking about character. Fortunately, we do not have to go through them all here or try to sort out which is the correct list. Because despite some differences of opinion, there is broad agreement today about *most* of the virtues and vices. For instance, most writers on character would agree that honesty is a virtue, dishonesty is a vice, courage is a virtue, and cowardice is a vice. Other examples of widely accepted virtues include compassion, kindness, integrity, self-control, wisdom, gratitude, generosity, and fortitude. In this book

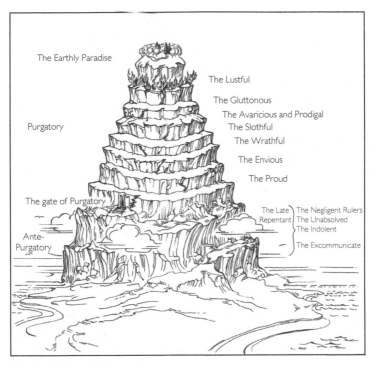

The Earthly Paradise

The Lustful

The Gluttonous

The Avaricious and Prodigal
The Slothful

The Wrathful

The Envious

The Proud

Purgatory

The gate of Purgatory

The Late | The Negligent Rulers
Repentant | The Unabsolved
| The Indolent

Ante-
Purgatory

The Excommunicate

Figure 1.2 Dante's Mount Purgatory

I will focus only on relatively uncontroversial examples of virtues and vices like these.[7]

To sum up, your character includes your own unique collection of characteristics or traits that are centrally important to who you are and how you act. Those can be grouped into the moral character traits and the nonmoral ones. Our focus is just on the moral category. Traditionally, these traits have been organized into the moral virtues and vices. Figure 1.3 puts these pieces together.

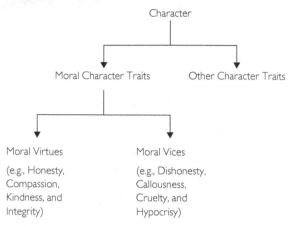

Figure 1.3 Two Types of Moral Character Traits

More on the Virtues

To better understand moral character, we need to understand virtue. What is a virtue? Think about your best friend again and suppose her character includes the virtue of honesty. What makes you think that she is honest? Or take your favorite superhero, in my case Batman— what makes him so heroic? Or think of examples of compassionate people. Maybe Jesus, Mother Teresa, or Gandhi comes to mind. What do they have in common when it comes to helping others?

Let us stick with the example of compassion for a while. One thing about a compassionate person is that she usually helps others in a time of need. Maybe she makes a donation to charity or visits a sick friend in the hospital. To examine this in practice, suppose Beth is browsing the Internet one day when she reads a story about refugee resettlement in her hometown and how the local community can partner together to help. Her interest is piqued and she quickly decides to gather clothes and home goods. A few days later, armed with a carload of donations, she arrives at the local collection point where items are being distributed to the refugees.

Now here is a question. Suppose this is all we know about Beth. Would her action *by itself* be enough to conclude that she has the virtue of compassion? It does seem like good *initial* evidence, but I think we can agree that it is *not enough* evidence. In other words, we can agree that there is more to having a virtue than just performing one good action.

To illustrate this, let me add some further details to the story. Suppose that when Beth arrives at the collection point she acts in a prideful manner. She boasts of her large collection of donated goods and arrogantly distributes them to the families. She even pauses to take selfies of "helping the refugees" and posts them to social media.

Obviously this does not seem to be very compassionate on her part! So what is missing from the original story? The answer is that a virtuous person not only does a good action, but also does it *in a way that is appropriate to the circumstances*. This could mean that Beth assumes a posture of humility when interacting with others and politely asks the families if they would be interested in any of her donations.

Okay, so suppose we change the story and say that Beth did just this. Would that be enough for Beth to qualify as a compassionate person? Again, I think we can agree that it would not. For here is another fact about Beth that I conveniently left out. Despite this one helpful action, it turns out that during the preceding and subsequent months she has ignored the needs of others. She laughed when a classmate dropped some papers. She scoffed at a request from her brother for help with a big test. She pretended that she did not hear the bullying of a friend that was going on at the schoolyard. And so on, time and again.

Beth hardly sounds like a shining example of compassion. What is missing? Clearly a virtuous person acts well in a *wide variety* of different situations. For Beth to be compassionate, she needs to be *reliably* helpful when relevant needs arise, whether that is at work, at home, at school, at the mall, at the grocery store, and so forth.

Of course, if Beth is *always* helping others, then she could hardly get on with her own life. There are simply too many needs and too many opportunities to help that arise each day. Just think about all the homeless and hungry, or the damage caused by natural disasters. The idea is *not* that a compassionate person has to always help whenever a need arises (her money would be all gone in a day and she would be completely exhausted too!). Rather, the idea is that her life exhibits a *pattern* of helping others in a variety of circumstances, and in a way that is appropriate for those occasions.

So let's change our story once again and suppose that over the course of the month Beth does exhibit such a pattern of helpfulness. Surely *now* we have said enough for Beth to qualify as compassionate. Haven't we? I am afraid that we have not. Return to the example of collecting supplies for the refugee families. Suppose she does it in a considerate way, but her motivation for helping the families is only so that she can get extra credit on a class assignment. Or so that she can put this down on her college application. Or so that she can relieve a feeling of guilt for something she had done wrong earlier in the day. Then, even though her *action* is admirable, her *motivation* is not. It is purely self-serving or egoistic.

To see this more vividly, imagine that *you* were in the refugee's position. You have lived in horrible conditions for years and have just managed to escape further persecution by fleeing your country. Now you have to navigate a new country, culture, and language. Here comes a seemingly nice woman who is generously offering you things that you need for your new home. Initially you have a very favorable impression of her character. She seems like a compassionate person who is genuinely interested in your situation. But then you ask her why she has gone out of her way to help you. And in a moment of honesty she says: "Oh, I just wanted to make my college application look better." I suspect you would be taken aback, maybe even left speechless. In my case I would likely be hurt and angry.

Now you might still be grateful for her help, and the clothing and kitchen supplies are badly needed. Yet at the same time, it is hard to praise her. The reason for this is simple. She does not really care about you. She is not ultimately concerned about your story or your well-being. Rather, what she really cares about is—herself. You are just a convenient means to her own ends.

A compassionate person, on the other hand, is different. If Beth had the virtue of compassion, then when she helps you she would be doing so for the right reasons. In this case, she would care about your well-being for its own sake and want what is best for you, *even if* she does not benefit in the process. This is *altruistic* motivation, not egoistic motivation.

Do not mistake any of this for extreme self-denial, as if the compassionate person can't derive any pleasure or enjoyment from assisting others. Rather, the compassionate person's central goal when helping another person is to do what is good for that person, rather than what is personally beneficial. At the same time, she *may also* find happiness for herself in the process of helping, even profound depths of joy.

But doesn't that sound like a contradiction? How can both of these things be true—that she can be focused on the good of another and also feel pleasure, satisfaction, or joy in the process? Here is an analogy that I like to use in my classes which shows how this is possible. When I drive my car, my goal is naturally to arrive at my destination. That is why I get in my car—it is the goal I am ultimately aiming for. At the same time, a *by-product* (or side effect) of my driving is that I enjoy the breeze on my face as I drive with the window down. Now my goal in driving is not to feel the breeze. Yet it is still true that when I drive I have this experience as a by-product, even though it is not part of my goal.

Similarly, Beth's goal, if she is compassionate, is to help alleviate some of the refugees' burdens as they transition to their new homes. At the same time, she can take great satisfaction herself in doing this, as the satisfaction is a by-product of her action and not the goal in the first place. So the life of virtue can be quite pleasing after all, even if in most cases it also involves putting other people's needs before one's own.

What is the lesson of all this? Quite simply that mere behavior, no matter how admirable and consistent it might be, is never enough by itself to qualify us as compassionate people. Over the course of a given month, Beth might do all kinds of helpful things, including assisting local refugees. Yet if she *only* does them with the goal in mind of benefiting herself—say, in order to make herself feel better or to impress a college admissions committee—then despite how positive the actions themselves are, we do not yet have a case of a compassionate person.[8]

What goes for compassion goes for the other virtues as well. An honest person would not reliably tell the truth only to make a good impression on others. A loyal person would not stand with her friend during difficult times, only in the hope of borrowing money from her later on. A person of integrity would not stand up for what is right solely in order to relieve his feeling of guilt. Having our heart in the right place matters to virtue, just as behaving well does.

There is another lesson here. It is often really hard to tell whether someone is truly virtuous. While we can study people's behavior, it is challenging to figure out what their underlying motivation is for that behavior. This is illustrated in figure 1.4.

Figure 1.4 One Action with Different Motives

Here we have the same person performing the exact same action of writing a large check to charity. What a generous person he must be! But wait. Why is he doing this? As we can see, his motive could vary even though the action itself is the same. In the first three examples, egoistic motives are at work, and his writing the check does not spring from the virtue of generosity. Only the fourth case looks like it could qualify, since there the motive is ultimately concerned with the good of other people.

So appropriate motivation is needed along with appropriate behavior in a variety of situations, in order for a person to qualify as compassionate. Now, is *that* enough? Almost, but surprising as it might be, we are still not quite there yet. To use Beth in our example just one more time, let us suppose that she demonstrates appropriate helping motivation and behavior over the course of two weeks. Yet suppose as well that this is unusual for her. Normally she is very self-absorbed, but for whatever reason she has had an onrush of feeling for the suffering of others that has led her to act in this way. Unfortunately, though, these feelings soon disappear, and sure enough she is back to her old ways.

That is not how the virtues are supposed to work. A virtue, when it is acquired, becomes a relatively stable feature of our characters and leads to relevant motivation and behavior over an *extended* period of time. If Beth is compassionate, then we can expect her to be like that for some time, whether it is months or years, barring radical changes or momentous events in her life.

This is not to say that the virtues, once acquired, become permanent fixtures in our characters. We can gradually lose them. Rather, the point is that, so long as one has a virtue, one is expected to exhibit that virtue reliably over time, both in the short run and in the long run.

Here ends our tour of the standards of virtue.[9] What has hopefully become clear is that there is a lot required in order to have a virtue! To help organize things, the bullet points in Figure 1.5 summarize the various features outlined above. Perhaps there are others too—I do not claim that these are all of the features of a virtue, but only that these are the central ones.

When I think about the features of a virtue, the one thing that strikes me above all else is this—it is *really hard* to be a virtuous person, someone who truly has all of the virtues needed for every area

- Leads to good actions that are appropriate to the particular situation.
- Leads to actions that are performed in a variety of different situations relevant to the particular virtue.
- Leads to actions that are done for the appropriate reasons or motives.
- Leads to a pattern of motivation and action that is stable and reliable over time.

Figure 1.5 Central Features of a Virtue

of the moral life. Indeed, it is really hard to have *just one* of the virtues, such as compassion. In this respect, the virtues resemble other difficult achievements, like becoming a chess master or a major league baseball player.

This is not to say that no one is virtuous, and I will discuss that topic in the second part of the book. It does mean, though, that becoming virtuous is not something that can happen overnight. However these character traits are acquired, for most of us it is a slow and gradual process.[10]

More on the Vices

So much for the virtues. How about we spice things up a bit with the vices? Let's talk about lust, greed, and cruelty.

Sorry to disappoint, but what I have to say here about the moral vices is very brief. Turns out that they share the very same features that the virtues do. The main difference is that they are oriented in the opposite way.

Suppose Sam has the vice of cruelty. Then he is likely going to try to hurt others, and not only in one situation either. Nor for a short period of time. Rather, he will exhibit a pattern of doing harm consistently across various situations and over time. He might, for instance, repeatedly kick the neighbor's dogs and also abuse his wife. This is because, let us suppose, he just enjoys delivering pain. Or he likes watching others suffer. Or he has a lot of anger and bitterness toward people. His life, then, reliably exhibits the pattern of bad actions and negative motives that are the trademarks of a cruel person. Much the same is true of the other vices—they have the same features listed in the bullet points, but their focus is in a morally negative direction.[11]

Having said this, I do want to highlight one very surprising aspect of the vices. Like virtuous people, the vicious often do *good things* for others. Why is that, if they are ultimately motivated in a way that does not help but harms?

If we think about it for a moment, the answer is not hard to find. There are all kinds of rewards in our society for doing nice, helpful things. You are thanked. Or maybe written up in the newspaper. Or look good in front of your friends. Or perhaps impress a cute girl or guy. Or advance in your career. The list is long.

In addition, there are all kinds of penalties in our society for getting caught being vicious. Jail time and fines are the obvious ones, but we can also fear alienating our friends, being fired from our job, or losing our spouse. So while a cruel person might like, for instance, to abuse animals, clearly if he has some degree of common sense he would not hurt a dog when the neighbor is watching.

Hence a vicious person can often behave admirably *when he believes other people are watching*. The real difference in behavior between the virtuous and the vicious emerges when they think they are not being observed. That is when our true character comes to light. As the inspirational writer H. Jackson Brown said in a now famous quote, "character is what we do when we think no one is looking."[12] How right that is.

Plato raised this very issue over two thousand years ago. In Book II of *The Republic*, Socrates is listening to his brother Glaucon question whether it really is good to be a virtuous person. In the course of his argument, Glaucon recounts the famous myth about the Ring of Gyges:

> . . . a shepherd [was] toiling in the service of the man who was then ruling Lydia. There came to pass a great thunderstorm and an earthquake; the earth cracked and a chasm opened at

the place where he was pasturing. He saw it, wondered at it, and went down. He saw . . . a hollow bronze horse. It had windows; peeping in, he saw there was a corpse inside that looked larger than human size. It had nothing on except a gold ring on its hand; he slipped it off and went out . . . while he was sitting with the others, he chanced to run the collet of the ring to himself, toward the inside of his hand; when he did this, he became invisible to those sitting by him, and they discussed him as though he were away.[13]

Such a ring allowed the shepherd to disappear from the eyes of the world. It also helped to reveal his true character. So what did that character look like? Was it virtuous or vicious? Here is the end of the story: "He immediately contrived to be one of the messengers to the king. When he arrived, he committed adultery with the king's wife and, along with her, set upon the king and killed him. And so he took over the rule."[14] Not good at all.

The creators of the movie *Hollow Man* certainly seem to have read about the Ring of Gyges and used it as the basis for their film (it is not a good film, I might add, which is a shame because the premise is so interesting). In a medical experiment gone wrong, Kevin Bacon's character is made invisible. While his footprints still show up in the dirt and you can see his profile in the rain or snow, for the most part he can come and go as he pleases without anyone observing him. With such great power and opportunity, his character is put to the test. It is quickly revealed to be corrupt, as he goes on a rampage of rape and murder (sorry for the spoiler).

The main point of these examples is that if a person acts well when around others, that does *not* automatically tell us whether he is virtuous or vicious. Sometimes true character is a very hard thing to detect. As a result, we are blindsided by his behavior, and shocked when out of the blue his vices rear their ugly heads. How often do we see this with prominent politicians, athletes, or celebrities? They can seem like such upstanding people. Then one day they get caught and a whole bunch of nastiness is discovered. Think of Tiger Woods, for example.

Remember, one morally positive action does not automatically mean an underlying virtue. So too we cannot conclude from one morally negative action that it automatically signifies an underlying vice. It is the pattern of behavior that counts as better evidence for either virtue or vice. Again, it is not the pattern of behavior *in public* that is truly revealing, but what happens behind closed doors.

That's why Tiger Woods is such a good illustration. At his prime, he was the most popular player in the game of golf and seemed destined to go down as the greatest golfer who ever lived. To most of us he appeared to be a very upstanding, decent guy. He worked hard, played by the rules, and was devoted to his family. Then he got caught, and his true character began to emerge. Woods did not simply have a single sexual encounter with another woman while he was married. Awful as such an event certainly is, it would not support the existence of an underlying vice all by itself. Instead, the evidence was much more damning—sexual escapades, repeated over and over again, with numerous women for several years. His behavior followed a clear pattern and was consistent and reliable across time and across situations.

It was also not public. Again, publicly it would have been hard to tell him apart from a model husband. Clearly he knew that carrying out his exploits publicly would have been too damaging to his endorsements and to his public image (not to mention his wife). So instead the affairs were conducted in secret. Until, of course, everyone came to find out all about them.

So for a person with a vice, it may not be easy for others to point to his behavior and say—aha!—there he is being cruel, or lustful, or dishonest. The vicious behavior might all be happening in secret—say, with Internet pornography or tax fraud or animal abuse (Michael Vick might come to mind here). Yet at the end of the day, what ultimately matters is *not* whether people observe our bad behavior or whether we can get away with it undetected. What ultimately matters is what is in our hearts, or as philosophers like to say, how we are *disposed* to think and act on moral matters.[15]

In fact, we can be vicious for a long period of time without ever doing anything wrong in public *or in private*. A cruel person might be strongly disposed to hurt animals but not come across any for several days. That does not mean his cruelty goes away during that time. No—the cruel disposition is still there, just waiting for the right situation.

The same point holds for the virtues as well—ultimately they are to be found in our hearts and have to do with how we are disposed to think and act. Virtuous people like Socrates or Paul or Desmond Tutu might not have had many opportunities to act compassionately during the time they were imprisoned, as all three of them were at one point in their lives. That does *not* mean that their compassionate characters ceased to exist during that time. Rather, their dispositions to help others remained with them all along.

To summarize, then, the vices are character traits which can lead us to think and act in morally awful ways when the situation presents itself. But the vices are often very hard to detect, since clever people who have them can still act just like the virtuous do in public. What is in a person's heart is what really matters to character, not how she presents herself to the world.

A Third Approach to Character?

Earlier I said that the moral character traits are divided into the virtues and the vices. This is how we normally think about character. We tend to believe that our close friends are honest, this politician is a cheat, that Hollywood actor is selfish, this policeman is courageous, that businessperson is generous, and so on.

This does not mean, by the way, that if one of our friends has the virtue of honesty, then he *also* must automatically be compassionate, courageous, wise, just, humble, generous, and gracious. Aristotle famously held that in order to have one of the virtues, you must have all of them. This became known as the doctrine of the "unity of the virtues."[16] Most philosophers today think that this doctrine is false. It sure seems that someone could be honest but also lack the virtue of generosity. Or be courageous but not humble. Or be compassionate toward others but not gracious when receiving help from them.

Regardless of whether Aristotle is right or not about the unity of the virtues, when it comes to thinking about character, the virtues and vices still rule the day. Again, take a moment and think how you would describe your best friend or your spouse. I bet I know what that list looks like—it is a list of virtues (and, hopefully, few vices). Now take a moment and list in your head the features of your least favorite politician. I bet there will be a long list of vices, and not many virtues.

One of the main goals of this book is to challenge the wisdom of using the virtues and the vices to describe other people. I believe that:

> Most people do not in fact have any virtues, and most people do not in fact have any vices.

Something else is going on in our characters, something that until very recently has not been appreciated much at all.

I will not say any more for now about what that something is. Let me only stress that the issues we are talking about here are not just part of some abstract academic discussion. So long as we continue to assume that people are honest, or cruel, or compassionate, or selfish, we are going to continue to make mistakes in understanding their character.

This happened recently at the university where I teach. Unfortunately for Wake Forest University, it was a hard lesson.

Tommy Elrod was, by all accounts, revered for his character. He was a family man, a regular churchgoer, and a generally well-liked individual.[17] Elrod was long associated with the university, having spent his undergraduate years playing football for the school and subsequently coaching the football team for eleven years. But as things often go, in 2014 there was a head coaching change and Elrod was not retained by the new coach. He seemed to land on his feet just fine, becoming a Wake Forest football radio analyst and gaining employment in the school's investment management office.[18]

Then, in one of the most bizarre stories in college football, in 2016 it emerged that he had been sharing sensitive information about the team's game plan with upcoming opponents (three in particular—Louisville, Army, and Virginia Tech). Shock and dismay would be one way to describe the fallout this caused on campus.

"It's incomprehensible that a former Wake Forest student-athlete, graduate-assistant, full-time football coach, and current radio analyst for the school, would betray his alma mater," Wake Forest head coach Dave Clawson said. "We allowed him to have full access to our players, team functions, film room, and practices. He violated our trust which negatively impacted our entire program."[19]

When we make mistakes about people's character, they can lead to disappointment, confusion, and betrayal. The Wake Forest University community knows this well.

In more extreme cases, these mistakes can cause significant pain, suffering, and even death.

Notes

1. One of the research projects we funded through the Character Project demonstrated this experimentally. See Goodwin et al. 2015.
2. See Conquest 2007.
3. Naturally you might wonder what the definition of "morality" is and how I know whether a character trait belongs in the moral category or not. I wish I knew the answer to these questions too! Frankly, no one has been able to come up with a very good answer. Instead, it is more a matter of knowing it when you see it.
4. Aristotle 1985.
5. Galatians 5:22–23, NIV translation.
6. For readers interested in studying the vices in more detail, I recommend Taylor 2008 and DeYoung 2009.
7. This is how I plan to sidestep the foundational question in ethics of whether morality is "objective" or just a human creation and so "relative" to what we think.

    Relativists would say that whether something is a virtue or a vice is a matter of human opinion. One person might think humility is a virtue; the next person might think arrogance is a virtue. There is no truth of the matter that says who is right and who is wrong.

    Like the majority of philosophers, I am an objectivist when it comes to morality, and so I think there *is* a standard independent of us that says whether humility is or is not a virtue. But trying to sort this debate out would require a long discussion that would sidetrack us from the main focus on character. So instead, as I indicated above, I will focus on examples of widely accepted virtues and vices, and make claims about them that I hope will be plausible for readers regardless of where they think morality comes from.

8. The same would be true if she *primarily* does these helpful things to benefit herself. In other words, even if some altruistic motivation is present, if it is not the main factor leading to the helping, then that still would not be compassion.

9. For those interested in going deeper, I recommend Hursthouse 1999: chapter 6.

10. Perhaps not for everyone. In other words, perhaps there are some cases where a person can undergo a quick and significant change in character. Saul on the road to Damascus is one such example. For the biblical account of his conversion, see Acts 9:1–19.

11. Here is a bit of a wrinkle to this picture. Some vices arise not because of what a person does, but because of what a person *doesn't do*. Ebenezer Scrooge, for instance, is a vicious person (in part) because he doesn't help those who are clearly in need and are deserving of his assistance, like the Cratchit family. His traits of callousness, selfishness, cold-heartedness, miserliness, and greed lead to his being negligent of others. These are what we might call more "negative" vices, since they have to do with neglecting or not doing something, in contrast with more "positive" vices that have to do with actively going out and harming other people. Thanks to Walter Sinnott-Armstrong for discussion here.

12. Brown 2000.

13. Plato 1968: 359d–360a.

14. Plato 1968: 360a–b.

15. In addition, to count as vicious thoughts, they have to be under our control to some extent. Thoughts about hurting others that arise, say, only through mental illness would not be part of a person's vicious character and would not be morally blameworthy either.

16. The expression is not used by Aristotle himself, but for the idea see Aristotle 1145a1–2.

17. http://www.journalnow.com/townnews/literature/ed-hardin-tommy-elrod-s-tale-is-a-sad-story/article_132e856c-9a67-5a26-8b76-a154ead4be04.html. Accessed February 15, 2017.

18. http://www.journalnow.com/sports/wfu/my_take_on_wake/my-take-on-wake-so-just-who-is-benedict-elrod/article_d48d7b68-c22d-11e6-8645-a7f498691019.html. Accessed February 15, 2017.

19. http://www.journalnow.com/sports/wfu/football/elrod-member-of-wake-forest-football-family-source-of-leaked/article_2aab2610-760e-5d7a-9ae0-286bc6b8902c.html. Accessed February 15, 2017.

2 | WHY BOTHER DEVELOPING A GOOD CHARACTER?

My three-year-old son is in the "Why?" stage.

"Daddy, why should I pick up my toys?"
"Because I don't want you to leave a mess in the playroom."

"Daddy, why can't I leave a mess?"
"Because that's not what good boys do."

"Daddy, why should I be a good boy?"
"Well . . ."

How do you answer a question like that from a little child?

I could try "Because I said so." But that is not very satisfying. Or perhaps "Just wait fifteen years and then you can take my ethics course." No, I can't say that.

While he stumped me for the moment (he does that a lot), down the road if he ever does want to talk about this again, I would start with the question itself, "Why be good?" Not "Why do good things?" The question is about being a certain kind of person, a person of good moral *character*. What does that involve?

Fortunately, we have already covered that ground in the previous chapter. It involves being someone who is honest, courageous, compassionate, humble, and so on—in a word, someone who is *virtuous*.

Now the question is why we should bother to become someone *like that*. Why care about becoming a virtuous person, and does developing a better character even matter?

There are a lot of different answers I could give. Here in this chapter I briefly mention the four I plan to tell my son when he is old enough.

I should note an important assumption lurking behind the question itself. It is that we are *currently not* good people, or people with a virtuous character. It wouldn't make any sense to ask why we should become virtuous people if we already are.[1]

I suspect that many readers will be fine with this assumption. Just watch the nightly news, or read a history of the twentieth century. It is hard to come away with warm, fuzzy feelings about most people's character. I agree. In the chapters to come, we will investigate this topic more systematically with the help of the best psychological studies on moral behavior. By the end of chapter 7, we will have a much clearer picture of what is really going on in most people's characters. At that point we can confirm it is not the virtues.

So good character is one thing. Our actual character is another thing. The question for us here is: why should we care about trying to bridge the gap? Let me begin with three stories of people who actually succeeded in making it across the character gap.

Courage in the Sewers

It was 1943, and the Nazis were exterminating all the people in a Jewish ghetto formed in the Polish city of Lvov. Thousands of men, women, and children were being rounded up and killed in the streets. A lucky few escaped immediate execution by being sent off to one of the work camps, but that still meant certain death in a matter of a few weeks. The situation was extremely bleak.

Ignacy Chiger, a Jewish maintenance foreman, had known what was coming. So with the help of a few trusted friends, he had been working for weeks digging a tunnel from a first-floor bedroom down to the main sewer system. When the killing started, dozens of people poured into the tunnel to escape.

The hope was that they would only have to remain in the sewers for a few days. But their hope quickly vanished. The Nazis set up permanent patrols all over the city and shot anyone who emerged from a manhole. Chiger and his group of twenty friends, family members, and even complete strangers were going to starve to death.

Enter Leopold Socha, a Polish sewer worker. He had discovered the tunnel when it was being dug, but rather than turn Chiger over to the Nazis, he helped with the planning. On the day of the escape, he navigated Chiger's group, including his wife, Paulina, and daughter, Kristina, through the darkness of the sewer tunnels to safety:

> They moved down the narrow pipe, struggling against the flow of water; and then turned into another pipe. They followed this a little way and emerged through the rear wall, into another of the elliptical tunnels. They were safe. "After that, I was certain that he would be our guardian, that he would look after us," was one of the few positive thoughts Paulina could recall from those hours.[2]

Then Socha began to take care of them:

> The following morning, Socha returned with his softly hissing lamp. With him he carried two workmen's bags, normally

weighed down with rough heavy tools, but that morning they were filled with bread and potatoes. With this he planned to feed the multitude, passing out fists of torn bread.[3]

But there was only so much one can do to make life comfortable in a sewer. Here was their first of what became five different homes:

There were municipal toilets in a square nearby, which had been a public disgrace—even above the ground. Every time the toilets were flushed a new wave of excrement passed down the trench and sometimes overflowed across the floor. They settled down on the stones, shivering in a howling wind, while rats scuttled about their feet. So, here was their first home in the sewers: cold, wet, and reeking of shit.[4]

The group never would have made it without Socha, and he had to undertake enormous risks in the process. If his role were ever discovered, he and his family would be immediately killed, along with the group of Jews. In addition, each day the work of delivering food to the Jews was extremely demanding:

We could hear them making their way through the mud and water for about half an hour before they arrived. With bags under their arms and the carbide lamp suspended from their teeth, they crawled for a kilometer through a "Forties" pipe [sixteen inches in diameter] arriving breathless and exhausted.[5]

Socha didn't do this out of bitterness or resentment, but rather out of concern for these people:

Then the familiar shuffles would announce Socha's arrival. The sight of his beaming face, illuminated by a row of shining teeth, became something of a symbol of his beneficence. "He was like a guardian angel, just for me," recalled Kristina. "Something sent from another world to keep me safe." The fresh bread was placed in the canister and then he and Wroblewski would share coffee with them. Invariably Socha would share some of his lunch with the children.[6]

He became one of the group, a friend and trusted family member. "The moment he arrived, he would go to the children to see how they were and would spend time playing with them, producing little gifts that brightened their eyes."[7] For a time, one of the children, Chiger's daughter Kristina, was suffering from severe depression. Socha worried about her:

> He sat me on his lap and he began talking to me, quietly. He just told me stories and told me not to worry . . . "Someday soon, you will breathe the air and you will see the daylight. It won't be long, you'll be like the other children and you will see the daylight . . . I will help you, don't worry. I am always with you and Pawel. I'm always with you. . ."
>
> And he took me down the pipes, to a place where I could see daylight—probably a manhole—and he picked me up and held me up to the light and he said, breath the air and look! See the daylight. . .
>
> I think it was soon after that I began, slowly, to behave normally again. I started to talk and react and eat again.[8]

Even when the group ran out of money with which to pay him for the supplies, Socha did not abandon them.

They went down into the sewers on June 1, 1943. They came back up on July 28, 1944, when the Russians liberated Lvov. It took fourteen months, but ten out of the original group of twenty survived:

> One by one these creatures of the underworld clambered out into the sunlight, blind and helplessly weak. Tears streaked their faces ... everywhere staring faces, stunned, disbelieving, silently shaking their heads. And there, in the midst of all the chaos, Socha stood proudly, staring his fellow countrymen in the eye.
> "This is my work. All my work. These are my Jews."[9]

Thus we have an account of the heroic work of Leopold Socha as memorialized in Robert Marshall's book *In the Sewers of Lvov*.[10]

Honesty in the White House

In 1917, Alonzo Rothschild published *"Honest Abe": A Study in Integrity Based on the Early Life of Abraham Lincoln*. The book begins with these words:

> He who seeks to understand the character and achievement of Abraham Lincoln must begin with a study of the man's honesty. At the base of his nature, in the tap-root and very fiber of his being, pulsed a fidelity to truth, whether of thought or of deed, peculiar to itself. So thoroughgoing was this characteristic ...[11]

I suspect that no one has heard of Leopold Socha. But everyone has heard of Abraham Lincoln. His character had many virtues, but Lincoln's honesty stands out the most.[12]

Here are two examples from early in his life while he served as a store clerk:

> Lincoln could not rest for an instant under the consciousness that he had, even unwittingly, defrauded anybody. On one occasion, while clerking in Offutt's store, at New Salem, Ill., he sold a woman a little bill of goods, amounting in value by the reckoning, to two dollars six and a quarter cents. He received the money, and the woman went away. On adding the items of the bill again, to make himself sure of correctness, he found that he had taken six and a quarter cents too much. It was night, and, closing and locking the store, he started out on foot, a distance of two or three miles, for the house of his defrauded customer, and, delivering over to her the sum whose possession had so much troubled him, went home satisfied.
>
> On another occasion, just as he was closing the store for the night, a woman entered, and asked for a half pound of tea. The tea was weighed out and paid for, and the store was left for the night. The next morning, Lincoln entered to begin the duties of the day, when he discovered a four-ounce weight on the scales. He saw at once that he had made a mistake, and, shutting the store, he took a long walk before breakfast to deliver the remainder of the tea. These are very humble incidents, but they illustrate the man's perfect conscientiousness—his sensitive honesty—better perhaps than they would if they were of greater moment.[13]

It was already at this early stage in his life that he acquired the name "Honest Abe," as we know from one of the first collections of stories about Lincoln:

Every one trusted him. It was while he was performing the duties of the store that he acquired the soubriquet "Honest Abe"—a characterization that he never dishonored, and an abbreviation that he never outgrew. He was judge, arbitrator, referee, umpire, authority, in all disputes, games and matches of man-flesh and horse-flesh; a pacificator in all quarrels; everybody's friend; the best natured, the most sensible, the best informed, the most modest and unassuming, the kindest, gentlest, roughest, strongest, best young fellow in all New Salem and the region round about.[14]

This pattern of honest behavior would continue in other situations. For example,

Lincoln was, by every account, extremely honest and upright in his business dealings and in his work as a lawyer. In New Salem he owned a small store in 1832 with William Berry. The business went broke the next year, largely on account of Berry's drinking. When Berry died not long afterward, leaving practically no estate, Lincoln was saddled with the burden of paying off the store's debts by himself. These debts totaled $1,100—a very large sum of money at the time. This debt was a huge burden to a young man trying to rise in the world. He jokingly referred to his debts from the store as his "national debt." . . . Lincoln was paying off his debts as late as 1848. His determination to pay the debts fully earned him the respect of his contemporaries and contributed to his reputation for honesty and fairness.[15]

And his honesty was not limited just to his business dealings. We see it on display in the courtroom too:

I remember one case of his decided honest trait of character. It was a case in which he was for the defendant. Satisfied of his client's innocence, it depended mainly on one witness. That witness told on the stand under oath what Abe knew to be a lie, and no one else knew. When he arose to plead the case, he said: "Gentlemen, I depended on this witness to clear my client. He has lied. I ask that no attention be paid to his testimony. Let his words be stricken out, if my case fails. I do not wish to win in this way."[16]

Lincoln's honesty would continue throughout his life, including during his years as president. As William Henry Herndon, a friend of Lincoln's and his junior partner in law, wrote in his biography, "In the grand review of his peculiar characteristics, nothing creates such an impressive effect as his love of the truth. It looms up over everything else. His life is proof of the assertion that he never yielded in his fundamental conception of truth to any man for any end."[17]

Compassion in Haiti

Tracy Kidder's 2009 book *Mountains beyond Mountains* introduces us to the life of Dr. Paul Farmer, who was one of the founders of the international health organization Partners in Health. Farmer and some of his friends began their work in Cange, Haiti, in 1985, and Kidder recounts what has become of the healthcare clinic they started:

Zanmi Lasante has become a very large public health and medical system, a system that sends about nine thousand children to school each year and has created schools where there were no schools, that employs nearly three thousand Haitians, that feeds many thousands of people each day, that has built hundreds of houses for the poorest patients, that has cleaned up water supplies in dozens of locales . . . The system now directly serves about three million impoverished Haitians, about one seventh of the country, and the real numbers are much larger . . . All the care is still first-rate and all of it is still essentially free to patients. And all but a handful of the staff are Haitian.[18]

Over time, the work of Partners in Health expanded beyond Haiti, to include Peru, Russia, Malawi, Lesotho, Rwanda, and Burundi. Kidder reports that

PIH now directly serves about 2 million patients . . . PIH still spends only about five percent of private donations on administration. Their work is geographically disparate, to say the least, but their general aim is the same everywhere: to relieve and prevent suffering . . . The organization now has on the order of 6,500 employees. The overwhelming majority come from the impoverished countries where PIH is working. Fewer than one hundred of the employees come from the United States.[19]

These are tremendous accomplishments that can be directly traced back to the vision and hard work of Farmer and his friends.

But amid all the statistics it is easy to lose sight of Farmer the person and how he cares for his patients. In Haiti, for example, here is how Farmer once treated a patient named Ti Ofa who had AIDS:

"Anybody can catch this. I told you that already," Farmer says. He opens a drawer in his desk and takes out a large plastic bottle. It contains indinavir, one of the new protease inhibitors used for treating AIDS.

No one else, not at this time, is treating impoverished Haitians with the new antiretroviral drugs. Indeed, almost no one in any poor country is treating poor people who have the disease . . .

Farmer leans closer to him. "I don't want you to be discouraged."

Ti Ofa looks up. "Just talking to you makes me feel better. Now I know I'll sleep tonight." He wants to talk and I suppose he knows he's welcome to do so. "My situation is so bad. I keep hurting my head because I live in such a crowded house. We only have one bed, and I let my children sleep on it, so I have to sleep under the bed, and I forget, and I hit my head when I sit up. I don't forget what you did for me, Doktè Paul. When I was sick and no one would touch me, you used to sit on my bed with your hand on my head. They had to tie up the dogs in the village, you walked around so late to see sick people."[20]

This is not an exceptional case, by any means. Farmer invests a tremendous amount of time in getting to know his patients and caring for them as real people. Indeed, this is the kind of work that he loves to do the most.

As another example, Farmer once took a seven-hour trip on foot to visit two of his patients. Stopping at one of their huts, Kidder says:

I estimate the hut to be about ten feet by twenty, and I count ten souls who live in it. Farmer gazes at the hut. "Well, I guess I don't need to do a house inspection." He stares at it some more. "On a scale of one to ten, this is a one." . . .

"I'm glad we came, because now we know how grim it is and we can intervene aggressively."

I know what this means: a new house with a concrete floor and metal roof, further arrangements for improving the family's nutrition, school tuition for the kids. Here's a good deed in progress, and a perfect example of the Farmer method. . .

I am aware of other voices that would praise a trip like this for its good intentions, and yet describe it as an example of what is wrong with Farmer's approach. Here's an influential anthropologist, medical diplomat, public health administrator, epidemiologist, who has helped to bring new resolve and hope to some of the world's most dreadful problems, and he's just spent seven hours making house calls. How many desperate families live in Haiti? . . .

I can imagine Farmer saying he doesn't care if no one else is willing to follow their example. He's still going to make these hikes, he'd insist, because if you say that seven hours is too long to walk for two families of patients, you're saying that their lives matter less than some others', and the idea that some lives matter less is the root of all that's wrong with the world . . . "That's when I feel most alive," he told me once on an airplane, "when I'm helping people." . . . This matters to him, I think—to feel, at least occasionally, that he doctors in obscurity, so that he knows he doctors first of all because he believes it's the right thing to do.[21]

Farmer genuinely loves his patients. He cares about them so much that he pushes himself to the limit: "Many times when I looked inside his house, his bed appeared unused. He told me he slept about four hours a night but a few days later confessed, 'I can't sleep. There's always somebody not getting treatment. I can't stand that.' "[22]

First Reason: Virtuous Lives Are Admirable and Inspiring

I chose these three examples because they resonate deeply with me at this particular moment in my life. But there are so many others I could have chosen instead: Harriet Tubman, Mother Teresa, Sojourner Truth, Confucius, and Socrates are all exemplary for their characters too, and in very different ways.

But what does this have to do with our question, "Why should we care about becoming better people?" The lives of these people, in my mind, provide an answer.

Not in the usual way, the way you would expect a philosopher like myself to get excited about. We didn't see any fancy arguments in the last few pages. No premises trying to persuade our minds that we had better get to work on our characters.

No, it is the *very lives themselves* of these exemplary individuals that can make us care. When we read more about those lives—much more than the brief snippets I have space to offer here—we see something that is so powerful in its goodness that it can evoke an emotional response in us.

Thus the first reason to care about becoming better people is an emotional one. Hopefully most readers will find themselves in awe of how Leopold Socha crawled through the sewer pipes every day to deliver food to the Jews he was protecting. And they will deeply admire how Paul Farmer traveled for seven hours to visit two destitute families in a remote village of Haiti.

Admiration is not all that typically happens. I can admire a beautiful painting or a fine wine, but it won't change my life very much. When it comes to examples of great virtue (and this includes examples from fiction as well as real life), another emotion becomes involved. It is what psychologists call *elevation*.

When I feel elevated, I experience an emotion of being uplifted and inspired. My heart is energized. There are often "physical feelings in [my] chest, especially warm, pleasant, or 'tingling' feelings."[23]

I deeply admire what Socha did in protecting the Jews hiding in the sewer. I also feel inspired by his courageous and compassionate actions. I feel uplifted and, most importantly for our topic here, I want to become more like *that*. Not only do I view him in such a positive light, but I also want to become more like him. I want, in other words, to become a better person, one who can so freely and generously help those in need.

If you have seen the movie *Pay It Forward*, you will recognize immediately the power of elevation. The main character is a seventh-grader named Trevor who has to complete an assignment for social studies. But it is a daunting assignment—he has to come up with a new plan to make the world a better place. What Trevor discovers is ingenious. Whenever someone helps another person, he or she has to add the requirement that instead of paying "back" the helper, the person who was helped has to "pay it forward" to someone else in need (with the same requirement of course). Doing good becomes something that snowballs, and also triggers feelings of admiration and elevation in those who see what is happening. In fact, at the end of the movie, hundreds of people who didn't know Trevor at all come forward to honor him for starting this movement and for how they felt inspired to become better people.

Now people you have never met, and indeed *can* never meet (like Leopold Socha and Abraham Lincoln), may not have a powerful emotional impact on everyone. Hopefully there is someone in your life—a grandparent perhaps, or a community leader, or a neighbor down the street—who has displayed remarkable virtue in an area of her life. You can admire what she has done and feel inspired to become more like her.

The "more like" is really important. The goal is not to actually become that person. In many cases, we could never do that anyway. I will never be president of the United States, and I am too old to start my education over again and train to become a doctor. Obviously, being a sewer worker during the Holocaust has no immediate parallel in the lives of most people.

The point is not to try to become Paul Farmer. It is to become *more like* Paul Farmer. It is, in other words, to be more intentional in helping the poorest people in the world, whatever that help might look like—and to do so in a way that is richly interpersonal, focused on their specific needs as a person, rather than as a mere statistic. It is *as if* he were in our position in life, with our resources and abilities, facing the very obstacles that we face, confronting the suffering that we see, and so on.[24]

So too the point is to become *more like* Abraham Lincoln. It is, in other words, to become more intentional in telling the truth and in not cheating other people. This would include at work, at parties, at home, and on social media, even though lying or cheating might be "fun" or make us look better in front of our peers.

Finally, it is worth stressing that the people we admire most and who inspire us are not perfect, even in the area of their lives where they are the most virtuous.[25] Hence we read about Socha: "For the most part he was cheerful and eager to please, but when slighted he could become furious."[26] Furthermore, Chiger claims that what motivated Socha to help was "repentance for all the crimes he committed during his very stormy and unethical past. It was contrition, a plea for the forgiveness of God. It was his greatest mission . . . He believed it was a way of snatching his sins from his soul, just as he was snatching us from certain death."[27] But that might not be the most virtuous kind of motivation to help someone.

Again, the point is not to be inspired to become exactly like these people. It is to *become more like them, in the ways in which they are virtuous.* When we study the lives of people like Socha, or we spend time with our saintly grandmother, we can be moved by what they did and who they are as people. Our emotional response to their lives is all the reason we need to work hard at becoming better people.[28]

But it is not all the reason there is to do this. Here are some additional important reasons.

Second Reason: Good Character Typically Makes the World a Much Better Place

Think about all the good that compassionate people have done in the world, and contrast this with all the harm caused by those full of cruelty and hate. What world would you rather live in? And what kind of people do you want your children to become—people who grow up to make the world a better or a worse place? Surely it is the former. But if that is what you want for your children, why wouldn't you want the same thing for yourself, right now? There is always time to change our character. It is never stuck in the mud, but is improvable, at least slowly. So just as we want our children to grow up to make the world a better place, so too should we want ourselves to "grow up" to the fullest, morally speaking.

Consider Paul Farmer. Because of his compassion, it is no exaggeration to say that tens of thousands of lives have been saved from the world's deadly diseases. The good character of this one person has made the world a much better place. If only there were many more Paul Farmers in the world.

Contrast this with the horrors caused by someone with a cruel character. For instance, here is what we learn about the Nazi commander of the work camp near where Leopold Socha was maintaining the sewers:

Sometimes, if a new transport arrived carrying women and children, he had them brought up to his villa and, as he had no use for the children, had them thrown into the air while he took aim and shot at them from the verandah. He often did this in the presence of his little daughter who used to applaud his successes.

On other occasions he used to take aim at a labour squad on the parade ground, trying to remove a nose or an ear or a finger. After this, he would move amongst the prisoners to extract the wounded. He would then march them to the other end of the parade ground and finish them himself with a bullet in the skull.[29]

Why would we want to live in a world with such misery caused by vice?

So a second reason to care about becoming better is that a good character typically makes the world a better place.[30]

Third Reason: God Wants Us to Become Good People

What if you believe in God, say the God of Judaism, Christianity, or Islam? Then you have another powerful reason to care about becoming a better person. For these religions hold that God created human beings to be a certain way, which includes having a good character. We regularly fall short of this good character, but God does not want us to remain complacent about that fact. We are supposed to take steps (perhaps with God's assistance) to get closer to how we were designed to be in the first place.

So if you are a sincere believer in one of these religions, it is probably obvious that you should care about becoming virtuous. You should also care about becoming virtuous *for the right reasons*. No doubt some believers in these faith traditions are motivated simply by trying to get rewards for themselves in the afterlife. This kind of motivation is purely self-interested or egoistic. At the end of the day, all they really care about is themselves. Can you really become a compassionate person (who cares about others for their own sake) or an honest person (who cares about the truth for its own sake) or a just person (who cares about what is fair for its own sake) if self-interest is all you have to go on? I do not think so.

Religious believers might be motivated in a different way, however. Someone who works at becoming a better person because he loves God and believes that God wants him to become better is not being self-interested. He is caring about something larger than himself. Similarly for the religious believer who is motivated to become better out of gratitude for what God has done for human beings, or out of a sense of admiration, reverence, or trust.[31]

What if you do not believe in the God of Judaism, Christianity, or Islam? Well, character matters a great deal in other major world religions too. Hence in the *Analects* we read:

> The Master said: "The rule of virtue can be compared to the Pole Star which commands the homage of the multitude of stars without leaving its place."[32]

> The Master said: "A man who finds benevolence attractive cannot be surpassed."[33]

> "Make it your guiding principle to do your best for others and to be trustworthy in what you say."[34]

So if you practice Confucianism, or any other religion that praises the development of virtue, you will also have a powerful reason to care about becoming a better person.

What about those who reject all forms of religion? Then clearly this section will not have as much to offer. Still, there is this. A *chance* remains that a divine being exists who wants people to have good characters. After all, no one has ever succeeded in proving, with 100% certainty, that no divine being exists. Given this chance, perhaps it is better to err on the side of caution and work at improving yourself, just in case.[35]

Hence we see a third reason to care about becoming better, one that speaks powerfully to most religious believers, but also one that might be of interest to nonbelievers too.

Fourth Reason: A Good Character Can Be Rewarding

Yes, seeing someone live a virtuous life might be inspiring. Having a good character might make the world a better place for other people. Becoming virtuous might be what God wants me to do.

But . . .

What about the daily grind of life on this earth? Wouldn't becoming virtuous simply drain all of the joy out of my life? Others might benefit, sure, but how is it any good *for me* if I am run into the ground in the process?

That's a natural reaction to have. Yet it seems that this is *not* what typically happens to virtuous people. Consider the caring doctor Paul Farmer again. You might think that his compassion would run him into the ground. After all, he barely sleeps. He travels all over the world to help with various health crises while rarely seeing his family. He goes on seven-hour treks to visit patients in remote villages. Yet, from Kidder's portrayal of him, Farmer seems strangely vibrant and energetic, more alive than the rest of us are. It turns out that treating patients is when he is the happiest, the most joyful. As we saw him say already, "That's when I feel most alive . . . when I'm helping people."

Becoming virtuous can help improve our lives in two different ways, actually. It can be a source of joy and contentment, as in the case of Farmer. The virtues are also a way of shielding ourselves from emotional and other hardships. A deeply virtuous person is not seriously tempted to cheat on her spouse or her taxes, for instance. She is thus spared the emotional baggage of wrestling with those choices. Plus she does not have to experience all the guilt, shame, or embarrassment that might come with actually cheating. Not to mention various punishments, whether they be fines, divorce, or even imprisonment for tax evasion. Avoiding these consequences is itself a big positive.

That strikes me as good common sense. Research in psychology is taking common sense one step further these days by rigorously showing how becoming good is also linked to what is good for us. Here are some general findings with respect to three important virtues:

Gratitude: Increased gratitude is related to better health, greater optimism, more positive mood, higher work satisfaction, better school achievement, and increased life satisfaction.[36]

Hope: Increased hope is related to increased life satisfaction in the present and the future, better school achievement, higher work satisfaction, and decreased anxiety.[37]

Honesty/Integrity: Increased honesty and/or integrity is related to decreased aggression, higher GPA, and increased performance for top-level business executives.[38]

Needless to say, these look like very important benefits.

Let's delve into this research just a little bit to get a feel for what researchers are up to. Take integrity and increased performance by business executives. John Sosik at Penn State University and his colleagues focused on assessing the characters of a number of top-level executives (like CEOs and CFOs). Each executive had to be rated on a measure of integrity (among other traits) by two employees who directly reported to the executive at the company. In addition, a boss or a member of the board would provide a rating of the executive's performance. This consisted of five questions, with a 1 to 5 scale for responses:[39]

1. How would you rate this person's performance in his or her present job?
2. Where would you place this person as a leader relative to other leaders inside and outside your organization?
3. What is the likelihood that this person will derail (i.e., plateau, be demoted, or fired) in the next five years as a result of his or her actions or behaviors as a manager?
4. To what extent does this individual contribute to the overall effectiveness of this organization?
5. Rate this person's overall level of effectiveness.

The results were clear in showing that an executive's level of integrity, as measured by the two direct reports, significantly predicted how high his or her performance rating would be.[40] The higher the integrity, the higher the performance rating. Why? As Sosik writes, "Without integrity, executives are not likely to make sound decisions and receive the levels of trust, support, and communication from associates required to exert effective social influence within organizations."[41]

Now let's switch to gratitude. The leading expert in psychology on gratitude, Robert Emmons at UC Davis, teamed up with Michael McCullough at the University of Miami to run a series of gratitude studies that tried to determine what good outcomes gratitude can bring about.[42] Let me just mention their first study. They put some of the 192 undergraduates participating in the study into a gratitude condition:

> There are many things in our lives, both large and small, that we might be grateful about. Think back over the past week and write down on the lines below up to five things in your life that you are grateful or thankful for.[43]

Other students were put in a hassle condition:

> Hassles are irritants—things that annoy or bother you. They occur in various domains of life, including relationships, work, school, housing, finances, health, and so forth. Think back over today and, on the lines below, list up to five hassles that occurred in your life.[44]

And still others were put in an "events" condition, which was basically a control group. In addition to their designated task, the students in all three conditions had to answer a variety of other questions as well. They completed ten of these weekly reports during the course of the semester.

Emmons and McCullough discovered a number of interesting results. Students in the gratitude group on average rated their lives during the past week much higher than did students in the other two groups. Same with their expectations for the week ahead. Strikingly, they also reported fewer symptoms of illness than did their peers in the other groups, and compared to the hassle group, they claimed to exercise 1.5 additional hours in a given week![45] These are important benefits indeed.

Let me draw a halt to reporting on these studies. But before we wrap up, all this talk of self-interest might raise a natural question about virtue. We already saw in the last section that if you are doing good things primarily to benefit yourself, then that will prevent your becoming a virtuous person. Which is true. If Paul Farmer is mainly helping people in Haiti to make himself feel good, then he is not truly compassionate. If Abraham Lincoln is telling the truth to improve his reputation, then he is not truly honest. If Leopold Socha is protecting the Jews to compensate for his own guilt, then he is not truly caring.

At this point, we need to recall the distinction between a goal and a mere by-product. When I drive my car, my goal is to get to my destination, but a by-product (or side effect) of driving the car is that I enjoy a pleasant breeze. Rewards can work the same way with a virtuous person. The *goal* of someone who is compassionate is to help those in need. Period. However, a *by-product* of helping others could be feelings of joy, happiness, and contentment. While the focus is on the other person, some nice benefits can come along for the ride.

While it is hard to know for sure, I would like to believe that this is what is happening with Paul Farmer. It can be true both that he feels most alive while treating his patients, and that this feeling is not *why* he treats his patients. He treats them because they are dying or seriously ill, but a by-product is that he can feel very good too when they are healed.

Benefits for oneself, as by-products, serve as the fourth reason for becoming good.

Conclusion

I look forward to talking some day with my son about these and other reasons for becoming a good person. For now, I still need to think of what to say to him the next time he asks me why he should be a good boy.

Notes

1. Although even in that case, there is an important question someone might ask about why bother continuing to do what is needed to *maintain* a good character.
2. Marshall 2013: 64.
3. Marshall 2013: 69.
4. Marshall 2013: 78.
5. Marshall 2013: 92.
6. Marshall 2013: 125.
7. Marshall 2013: 159.
8. Marshall 2013: 182–183.
9. Marshall 2013: 224.
10. The end of Socha's life was a powerful display of his character as well. Just a year after the war was over:

   Socha and his daughter Stepya were out together riding their bicycles. As they peddled down a steep hill, Socha saw a Russian army truck careering madly across the road in Stepya's path. He desperately peddled ahead, overtook his daughter and knocked her safely out of the path of the truck. Within the same instant, Socha had collided with the juggernaut and under the mangled bicycle frame, Socha's broken body lay lifeless. "He had fallen over a drain in the street, and his blood flowed freely into the sewer," wrote Chiger (233).

   His courage never failed.
11. Rothschild 1917: 1.
12. For a careful discussion of Lincoln's character and virtues, see Carson 2015.
13. McClure 1879: 22–23.
14. McClure 1879: 31.

15. Carson 2015: 260–261.

16. Stevens 1998: 142.

17. Herndon and Weik 1949: 487.

18. Kidder 2009: 304.

19. Kidder 2009: 306–307.

20. Kidder 2009: 30.

21. Kidder 2009: 295.

22. Kidder 2009: 23–24.

23. Haidt 2003: 282. For more on the psychology of elevation, see Haidt 2000; Algoe and Haidt 2009; and Aquino et al. 2011.

24. Thanks to Nate King for this last way of putting the point.

25. Perhaps I should say "are typically not perfect." In some religious traditions, inspirational figures such as Jesus are considered to be morally perfect or very close to it.

26. Marshall 2013: 93.

27. Marshall 2013: 167. The portrait of Farmer painted in Kidder's book isn't entirely positive either, as, for instance, Farmer's work seemed to take a toll on his family life.

28. I don't think of emotions as just brute causes pushing us to feel and do things. I think of emotions as, when all goes well, providing us with good motives or motivating reasons to do things.

29. Marshall 2013: 143.

30. A critic might say—wait, all this shows is that good *behavior* makes the work a better place. It doesn't show that good *character* does, if that also means having good motivation behind the behavior.

    But good behavior, supported by good motivation, would seem to make the world a better place *more reliably*. Yes, good behavior can stem from the pursuit of self-interest, too, as we saw in the last chapter. But what happens when it would not be in one's self-interest to act well? Virtuous motivation, on the other hand, will lead to good behavior regardless of whether it is in our self-interest or not.

31. We will return to this topic at greater length in chapter 10.

32. Confucius 1979: 2:1.

33. Confucius 1979: 4:6.

34. Confucius 1979: 1:8.
35. If this sounds like reasoning Pascal used in his famous Wager, it should. For a very helpful overview of Pascal's Wager, see Lycan and Schlesinger 1989 and Rota 2016.

   Of course, there is also a *chance* that there is a divine being who wants people to become as cruel, dishonest, and mean-spirited as possible. That chance has to be acknowledged as well, and using the same line of reasoning, it may be the basis for working toward a bad character.

   Do these two chances of a virtuous and a vicious God simply cancel each other out? It is not clear that they do. There seems to be a *higher* chance that a God exists who likes good character rather than bad. Again, the major world religions show a remarkable degree of agreement on the importance of traits like honesty and compassion, even if they understand them in somewhat different ways. There are no major religions that I know of which promote the development of cruelty and dishonesty in the characters of their followers.

   Admittedly, if we had lived at other times, and were only familiar with, say, the jealous and bickering Greek gods, then there might not seem to be a higher chance that a God exists who likes good character. But today we have a much richer appreciation of the major world religions and can see for ourselves whether most of them affirm such a God (or gods).
36. See McCullough et al. 2002; Emmons and McCullough 2003; Peterson et al. 2010; and Wagner and Ruch 2015.
37. See Park et al. 2004; Shimai et al. 2006; Park and Peterson 2008; Peterson et al. 2010; Proyer et al. 2011; Buschor et al. 2013; and Wagner and Ruch 2015.
38. See Park and Peterson 2008; and Sosik et al. 2012.
39. Sosik et al. 2012: 373.
40. Sosik et al. 2012: 375. This is a correlational finding, as are most of the results in this research. Alas, such correlational studies cannot tell us about causation, and so we don't know if the virtues in question are bringing about the beneficial results for the person (although see Sosik et al. 2012: 379).
41. Sosik et al. 2012: 377.

42. Emmons and McCullough 2003.
43. Emmons and McCullough 2003: 379.
44. Emmons and McCullough 2003: 379.
45. Emmons and McCullough 2003: 381.

PART II

What Does Our Character Actually Look Like Today?

3 | HELPING

We have spent some time developing an understanding of virtue. We have also seen why it is so important to work hard to become virtuous people ourselves. But what does our own character actually look like right now? What about our friends and families, or the strangers at the mall or the ballgame? How good is our character when it is put to the test?

Maybe most of us *already are* virtuous people. If so, we can be content with our good character and reap the benefits that were mentioned in the last chapter. But do you really believe that, especially these days? Even a quick glance at our recent history shows two world wars, the purging of twenty million people in the Soviet Union and forty-five million more in China, widespread apathy to massive starvation throughout the world—the list goes on and on. Or we can just look tonight at the news—as I write this, ISIS is beheading American journalists and terrible conflicts are escalating in the Ukraine, Israel, Iraq, Libya, Afghanistan, and Syria. Hardly things to pat ourselves on the collective back for and praise the virtue of human beings in general.

Obvious as it might seem, though, we should *not* jump to the conclusion that we are moral failures. It could be that most of us are indeed good people, while a few "rotten apples" get a lot of attention in the media as they carry out atrocities. Besides, we all know that the media tends to focus on negative stories and does not give as much attention to sacrifice, selflessness, and love.

Instead of looking to the news, a more careful way to examine our characters and put them to the test is by performing controlled psychological experiments. Ideally these experiments would observe people's moral behavior in the course of their ordinary lives, *without their even knowing that they are part of a study*. If that is not possible, then at least they should be observed in a laboratory context that is as realistic as possible.

Such studies will be our focus in the next four chapters as we look at some of the fascinating research that has been done by psychologists. In these chapters we will specifically examine our tendencies to help, hurt, lie, and cheat.

Would You Help in a Mall?

It is a Saturday afternoon and you are enjoying a walk alone in the local shopping mall, peacefully window shopping. You notice a woman carrying a grocery bag with a tear in the bottom. Candy is slowly falling from the tear, yet the shopper seems to have no idea what is happening. No one else is around who might point this out to her. What do you think you would do?

Help the shopper, of course! Maybe you would pick up the candy. Maybe you would call out to her. Surely you would do *something*. Wouldn't you?

In fact, you are probably thinking, wouldn't *most people* in that situation let the shopper know about the tear? It is obvious that there is something wrong. It would be a trivial matter to address this, just a few seconds of anyone's time. Besides, usually people in a mall are not in any rush to begin with. The shopper would be very thankful. And helping is what society (and our mother!) expects us to do.

According to a study performed by Cornell University psychologist Dennis Regan and his colleagues, most people did the exact opposite. Regan had an actor, or what psychologists call a "confederate," play the role of the shopper with the torn bag. He then secretly watched how people in a mall behaved when they saw her bag leaking candy. Of twenty adults, only three did anything to help. Seventeen just continued on their way as the candy fell.[1]

When I present this result to people, they are always surprised. Maybe there was something defective about the experiment? Maybe the actor was not doing a good job? Or maybe there happened to be a lot of "bad people" that day in the mall?

Maybe, just maybe, this result is not so abnormal at all. In fact, during the past sixty years there have been hundreds of studies in psychology that examined whether people would help in various situations. Many of these studies found that most people *did not do anything*, even when the help required would have been fairly easy.

That sounds rather depressing, doesn't it? Fortunately the story is not quite so bleak. There are also many studies that discovered how willing people are to do difficult and demanding acts of kindness, with the best interest of the other person (and not themselves) in mind.

Hence this chapter will take us on a journey through some of the best and some of the worst sides of our characters when it comes to helping others. By the end of this journey, we will see why most of us do not have the virtue of compassion ... but we are not Scrooges either.

Are You Feeling Guilty Today?

I actually left out quite a bit of the Regan study. Before they came across the leaking candy, each of these shoppers had first spent some time with a guy asking to have his picture taken. This was also an actor working for Regan, and he always mentioned that his camera was rather sensitive (it looked pretty expensive too). Lo and behold, when each shopper used the camera, the shutter failed. No worry. The guy said the camera "acts up a lot," and that they had done nothing wrong. A few stores later, here comes the woman with the torn bag of candy.

Would this earlier camera incident make any difference to whether you would help? Does it change what you predict most people would do when they notice the candy? I doubt it. Each person was let off the hook about the broken shutter, so no guilt should be involved. It is a shame this happened to the camera owner (sorry for him!), but it is likely not going to bother many people for very long. Plus, it does nothing to morally justify or excuse ignoring the spilled candy.

Okay, so much for these twenty participants. It probably seems strange that Regan went through all this trouble with the broken camera. What was the point? We will see in a moment, as these participants were actually functioning as the *control group*. Regan was much more interested in twenty different people in the same mall. They were going to be part of the *experimental group* (although of course no one in either group ever realized that they were in a study!).

Regan introduced just one change to the situation for the experimental group. Now the camera owner blamed the shoppers, saying that they must have done something wrong when they were taking the picture. The camera is jammed, it needs to be fixed at significant expense to the owner, and it's all the shopper's fault.

What are your expectations now? Do you think these shoppers who have been blamed for the camera malfunctioning would be more or less willing to help the woman with the torn bag, as compared to the control participants? The difference ended up being dramatic:[2]

55% of these participants helped (eleven out of twenty)

versus

15% of the controls

Why would that be?

A plausible explanation has to do with guilt. Guilt is an emotion we often feel whenever we do something (or do not do something) that goes against the standards we have set for our behavior.[3] Just think about the last time you forgot to do something really important for your best friend that she asked you to do. What powerful feeling did you experience afterward? It was almost certainly a feeling of guilt. In the broken camera group, many shoppers likely felt guilt for having broken someone's expensive camera (or so they thought). Soon afterward they saw an opportunity to help, and their feelings of guilt somehow made a difference in lending a helping hand.

So it seems that Regan found a connection between guilt and increased helping. He was not the only psychologist to do so, as dozens of other studies have revealed the same connection.[4] Why does guilt seem to have this effect on helping? What is going on in our mind that would explain this relationship?

While most psychologists are in agreement that there is a direct relationship between guilt and helping, there is no consensus at this point as to why. One model, though, which seems to be increasingly popular is the *guilt-relief model*.[5] The idea is that when I break a stranger's camera or knock over his books, I not only tend to feel

I am feeling guilt about something I did.

I want to relieve my guilt.

Here is a chance to help someone and thereby relieve my guilt.

So I experience increased motivation to help.

So I am more likely to help than I would have been otherwise.

Figure 3.1 The Guilt-Relief Model

guilt, but I also want to eliminate or at least reduce my guilt. Helping can be a great way to do so. By helping, I can make myself feel better, so it is only to be expected that guilt could give a boost to helping. Figure 3.1 outlines this idea visually.

So be on the lookout the next time someone asks you to help while you are still feeling guilty. This is a perfect time to stop for a moment and reflect. Maybe you were saying something mean about a friend behind his back, and now that friend needs a ride to the airport or help moving a couch. Or you see an image of a starving child during a television commercial and then are given a chance to donate to famine relief. Or maybe you feel bad about not spending much time with your daughter recently, and she asks you to help her with her homework. Ask yourself, when the time comes, if you feel more inclined to help in these situations than you would ordinarily be. If so, then maybe that motivational boost is coming from a desire for guilt-relief.[6]

Rather than continue to explore guilt and helping further, let's see if a similar pattern shows up in other areas of the psychological research on helping.

Some Embarrassing Results?

You are starting a new volunteer organization to work for a really good cause in your neighborhood. You gather your leadership team together and spend hours brainstorming about how to get people to sign up to volunteer. You plan on doing the usual things, like building a website and posting about the organization on Facebook. But you also want to go a step further and have sign-up tables around town. Where should we put them, you ask? Should we have them outside grocery stores, like the Salvation Army does? How about at the high school, where there are young, energetic, and idealistic students? Or near the retirement community, where people tend to have more free time? Which of these, you wonder, would be the best place to get people to sign up to help?

I bet one place never crosses your mind—outside a crowded public bathroom! The psychologists Arnie Cann and Jill Blackwelder at the University of North Carolina at Charlotte thought that this might be a perfect location. In their study, people were leaving a bathroom when, three feet after exiting, they were approached by a stranger who said, "I am in a big hurry and I have a friend who needs these notes. I wonder if you could take them to her?" If the person said yes, she was told where to take the notes (roughly 130 feet away).

Any reasonably good experiment like this one is going to have a control group. These were people who were approached in the exact same way, but with the one change being that they were walking down a hallway instead of exiting a bathroom. Would you expect there to be much of a difference between these two groups? I suspect you know what is coming:[7]

	Agreed to deliver notes
Bathroom condition	80%
Control condition	45%

Here is another stunning difference, despite such a small change in the situation. What is going on this time?

We could again appeal to guilt. But that does not seem very plausible for a single-sex bathroom in a public building. Instead, a much more fitting emotion would be embarrassment. This emotion tends to arise when there is a clash between the public image that we want to project, and what happens when other people see us do something which undermines that image.[8] Most of us know what it is like to feel embarrassed when we trip and fall flat on our face in public. That goes against an image of being poised and coordinated. On the other hand, what about tripping and falling at your apartment when you are alone? Would you be embarrassed by that? Annoyed, perhaps, or angry, but I doubt embarrassed. Similarly when we discover that we have forgotten to button a certain button or zip a certain zipper. We are embarrassed when other people discover this for us, because we are coming across as, among other things, absent-minded. We are not embarrassed, though, when we discover it on our own before we have even left the house for the day.

So too does embarrassment arise in the situation that interested Cann and Blackwelder—going to the bathroom within earshot of others. What they found is that just as guilt can increase helping, so too can feelings of embarrassment. Other psychology studies have found the same thing, thus confirming that there is a connection here.[9]

But why? If anything, shouldn't feeling embarrassed make us more likely to *shrink* from other people and *avoid* helping them? Wouldn't I want to escape the situation as quickly as I can?

As with guilt, there is no one widely accepted explanation of the link between embarrassment and helping, but the *embarrassment-relief model* is a leading contender. The idea is that when we are embarrassed, we want to eliminate those feelings. Now, that may not necessarily mean helping someone. It could mean flight (running away with our hands over our face), evasion (deflecting the conversation quickly to another topic), offering excuses (this medicine makes me have uncontrollable gas), or humor (my strap always breaks at the worst time!). However, if the circumstances are right, it could also mean helping someone. In that case, I would *not* be shrinking away or escaping the situation. I would be proactively helping, but only so as to rid myself of my feelings of embarrassment. As with guilt, helping another person in need can sometimes be a great way to make ourselves feel better.[10]

Since this sounds very similar to what we already said about how guilt can increase helping, I don't want to spend much time on the embarrassment-relief model here. There is another side of the research on embarrassment, though, which has found some truly disturbing results. Here the focus hasn't been on embarrassment *relief*, but on embarrassment *avoidance*. In other words, the difference has to do with trying to make sure that one doesn't feel embarrassment in the first place, rather than with trying to do something to be free of the embarrassment one is already experiencing.

Indeed, avoiding embarrassment is at the heart of what became one of the most famous experiments in the history of psychology. In 1969 the Columbia psychologists Bibb Latané and Judith Rodin conducted their "Lady in Distress" study. Try to imagine what it must have been like if you were one of the volunteers. Suppose you thought you had signed up to be part of a market research survey, and on the appointed day you meet a female representative in a small room. While you fill out the forms, she goes to the next office. Four minutes later:

> . . . if [you] were listening carefully, [you] heard her climb up on a chair to get a book from the top shelf. Even if [you] were not listening carefully, [you] heard a loud crash and a woman's scream as the chair fell over. "Oh, my God, my foot . . ." cried the representative. "I . . . I . . . can't move . . . it. Oh, my ankle. I . . . can't . . . can't . . . get . . . this thing off . . . me." She moaned and cried for about a minute longer, getting gradually more subdued and controlled.[11]

Would you do anything to help, even if it meant just calling out loud to the representative to see if she was all right?

Latané and Rodin approached this question by dividing up the participants from the start into different groups. In one group, each participant was alone while filling out the survey forms. In another group, each participant was paired with another participant in the same room who was a complete stranger. A third group had each participant put in a room with a stranger, but this time the other person was actually an actor secretly instructed by Latané and Rodin to ignore the crash.

So now try to envision what you would do in each of these situations. It wouldn't make a difference, right—you would do *something* to help in *all* of them, wouldn't you? You might think so, but the answer seems to be—it depends. For here were the percentages of participants who helped:[12]

Alone	70%
Participant plus stranger	40%
Participant plus confederate	7%

Only 7% helped in the third group, even though a woman was clearly in a great deal of pain and needed assistance. So if you are like most people, you would have completely ignored her cries.

We will connect these results to embarrassment in a moment. But it is worth noting that this wasn't the only time such surprising results were found:[13]

Emergencies involving the participants. Compared to being alone, participants in groups are less likely to help when a stream of smoke is coming into the room where they are seated.[14]

Emergencies involving a victim in danger. Compared to being alone, participants in groups are less likely to help when hearing a man have an epileptic seizure,[15] a maintenance worker fall off a ladder in another room,[16] and a man cry out in pain from what seems to be a serious electric shock.[17]

Emergencies involving third-party criminal or immoral behavior. Compared to being alone, participants in groups are less likely to help when watching a thief steal cash from a receptionist's envelope,[18] observing young men steal a case of beer from a discount store,[19] and hearing a bully beat up a child.[20]

Nonemergency opportunities to help. Compared to being alone, participants in groups are less likely to help with knocked over computer disks,[21] accidentally dropped coins in an elevator,[22] and evaluating written work.[23]

Nor is this just a feature of an artificial laboratory environment. Remember the story from the preface about the death of Walter Vance? He was shopping at Target on Black Friday, had a heart attack, and was lying on the ground for a long period of time before anyone offered assistance. By then it was too late. This is a true story involving the same thought processes whereby people, in a group of strangers, did not do anything to help even when someone's life was at stake.

Why? What could possibly explain such atrocious behavior? I think the most plausible answer is still the one developed by Latané himself in 1968 along with his collaborator, John Darley, who at the time was teaching at NYU. They mention three important ideas: diffusion of responsibility, social influence, and audience inhibition.[24] That's more than we need to go into here, but I highly recommend their book, *The Unresponsive Bystander: Why Doesn't He Help?* if you want to pursue this fascinating research in more detail.

Based on their research, it seems likely that *audience inhibition* has the most to do with avoiding embarrassment. The idea is that the more people I think are watching, the more backlash there might be if I attempt to help someone only to find out that—whoops!—no help is really needed.[25] That would be an embarrassing situation, and one we definitely want to avoid getting ourselves into. This idea of audience inhibition is represented in figure 3.2.

Figure 3.2 Audience Inhibition and Helping

That is why there is also more helping in groups of friends than groups of strangers. Normally people are more at ease in front of their friends; messing up in front of them is safer in many ways than it is in the presence of strangers.

So contrary to what you might have predicted about your own behavior, we should come to recognize that if we were put in a room with a stranger, and the stranger did not respond to cries of—"Oh, my ankle. I . . . can't . . . can't . . . get . . . this thing off . . . me"—coming from the next room, it is likely that we would not help either. Maybe the stranger knows something I don't about what is going on with those cries. Maybe I am just imagining the sounds or not hearing things clearly. In any event, I really want to avoid making a fool of myself in the stranger's eyes.

A Brighter Side to Helping

At this point I have probably made you feel somewhat depressed. In these studies many people did not help with easy tasks like picking up candy or carrying papers. Sometimes they did not do really important things either, like checking on someone who just had a terrible accident. In addition, there seems to be something disturbing about this idea of helping to make your guilt or embarrassment go away. Is this really the best we can do?

Fortunately we can do much, much better. And we already have the means to do so embedded within our characters. In other words, most of us have a unique capacity to help others in powerful ways, and for genuinely caring reasons. What could such a tremendous capacity be?

It is empathy.

Imagine you are in college. One of your professors interrupts the class to announce some recent news about a fellow student named Katie Banks. The professor is about to play a radio interview, but before he turns the player on, he gives everyone these instructions:

> Try to *focus on the technical aspects*. Try to assess the effectiveness of the techniques and devices used to make the broadcast have an impact on the listener.[26]

Then you hear the interview with Katie. Her story is awful. Katie's parents and a sister have been killed in an automobile crash. There is no life insurance. Katie has a younger brother and sister, who she now has to support on her own. She needs help to finish her last year of college. Otherwise she will have to give her siblings up for adoption.

This is a bad situation. A really bad situation.

Fortunately, your professor is trying to help Katie out. He gives you an envelope with a letter from Katie. In the letter Katie talks about the ways she could use some help, such as "sitting with her younger brother and sister while she attended her night classes, fixing things around the house, providing transportation, making telephone calls, or stuffing envelopes for a fund-raising project."[27]

What would you do? I have no way of knowing. But the majority of students in a class where this was actually done decided not to volunteer any of their time:[28]

	Percent volunteered	Mean number of hours volunteered
Control group	37%	0.60

Keep in mind that this was not a complete stranger or someone living in another country. This was a real student, they were told, who lived right there on campus.

I thought we were supposed to get some encouraging news. Isn't this more of the same depressing stuff? It is. Now comes the uplifting part. These students were the control group. For a different group of students, the professor changed just two sentences in the instructions. Instead of focusing on the technical aspects, these students were told:

> Try to *imagine how Katie Banks feels about* what has happened and how it has affected her life. Try to feel the full impact of what she has been through and how she feels as a result.[29]

Could a two-sentence change make a real difference in behavior? It sure did:[30]

	Percent volunteered	Mean number of hours volunteered
Empathy condition	76%	1.33

This, to me, is striking. By taking this different perspective and trying to feel what Katie Banks was going through, these students were far more inclined to help, and to invest themselves in helping.

Clearly these instructions tapped into something psychologically powerful in the students. That would be empathy. Empathy is a complex emotion, and both philosophers and psychologists have been trying to understand it for a long time. At least in cases like this one involving Katie Banks, empathy seems to have two main components. First, I try to imagine what Katie is going through, what it would be like to be in her shoes. This is the *perspective-taking* component. Second, I actually feel some of what she is going through. This is the *empathetic feeling* component. Together, by trying to see things from her perspective and feel something like what she is experiencing, I can be inspired to help.

Figure 3.3 illustrates some of the main steps in this process. It seems that a number of the students went through these steps, whether they realized it completely or not.

The data reported above on volunteering to help Katie Banks is from real students at the University of Kansas. Here is a secret that those students did not know. There was no Katie Banks. She is a fictional creation of the psychologist C. Daniel Batson.

Batson is probably my favorite psychologist working today. For much of his career at the University of Kansas, he has tried to understand empathy and how it can affect human behavior for good and bad. In the process Batson has designed experiments that, to my mind, are wonderful models for how to test our character.[31]

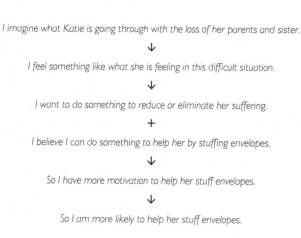

I imagine what Katie is going through with the loss of her parents and sister.

↓

I feel something like what she is feeling in this difficult situation.

↓

I want to do something to reduce or eliminate her suffering.

+

I believe I can do something to help her by stuffing envelopes.

↓

So I have more motivation to help her stuff envelopes.

↓

So I am more likely to help her stuff envelopes.

Figure 3.3 Empathy and Helping Katie Banks

Over the course of thirty years of research, Batson has found the same pattern repeated again and again in at least fifty different experiments. If people are made to feel empathy, they are more likely to help. Not just a little bit, and not just doing easy tasks. They are also more likely to help with very inconvenient tasks, in a time-consuming way. Now, that is some good news.

There is even more. Batson is known throughout the field of psychology, not just for finding a robust relationship between empathy and helping—other psychologists have done the same thing—but for his explanation of *why* the two are linked. At this point, you might be thinking—oh no, here comes another story about how helping makes us feel better and relieves our distress. Before it was helping that relieved guilt and embarrassment. Now, with empathy, it would be helping to relieve the distress we experience when we appreciate someone's suffering. This, in fact, is what some psychologists thought was the correct story to tell. Not Batson.

Instead he has supported what he calls the *empathy-altruism hypothesis*.[32] The key contrast here is between egoism (focused on benefiting yourself) and altruism (focused on benefiting other people). Imagine you are Katie Banks for a moment. Here is a student named Frank from your university who has come to help watch your siblings so you can go to your night classes (Frank will also show up in later chapters to help illustrate some of the other studies).

Frank proves to be extremely helpful, always showing up on time and doing a great job with the kids. One day, out of curiosity, you ask Frank why he volunteered to help. He tells you about that day in class when his professor played your interview and told everyone to really imagine what life is like for you and to feel the impact of what you have been through. Then Frank says one of the following:

So at that moment I decided to sign up so I could look good in front of my classmates.

So at that moment I decided to sign up so I would be able to feel better about myself.

So at that moment I decided to sign up so I would not beat myself up with guilt the next day.

So at that moment I decided to sign up because it is fun to help other people.

So at that moment I decided to sign up as my resume is looking a bit thin and I need a volunteer activity.

These sound like very different answers, but they all share one thing in common—they are all self-serving (egoistic). In every one of them, Frank is ultimately concerned about one person, namely Frank. Katie factors into this equation solely as a means to get Frank what he wants.

Now, you might expect that most people would answer in one of these ways, at least if they were being honest. What Batson found, over and over again, is that the experimental results were telling him a fundamentally different story. It is a story about altruism, not egoism. It is a story where, if Frank is answering truthfully and knowledgably, he would say something like:

So at that moment I decided to sign up so that I could help you out.

So at that moment I decided to sign up because I was concerned about you.

Period. Not to get some reward for himself or to avoid some punishment. Just to help out Katie, to try to relieve her suffering, to try to make her life better. Frank's ultimate focus here is on Katie, not on himself. This, in a nutshell, is Batson's empathy-*altruism* hypothesis.

If Batson's hypothesis is correct—and he has produced many studies in support of it and convinced many philosophers and psychologists alike that it is—then he would have succeeded in refuting one of the most famous ideas in human history. This idea, which goes by the name "psychological egoism," says that, at the end of the day, we are always motivated by our own self-interest in some form or other, even when we are helping someone in need.

Batson agrees that this idea is true in *many* cases. No doubt we often are led by self-interest to do all kinds of things, including helping. Just think, for example, of the various reasons why people make donations to charity, such as to get a tax deduction, and how they are often self-serving.

The remarkable story emerging from Batson's research is that we are not *always* like this. Most of us have some capacity to feel empathy, which can be strengthened over time. When we see the suffering of other people, we can be led to help them for their sake and not for our own. This is very encouraging news indeed.

What Does All This Mean for Our Character?

So outside a bathroom is a good place to find volunteers to help you do something. And if I injure myself, I had better hope that only one person is around to see it, rather than a group of strangers. Fascinating bits of trivia, you might say, but what does any of this have to do with character?

Quite a bit, actually. For experiments like the ones mentioned in this chapter teach us how good or bad we tend to be when it comes to helping others. In particular, we can offer a preliminary answer to these important questions:

Do most people, including our friends, leaders, and coworkers, have the virtue of compassion?

Or do most people have the vices of selfishness, indifference, and apathy?

First, though, we need to stop thinking like psychologists for a moment and start thinking like philosophers.

Let's begin with compassion, one of the most universally celebrated virtues there has ever been. Try to think of an example of an extremely compassionate person you have read about somewhere or even know personally in your life. Or consider the examples from the previous chapter of Leopold Socha and Paul Farmer. How does the behavior we observed in the studies above compare to their actions?

Not well, I think. For as we saw in the studies of guilt and embarrassment, the control group participants often do nothing. Similar results show up all over the place in psychology, such as in studies on helping and good moods, bad moods, anticipated blame, and even anticipated empathy.[33]

Wait, you might object. As you said in chapter 1, a compassionate person can't be expected to help *every time* someone is in need. Then she would be utterly exhausted in a few days and never get anywhere with her own life. So isn't this argument just too extreme?

I do not think so. True, we should not hold people to such an unreasonable standard for being compassionate. At the same time, a compassionate person will often attempt to help people with small problems that can be addressed quickly and with minimal time and effort.[34] So this is *not* saying a compassionate person has to donate all of his life savings to famine relief or spend all of his time with the poor. It is only saying that we should expect the life of a compassionate person to show a pattern of helping to address at least obvious and relatively minor needs.[35]

Yet even when it was as simple as spending a few seconds carrying papers or telling someone about a torn shopping bag, many control participants did nothing. As representatives of the population at large, they illustrate that many of us do not seem to have this virtue either.

But, you might say, these are such minor failures involving papers and candy. What really matters to the compassionate person is whether someone is *really* suffering, injured, or dying, not whether someone has dropped candy. The same people who ignored the candy might also go out of their way to help a friend battling a terrible ordeal.

I am not convinced. Go back to the example you came up with on your own of a compassionate person. What would she do when she sees a big stack of papers fall to the ground? Just ignore them? That is not what I would expect of my moral heroes.

Leave that aside. The more important point is to remember that there are plenty of studies where a lot more *is* at stake. The example I used was the so-called "bystander effect." This had to do with how being in a group of nonresponders can make it much less likely that someone will help in emergency situations.

Suppose, though, that you are *still* not convinced by these results about our general lack of compassion. Then here is an even more convincing reason. The pattern of *motivation* we see from these studies is not flattering, to say the least. After all, a compassionate person's motivation to help will not fluctuate wildly based on her guilt or embarrassment. Think again of your favorite example, such as Paul Farmer or Mother Teresa. Would Mother Teresa help the poor when embarrassed, but not otherwise? Or when feeling guilty, but not otherwise? Of course not.

But as we have seen:

> 55% of guilty versus 15% of control participants helped in Regan's study involving the broken camera and the torn bag.

> 70% of people alone versus 7% of people with a stranger helped in Latané and Rodin's study where a woman screamed as she fell off a chair in the next room.

As additional examples not mentioned already:

> 61% of people in a good mood versus 25% of control participants helped in a study by Robert Baron that which used the smell of cookies and cinnamon rolls in a shopping mall to induce the good mood.[36]

> 71% of people in a bad mood versus 33% of controls helped in a study by Frank Weyant involving volunteering for the American Cancer Society.[37]

Plus, when they do help, the motives look suspect. As we have seen, according to leading models of how guilt and embarrassment can boost helping, the motivation to help is self-centered. It involves eliminating our guilt and overcoming our embarrassment.[38] The same self-centeredness is present when helping to maintain our good mood, or to eradicate our bad mood.[39]

A compassionate person, on the other hand, is reliably altruistic in action *and* in motivation. The focus is squarely on improving another person's situation. The helper may benefit in the process. The helper may suffer in the process. But that is not the main focus. When we are altruistically motivated, we are not focused on ourselves.

Thus, by way of summary, it seems that most people will often not help with such apparently simple tasks as picking up dropped computer punch cards[40] or making change for a dollar.[41] When they do help, they might do so as a result of feeling guilty or embarrassed, thereby acting on motives that are not altruistic but self-interested. None of this is what we expect from a compassionate person. So I conclude:

Most people today do not have the virtue of compassion.

To be fair, I only claim that "most" people do not have the virtue of compassion. I do not say "all" people. In other words, the data is compatible with the existence of a *few* people who might have this virtue to some degree. For instance, 16% of the shoppers in the control group of Regan's study called attention to the torn bag leaking candy.[42]

Of course, since just one morally admirable action does not make someone virtuous, what we really need are studies that follow the same people around in many different moral situations in their lives and see what they end up doing. Unfortunately such "longitudinal studies" are almost nonexistent in psychology. They are very expensive, and take a lot of time. They also raise the challenge of how to monitor a person's ordinary life in an ethically respectful way, without at the same time having that person act differently knowing that he is being observed.

So there might be a fortunate few who have a virtuous character in this area of their lives. Most of us, on the other hand, have a long way to go to become compassionate.

If that is right, does it mean that most of us are therefore selfish, indifferent, and apathetic people? In other words, deep down are we just like Ebenezer Scrooge?

If it weren't for the previous section of this chapter, I might be tempted to say yes. But the empathy research changes things significantly. Here we see reliable patterns of helping in many situations. Here we see a willingness to help address even significant and costly needs. And, most important of all, here we see evidence for helping that is robustly selfless. None of that is what I would expect to find in a Scrooge.

Hence I conclude much more quickly this time that:

Most people today do not have the vices of selfishness, indifference, and apathy.

Just because we may not be compassionate people, does not mean that we are Scrooges either.

So we are left with a deep tension, if not the appearance of an outright contradiction. On the one hand, we have powerful capacities for doing good in the world, and for praiseworthy motives. On the other hand, we have powerful capacities for failing to do good in the world, and for suspect motives. Both of these aspects of our character are present in our hearts and they are both robust. We should not downplay them or ignore them.

For now I will just let them be. Let's see instead whether the same tension is revealed when we put other areas of our character to the test.

Notes

1. Regan et al. 1972.
2. Regan et al. 1972: 44.
3. This is not intended to be a strict definition of guilt, but rather a rough characterization of the concept. For instance, an additional element of guilt is that we fail to live up to our standards in a way for which we can be held personally responsible and accountable, at least in our own mind.
4. To read about more of them, see Miller 2013: chapter 2.
5. See, e.g., Donnerstein et al. 1975; Cunningham et al. 1980; and Lindsey 2005.
6. To be fair, the study by Regan does not point *only* in the direction of the guilt-relief model. Other interpretations of the results could be given. Here

I only want to suggest that the results of this study are what you would expect to find according to this model, and furthermore the guilt-relief model is gaining increasing support among psychologists.

Note that I haven't said much in *evaluating* this part of our psychology. That will come at the end of the chapter. But let me grant here that in some ways it would be a good thing if many people were motivated by guilt-relief, since that would increase the likelihood they will help others in need. Even if that's true, though, my concern is about whether it is a *virtuous* way of being motivated. More on that soon enough.

7. Cann and Blackwelder 1984: 224.
8. As with guilt, this is not intended to be a strict definition but a rough characterization of embarrassment.
9. For additional studies of embarrassment and helping, see Foss and Crenshaw 1978; Edelmann et al. 1984; and Gonzales et al. 1990.
10. See, e.g., Apsler 1975; Cann and Blackwelder 1984; and R. Miller 1996: 4.
11. Latané and Darley 1970: 58. For the original study, see Latané and Rodin 1969.
12. See Latané and Rodin 1969: 193–195 and Latané and Darley 1970: 60–63.
13. The text that follows is adapted from Miller 2013: chapter 6. The categories used follow Latané and Nida 1981. For useful reviews of this large literature, see Latané and Nida 1981 and Latané et al. 1981.
14. Latané and Darley 1968. For additional studies, see Ross and Braband 1973 and Latané and Nida 1981: 311.
15. Darley and Latané 1968 and Latané and Darley 1970: chapter 11.
16. Clark and Word 1972.
17. Clark and Word 1974. For additional studies, see Gottlieb and Carver 1980; Latané and Nida 1981: 311; and Tice and Baumeister 1985.
18. Latané and Darley 1970: chapter 8.
19. Latané and Darley 1970: chapter 8.
20. Latané and Darley 1970: 82. For additional studies, see Schwartz and Gottlieb 1980; Latané and Nida 1981: 311; and Chekroun and Brauer 2002.
21. Karakashian et al. 2006.
22. Latané and Dabbs 1977.

23. Petty et al. 1977b. For additional studies, see Petty et al. 1977a, Latané et al. 1979, Latané and Nida 1981: 311, 313, and Chekroun and Brauer 2002: 855.

24. For overviews, see Latané and Darley 1968, 1970; Schwartz and Gottlieb 1980; Latané and Nida 1981; Latané et al. 1981; and Cacioppo et al. 1986.

25. As Latané and Darley explained, "The bystander to an emergency is offered the chance to step up on stage, a chance that should be every actor's dream. But in this case, it is every actor's nightmare. He hasn't rehearsed the part very well and he must play it when the curtain is already up. The greater the number of other people present, the more possibility there is of losing face" (1970: 40). For additional discussion, see Miller and McFarland 1991; Prentice and Miller 1996; and Karakashian et al. 2006.

26. Batson et al. 1989: 929, emphasis theirs.

27. Batson et al. 1989: 930.

28. Batson et al. 1989: 931.

29. Batson et al. 1989: 929.

30. Batson et al. 1989: 929.

31. For a summary of his experiments and findings, see Batson 2011.

32. For extensive discussion of this hypothesis and the support he has found for it, see Batson 2011.

33. For an overview of this research, see Miller 2013.

34. As philosophers like to say, "Other things being equal." Obviously if you have broken your leg or are about to pass out, this would not apply.

35. If you are looking for some guidance in the form of a principle or checklist to tell how much you need to donate to charity or help others in order to count as compassionate, I'm afraid I don't have any such specific guidance to offer in this book. In fact, I'm not even sure we can come up with such a checklist in the first place.

36. Baron 1997. We will come back to this study in more detail in chapter 7.

37. Weyant 1978. The explanation for this surprising result is often taken to be that the helping was seen as a means of reducing the bad mood.

38. I noted that there are other competing models in the psychology literature that were not considered in this chapter. But as far as I am aware, none of these models involves altruistic or selfless motivation either. See Miller 2013 for the details.

39. See Miller 2013.

40. Konečni 1972.

41. Baron 1997.

42. Also, the claim in the text needs to be qualified to apply just to people in North America and Europe, since that is where the vast majority of the studies have been conducted. The results might be similar everywhere around the world, but that needs to be shown empirically first.

4 | HARMING

One day Frank came upon an ad for a new study that sounded really interesting. He could help some researchers at his local university learn more about how people perform under pressure. That could be really valuable information, he thought. Besides, he could make some easy money. So he eagerly signed up.

Today is the big day of the study. He meets one of the psychologists, who takes him to a room where they can talk. Frank learns that his job is to give a test to someone in the next room, while the psychologist watches over his shoulder. Here's the twist. Frank is told that the person in the other room is unemployed and must pass this test in order to get a job. Now the stakes are raised. This is a really important test, and someone's well-being hangs in the balance. I had better do a good job administering the test, Frank thinks to himself.

The test has thirty-two questions. He is instructed that, every time the job seeker gives a few wrong answers, Frank needs to make a negative and stressful remark. It starts off being a mild one ("Up to now, your test score is insufficient"). But when he hears this, the job seeker is clearly annoyed and lets Frank know it. Frank can also see a computer readout of the person's stress level after the remark. It has definitely gone up.

To be clear, this was never part of the deal when this unemployed man was applying for the job. He was never told that he would be getting stressful feedback during the test. He has been deceived, and Frank knows it.

This is starting to get bad, but Frank keeps going with the next question. After a while, it is time for another stress remark, and then later another one. The remarks get harsher and harsher:

> If you continue like this, you will certainly fail the test.
>
> According to the test, you are more suited for lower functions.

Things get worse for the poor job seeker. His stress level is rising, and clearly the more stress he is feeling, the worse he is doing on the test. If this continues, he will fail and lose his only chance at the job.

By the tenth stress remark, things are getting out of hand. The job seeker has "demanded that [Frank] stop making the remarks." He "accuse[s] the experimenter of having given him false information about the nature of the experiment and withdr[aws] his consent . . . After stress remarks 14 and 15, his response [is] one of despair."[1]

What is going on with Frank as things get dramatically worse for the job seeker? At times he shows some signs of conflict about what he is doing. He even asks the psychologist in the room with him whether he should continue. The psychologist, though, is very clear and matter-of-fact—"Please continue," he might say, or, "You have no other choice, you must go on." And so Frank does.

By stress remark 13, the applicant has failed the test. At this point, there isn't much need for Frank to continue to tell him about how badly he is doing. That doesn't stop Frank. He keeps going with the questions and the stress remarks, all the way to question 32 and, with it, the fifteenth and final stress remark. Then he stops.

Naturally, the job seeker is devastated. He has lost his chance at getting a job he desperately needs. Not only that, but he has been put through a terrible ordeal. He has been deceived, verbally abused, and reduced to a state of despair.

Frank knows all this. He is not happy about it either—watching the person suffer does not give him any sort of perverse pleasure. Indeed, he "intensely disliked making the stress remarks."[2] At the same time, he does not blame himself for what has happened. He is not primarily responsible, he thinks—any blame rests squarely with the psychologist in charge. After all, he is just "acting as the agent of the experimenter."[3] Not surprisingly, then, Frank is "extremely aloof towards the applicant."[4]

Now, here is the really scary part. Frank is not an unusual guy. He is not one of the "rotten apples." We are all like Frank. Most of us would do the exact same thing in this situation.

Aggression and Our Lack of Virtue

We know this because a study with this very setup was published in 1986 by the psychologists Wim Meeus and Quinten Raaijmakers. While Frank is our imaginary friend who takes part in a lot of the studies described in this book, there were many participants who actually went through the circumstances described above, including choosing to give every single stress remark. Indeed, given 15 possible remarks, the median used by participants was 14.81. It turned out that 91.7% of participants made all 15 remarks! So that means they used remarks 14 and 15, *even when they knew it was too late and the job seeker had failed the test.*[5]

The desire to obey what the psychologist said was so strong that most participants were, in effect, willing to deceive and verbally abuse someone in desperate need of work. Of course, these job seekers were really actors working for Meeus and Raaijmakers. But the participants did not know that.

This is just one in a long line of studies throughout the history of psychology looking at how people will behave aggressively when told to do so by an authority figure.[6] The most famous studies of all were conducted by the Yale researcher Stanley Milgram in the 1960s, and I will come back to them later in this chapter. In general, what this research has found are a number of very disturbing tendencies:

> Most people are willing to do terrible things under pressure from authority figures, even when they can easily opt out without any punishment.

> These same people tend to be upset about what they are doing, but not enough to stop them from doing it.

> If they had been asked beforehand about how they would act, they would never accept the idea that they would do these terrible things. Plus they would predict that most people in general wouldn't do them either.

Even worse, these discoveries mirror what has happened many times in real life.

The obvious example is the Holocaust. In fact, many of these studies of aggression done in the 1960s and 1970s were directly inspired by the question of how seemingly "ordinary" German citizens could become obedient executioners of the Jews and other minorities. More recent, and on a much smaller scale, are the human rights abuses that took place at the Abu Ghraib prison in Iraq. They have also been extensively discussed by psychologists.[7]

None of this paints a very flattering picture of our character. In the last chapter, we looked at helping other people, and the relevant virtue was compassion. Now we are looking at harming other people. The relevant virtue, then, would be a good character trait that keeps us from harming others when it is not justified.

The last bit is very important. Sometimes harming *can be* justified—say, when you are assaulted by a mugger, or when you shoot a terrorist in the leg to prevent him from detonating a bomb. Whatever this relevant virtue is, it wouldn't stop you from doing *those* actions, but it would work against unjustified harming.

Since we always have to remember that motivation matters too, this same virtue would restrain unjustified harming *for the right reasons*. If your child has an opportunity to beat up the awkward new kid at school, but chooses not to, that is a very good thing. If your child only held back out of fear of being expelled, that is not an example of a good reason. Not harming someone because you care about her or because it would hurt her or because it would violate her dignity or rights—these are examples of morally good reasons. Not harming someone only because you worry about being punished by the teachers or your boss or the police—these are not morally good reasons.

What is this virtue called? Unfortunately, the English language does not have a simple or familiar word for it. "Compassion" is often used for helping people. "Nonmalevolence" is what many philosophers would call it, but that is an unfamiliar word these days. When was the last time you heard someone use it? How about we just call it the virtue of "proper restraint."

Research like the study by Meeus and Raaijmakers shows, to my mind, that most of us do not have this virtue. Someone like Frank said terrible things to the unemployed person. Afterward he deflected responsibility for his actions onto the experimenter, even though he had the freedom to leave the study at any time. As I noted, examples of these forms of obedience to authority abound in many experiments and in real life.

Wait, aren't these pretty unique cases? Perhaps most of us would obey when authority figures tell us to harm others. But how often does that really happen in ordinary life? In fact, aren't we pretty good people when it comes to not harming others most of the time? Haven't I been too hasty jumping to the conclusion that we lack the virtue of proper restraint?

No, I do not think I have. And neither, I would venture to say, does Bryan Stow. Bryan, you might remember, was the forty-two-year-old paramedic leaving the first game of the baseball season at Dodger Stadium in March 2011. In the parking lot he was attacked by two Dodgers fans, Louie Sanchez and Marvin Norwood. They beat Bryan terribly, knocking out one of his eyes and disabling his tongue. Barely alive in a coma, he was left paralyzed with serious brain damage. What was his offense? Apparently it was simply because he was a fan of the rival San Francisco Giants.[8]

Now, of course I am not saying that we have all hurt other people as violently as Bryan's attackers hurt him. Most of us have never done anything *that* severe. Nor am I saying that most of us are even inclined or tempted to act that aggressively. It is an extreme case, I admit.

What I *am* saying is that we are disposed *to some significant degree* to act aggressively in many situations. Typically we do not end up acting aggressively, since we could go to jail, get fired from our job, lose custody of our children, or get beaten up in return. But the idea remains that, deep down in our hearts, the aggressive impulses are lurking, whether people are aware of them or not.

How do I know this? Aggression has not just been studied in the context of obeying people in authority. There are dozens of other studies that have further tested our characters to see what is going on when it comes to hurting other people. Let me mention just one. Leonard Berkowitz is currently a retired psychologist at the

University of Wisconsin–Madison. During his career, he became one of the leading researchers on aggression, and in a classic study he had each participant get paired up with a stranger (really an actor working for Berkowitz). Separately they had to come up with ideas to help improve the record sales and image of a singer. Then they were hooked up to shock machines in different rooms.

First the actor was told to evaluate the quality of the participant's ideas and shock the participant accordingly (so bad ideas = more shocks). This was rigged so that the participant would just get one shock (hence, a very mild result). Then it was the participant's turn to evaluate the actor's work and shock accordingly.[9]

As you might guess, there was a bit of retaliation by the participant to being shocked, but not much:[10]

Average number of shocks in return	2.60
Average duration of shocks (in thousandths of a minute)	17.93

Now Berkowitz made an important change, since this was his control group. For a second group of participants who would be in the more important experimental group, each time one of them took part in the study, the actor gave him or her seven (!) shocks.[11]

What do you think the participant would do when it was time to evaluate the confederate's work? Surprise, surprise, participants were pretty upset:[12]

Average number of shocks in return	6.07
Average duration of shocks (in thousandths of a minute)	46.93

They made sure that the other person would get some payback for their earlier shocks. These were way more shocks than what the actor deserved, and they were longer ones too.

This is not an isolated result, either. Psychologists have become very good at triggering aggressive behavior in the lab. Sometimes even direct insults have been used.[13] When provoked in different ways, participants have been more than willing to give intense blasts of noise[14] or provide bad evaluations of an experimenter[15] or of a job candidate.[16] In other cases, subtle environmental factors made harming go way up. These included the temperature of the room, a movie depicting a violent act, slides of weapons, the background noise level, violent video games, unpleasant odors, crowded spaces, ions in the atmosphere, and even ozone levels.[17]

Now think of your favorite virtuous person. When I imagine Jesus or Mother Teresa or Paul Farmer, I do not see how they could act like many people in these studies did. Surely a virtuous person would have the restraint needed to *not* verbally abuse an unemployed man and reduce him to utter dismay, even when pressured by a psychologist. Surely that same person would not give painful electric shocks over and over again to a stranger just because the stranger had shocked her aggressively. Surely odors, background noises, hot temperatures, and even direct insults would not call forth harmful responses like the ones we see repeatedly in the studies. A virtuous person would show more restraint.

I could keep going on and on about this, but I won't. I think we can all identify with these aggressive tendencies, both in ourselves and in people we know. We have all lashed out verbally in anger, yelled at a loved one in frustration, bad-mouthed a colleague behind his back, made fun of someone's unusual appearance or clothes, and wanted in our heart of hearts to hurt an enemy, a rival, or a competitor. On a broader level, what do we read in the newspapers or see on the news every day? The latest school shooting, armed robbery, sexual assault, military invasion . . . and so on down the list.

The virtue of proper restraint is rare at best. I don't think we need much convincing of that. The only debate here, it seems to me, is about whether most of us have the opposing vice of cruelty. To find the answer, we need to go back in time to arguably the most famous experiment ever conducted in psychology.

Milgram Then and Now

If you know anything about the Milgram studies, they seem like a bizarre example to use to illustrate a *lack* of cruelty. Indeed, they are perhaps the best illustration in psychology of how cruel we are capable of being. After all, now we are talking about *actually killing an innocent person.*

I need to ask for your patience. What I have in mind should become clear soon enough. For now, let's first present the basic Milgram setup.[18] Here is our friend Frank. Imagine that he is supposed to serve as a teacher in charge of administering a test to a learner (who, of course, is actually an actor, but Frank doesn't know that). In the most famous version of the study, the learner is in another room, and Frank can hear him loud and clear. (Does this sound familiar? It should. Meeus and Raaijmakers's stress remark study was based directly on Milgram's work.)

For every wrong answer by the learner, Frank is supposed to use a shock generator to deliver an electric shock of increasingly greater strength, starting at 15 volts (labeled a "slight shock") and going to 450 volts ("XXX"). Beforehand Frank himself experienced what 45 volts feels like, so he knows a bit about what the learner will go through and is convinced that this is serious business. But what Frank does not know is that the situation is rigged so that the learner will end up getting about 75% of the answers wrong. This guarantees that Frank is faced with the difficult decision of whether to continue the process of delivering more and more painful shocks as time goes on.

The third person involved in this bizarre situation is the "experimenter." He is in the room with Frank, looking rather official wearing a technician's coat. If Frank resists or complains in some way, this experimenter responds by saying, "Please continue." This is the first of four prods used if Frank continues to object; the last one is "You have no other choice, you *must* go on."[19] If Frank puts up a fight, the experiment is over, unless Frank continues and eventually turns the dial all the way up to the 450-volt level.

Stunningly, that's the way the experiment usually ended. For Milgram found that 65% of people like Frank were willing to give what was (to their eyes) the deadly 450-volt, XXX shock; 80% went to the 270-volt level.[20] Even this is bad enough, since at that point the learner would be screaming in agony, demanding to be freed from the test: "Let me out of here. Do you hear? Let me out of here." *Plus,* Frank already knows of the learner's heart condition. Even at 150 volts the learner started saying things like "That's all. Get me out of here. I told you I had heart trouble. My heart's starting to bother me now."[21]

How can this situation be so effective in taking ordinary people and, over the course of just a few minutes, transforming them into willing killers? Well, here are a few things that did *not* make a difference: the type of building (i.e., Yale University's psychology lab or an ordinary office building),[22] the sex of the participants,[23] or the country where the study was being done.[24] Nor, it turns out, the fact that this research was from the 1960s. For there is good reason to think that similar results would hold today as well.[25] Indeed, one of the teams we funded through the Character Project tested this very thing.

For a long time, it has been difficult to replicate the Milgram studies. Because of the potential for lasting psychological trauma, ethics committees have banned such research for decades (for good reason). But the psychologist David Gallardo-Pujol and his team at the University of Barcelona came up with a clever alternative. Rather than having a real human being "receive" electric shocks, Gallardo-Pujol created computer-generated avatars in a virtual reality cave who would serve as the learners instead. Figure 4.1 shows how he set up the situation.

So now when Frank comes into the lab, he uses a real shock generator and there is a human experimenter standing next to his seat (although interestingly Gallardo-Pujol did not have the experimenter give any of the verbal prods like "Please continue"). But he

Figure 4.1 The Virtual Reality "Learner" in Gallardo-Pujol's Replication of the Milgram Studies

also sees an avatar and observes it "react" in "pain" to the electric shocks when it gives a wrong answer.

To be clear, there is no doubt in Frank's mind that this is *not* a real human being. At the same time, the technology is quite sophisticated, and it is very uncomfortable watching the avatar cry out in pain. I have seen video recordings of the study. Even though I was in North Carolina watching a recording of a virtual reality simulation in Barcelona, I couldn't help but be very disturbed.

Lo and behold, the participants in this study, who were adult males from Spain, showed the same pattern of shocking to the XXX level as did Milgram's original participants—72% were fully obedient.[26]

I think it is safe to say that thanks to the work of Milgram, Gallardo-Pujol, and many other psychologists, we have good evidence for the following observation:

> Most of us have characters which, when put to the test, lead us to obey people we see as legitimate authority figures. Our desires to obey can become so strong in certain situations that we will intentionally kill an innocent person.

This is worth emphasizing again. I am not talking just about those people Milgram studied fifty years ago. I am talking about the person working in the office across from you, or driving the cab, or teaching your class, or sleeping in your bed. They would most likely inflict terrible pain and potentially even kill someone if they were placed in that kind of situation. You and I would too.

This is deeply puzzling. For we are being asked to go against what we have always believed—that we should never deliver terrible pain to an innocent person.[27] That principle is already hard enough to ignore. In addition, there are severe physical and economic risks with obedience too, including the possibility of being arrested for manslaughter. Then there can be psychological costs, such as anticipated guilt and shame, loss of self-esteem and good mood, and increased anxiety and stress, which should not be underestimated. Wouldn't all these various costs, together with our belief in the clear immorality of what we are doing, be enough to stop us from going all the way to the XXX level? You might think so. For many of us, it turns out that they are not.

A long story is needed to sort all this out. One thing is going to be a central part of that story—displacement of responsibility.[28] The more Frank puts the responsibility for hurting the learner on the experimenter ("I'm just doing what I am told." "He's the one to blame, not me"), the more willing he is to shock. The more Frank takes responsibility himself for hurting the learner, the less willing he is to shock.

The participants said it themselves. Milgram describes one of the people who did stop early this way: "He still feels responsible for administering any shocks beyond the victim's first protests. He is hard on himself and does not allow the structure of authority in which he is functioning to absolve him of any responsibility."[29]

In contrast, another participant (the experimenter refers to him as "Teacher") shocked all the way to XXX. But several times he stopped to talk about personal responsibility:

SUBJECT: I refuse to take the responsibility. He's in there hollering!

EXPERIMENTER: It's absolutely essential that you continue, Teacher.

SUBJECT: (indicating the unused questions): There's too many left here; I mean, Geez, if he gets them wrong, there's too many of them left. I mean who's going to take the responsibility if anything happens to that gentleman?

EXPERIMENTER: I'm responsible for anything that happens to him. Continue, please.

SUBJECT: All right.

[later]

SUBJECT: You accept all responsibility?

EXPERIMENTER: The responsibility is mine. Correct. Please go on. (*Subject returns to his list, starts running through words as rapidly as he can read them, works through to 450 volts.*)[30]

In this case, the subject clearly resisted giving increasingly painful shocks. His words seem to reflect a deep psychological struggle as the study went on. Yet he found the wiggle room he needed, it would appear, by displacing his responsibility for the terrible shocks onto the experimenter with him in the room. Once that was done, he continued along to 450 volts.

Wait, weren't we supposed to be using Milgram's results to illustrate why most people are *not* cruel? If anything, it seems that we have just provided yet more evidence for why that's precisely how we *are* put together.

But not so fast.

Our Lack of Cruelty

Robert Alton Harris was a cruel person. Born in 1953, at the age of thirteen he was sent to juvenile detention for car theft. At twenty-two he killed his brother's roommate and was convicted of manslaughter. Animals were his more frequent victims: "He killed cats and dogs . . . and laughed while torturing them with mop handles, darts and pellet guns. Once he stabbed a prize pig more than 1,000 times."[31] But what eventually earned him the death penalty was the choice he made on July 5, 1978.

Together with his brother Daniel, Robert Harris planned to rob a bank. They commandeered a vehicle in which two boys were eating lunch and drove the car to a secluded location. Robert told the boys to start walking home, but "as the two boys walked away, Harris slowly raised the Luger and shot [one of them] in the back . . . [The boy] yelled: "Oh, God," and slumped to the ground. Harris chased [the other boy] down a hill into a little valley and shot him four times. [The first boy] was still alive when Harris climbed back up the hill . . . Harris walked over to the boy, knelt down, put the Luger to his head and fired."[32]

Now *that*, in my mind, is a cruel person. He helps to illustrate two important features of cruelty which show why we should think that most of us are not, in fact, like this too. The first is a general willingness to do cruel things, especially when one is given the chance to get away with them. Harris definitely demonstrated this willingness.

Of course, a cruel person needn't be cruel all the time, as we already saw in chapter 1. There is a big difference between a clever cruel person and a foolish cruel person. Harris was a clear example of the latter. If the boss is watching or the police officers are sitting at the next table, a clever cruel person with some degree of awareness wouldn't kick a dog or destroy property in plain sight.

But when the threat of punishment is clearly removed, and the "rewards" in the cruel person's mind are obvious, then we would expect to find him at his worst. If, for example, he uses technology that preserves his anonymity, like the now defunct social networking site Yik Yak that was very popular for a time on college campuses like mine, he might regularly write comments meant to tear people down.

Here's the surprising thing, though. In study after study, when there is an opportunity to be cruel and get away with it, *almost no one takes advantage of that chance.* This is where Milgram's work is relevant. He didn't just conduct the one study previously mentioned, even though it became by far his most well-known contribution; he actually conducted eighteen different variations of this study. In some of these versions, what is so remarkable is that *hardly any harm was done to the learner at all.*

For instance, in one variation there were no prompts from the experimenter. The participant was told that he or she was entirely free to choose the level of shock to give for every wrong answer. So if someone wanted to, she could give the XXX shock every single time. Instead, participants were remarkably gentle in their behavior. The maximum they gave only averaged to a 5.5 level of shock out of 30 levels, and thirty-eight out of the forty participants stopped the experiment entirely the very first time the learner strongly protested.[33]

This was not an isolated result. If participants were given commands from two experimenters at the 150-volt level that contradicted each other, *every one* of them stopped at that point or one shock level higher.[34] Or, in an interesting twist, suppose the *experimenter* was the one receiving the shocks, and now one participant administered the test to him while another participant took over the job of giving the four prods. Surprise, surprise—0% shocked all the way, and everyone stopped the test when the learner gave his first protest.[35]

The same thing was discovered by Meeus and Raaijmakers with their stress study involving the unemployed job seeker. They also had a separate group of participants serve in a control condition, where in this case they could choose to give as many stressful remarks as they wanted. Not one person delivered all 15 remarks, with the median being 6.75.[36] Many other studies have found similar results.[37]

None of this is what I would expect from a cruel person. These were all opportunities where clear license was given to inflict as much or as little pain as participants wanted to. Most people barely did anything at all.

That's not the end of the story. Recall Robert Harris. I said that he helps to illustrate two central features of cruelty. The first has to do with his willingness to act in terrible ways. The second feature has to do with how *comfortable* Harris was in doing them. We said that he reportedly laughed while torturing animals. After he murdered the two boys, "He smiled and told Daniel that it would be amusing if the two of them were to pose as police officers and inform the parents that their sons had been killed."[38] As he looked at the blood and tissue on his gun, he remarked, "I really blew that guy's brains out," and laughed.[39]

In a word, Harris acted wholeheartedly. He never seemed troubled by guilt, and did not show signs of inner turmoil or conflict. He just plowed ahead, and was content with the outcome. That's how cruel people are put together psychologically. They kick the dog when no one is looking, they bully classmates anonymously online (or in person!), or they destroy someone's art project behind her back. But they also do these things decisively, and have little difficulty afterward dealing with what they have done.[40]

Now consider this from Milgram: "After the maximum shocks had been delivered, and the experimenter called a halt to the proceedings, many obedient subjects heaved sighs of relief, mopped their brows, rubbed their fingers over their eyes, or nervously fumbled cigarettes. Some shook their heads, apparently in regret."[41] And in a famous passage, he writes, "I observed a mature and initially poised businessman enter the laboratory smiling and confident. Within 20 minutes he was reduced to a twitching, stuttering wreck, who was rapidly approaching a point of nervous collapse."[42] Is this what we would expect from a cruel person? I don't think so. Nor, again, is this specific to the Milgram studies.[43]

We tend to be more complicated people than someone like Robert Harris. Yes, we will do hurtful things in some situations. *But* we don't do them in others, even when no one is looking. Yes, when we do hurt others, we also tend to be motivated in problematic ways. *But* it is often a conflicted form of motivation, and afterward we wrestle with guilt and shame.

Hence I conclude:

Most people today do not have the virtue of proper restraint.

But at the same time, this is also true of us:

Most people today do not have the vice of cruelty.

Conclusion

We can see a pattern emerging. Our characters are rich and complicated, and are best understood as neither virtuous nor vicious. Rather, a deep tension has shown up once again. When it comes to hurting people, we have a frightening capacity to sometimes hurt, injure, and even kill innocent people. Side by side with this, we also have an impressive capacity to sometimes be gentle, calm, and controlled.

Once again, I won't try to make sense of this strange tension quite yet. Instead, let us continue to see whether a similar pattern emerges in still other areas of our moral lives.

Notes

1. Meeus and Raaijmakers 1986: 316.
2. Meeus and Raaijmakers 1986: 318.
3. Meeus and Raaijmakers 1986: 319.
4. Meeus and Raaijmakers 1986: 319.
5. Meeus and Raaijmakers 1986: 317.
6. For an overview, see Miller 2013: chapter 9.
7. See, e.g., Zimbardo 2007.
8. http://rockcenter.nbcnews.com/_news/2011/12/19/9554915-bryan-stows-friends-describe-brutal-attack-outside-dodger-stadium.   Accessed September 17, 2015.
9. I should also mention that Berkowitz made sure there was a 12-gauge shotgun and a .38 caliber revolver near the participant. Why? Nothing having to do with this study. The participant was told that these guns were being used in another study.
10. Berkowitz and LePage 1967.
11. Berkowitz and LePage 1967: 204.
12. Berkowitz and LePage 1967: 205–206.
13. For references and a list of commonly used forms of provocation designed to generate aggression, see Krahé 2001: chapter 1 and Bettencourt et al. 2006: 752–753. See also Anderson and Bushman 2002: 37.
14. Bushman and Baumeister 1998.
15. Berkowitz 1965.
16. Caprara 1987: 11.
17. For the slides of weapons, see Caprara 1987: 9. For noise level, see Baron and Richardson 1994: 177–179 and Geen 2001: 36–37. For violent video games, see Giumetti and Markey 2007. For the remaining environmental

factors listed, see Anderson 1987: 1161; Baron and Richardson 1994: 167–185; and Krahé 2001: 86–87. See also Carver et al. 1983; Baron and Richardson 1994: 167; and Anderson and Bushman 2002: 37–38.

18. In what follows I draw on Milgram 1974.

19. Milgram 1974: 21, emphasis his.

20. Milgram 1974: 60.

21. Milgram 1974: 56–57.

22. Milgram 1974: 61, 66–70.

23. Milgram 1974: 61–63. For other relevant studies, see Doris 2002: 47 and Burger 2009.

24. See, e.g., Brown 1986: 4 and Meeus and Raaijmakers 1986: 312.

25. See, e.g., Burger 2009.

26. Gallardo-Pujol et al. 2015: 662. Of course, we can't consider this to be a perfect replication of Milgram's work, since the avatar is not an actual human being.

27. Milgram 1974: 6, 41.

28. As Milgram writes, "The disappearance of a sense of responsibility is the most far-reaching consequence of submission to authority" (1974: 8).

29. Milgram 1974: 52.

30. Milgram 1974: 74–76.

31. Corwin 1982.

32. Corwin 1982.

33. Milgram 1974: 61.

34. Milgram 1974: 95, 105–107.

35. Milgram 1974: 95, 99–105.

36. Meeus and Raaijmakers 1986: 317.

37. For an overview, see Miller 2013: chapter 9.

38. Corwin 1982.

39. Corwin 1982.

40. To be fair, Robert Harris may have been a psychopath. I don't know enough about his life, and the mental evaluations he might have received while in custody, to say one way or the other. If he was a psychopath, then I should have chosen a different example. I imagine we all know, or at least have heard

of, someone who is cruel. All the same points above can be made using that person as our example instead.

41. Milgram 1974: 33. See also Milgram 1963: 375, 377; 1974: 42–43, 148, 153–164; and Miller 2004: 196.

42. Milgram 1963: 377. See also Miller 2004: 196, 215, 232.

43. As we saw, Meeus and Raaijmakers reported that the participants "intensely disliked making the stress remarks" (1986: 318).

5 | LYING

A story broke with a provocative picture of a man in boxer shorts who looked just like US Representative Anthony Weiner. It turned out that Weiner had indeed mistakenly posted the picture on his public Twitter account, instead of sending it privately to a female undergraduate from Seattle.

Initially Weiner denied sending the picture, claiming that this was all the work of a hacker. He said, "Maybe it did start being a photo of mine and now looks something different or maybe it is from another account."[1] However, pictures sent to other women emerged as well, and we all learned the truth soon enough. As a result, Weiner promptly resigned from Congress in 2011. At a news conference, he confessed: "Once I realized I had posted it to Twitter, I panicked, I took it down, and said that I had been hacked. I then continued with that story, to stick to that story, which was a hugely regrettable mistake."[2]

To make matters worse, even after his resignation his sexting behavior continued, and so did the secrecy and deceit. While running for mayor of New York City in 2013, he engaged in scandalous behavior with a twenty-two-year-old woman.[3] Then, in 2016, Weiner sent a terribly disturbing picture to another woman of him in his underwear next to his young boy, who was sound asleep.[4]

There is no doubt that Weiner lied, first and foremost to his wife. He was lying to the public too, since he said things to the cameras while knowing full well that they were bogus. He sent the pictures himself, and took them in the first place! Obviously in making these false statements, he was out to deceive people. He was willing to go to great lengths to try to preserve his image as a loyal husband who would never cheat on his wife. Weiner exhibited a pattern of consistent lying that was motivated by the wrong reasons. He looks like a clear example of a dishonest person.

The Anthony Weiner case helps to bring out two of the central features of lying. First, a liar makes statements which he knows to be false, such as "That is not me in those pictures," and, second, he does so on purpose, to deceive others. The *Oxford English Dictionary* (1989) summarizes this very nicely; a lie is "a false statement made with the intent to deceive."

To me, these two features get at the heart of lying.[5] Just think about the lies people tell to cover up a pornography addiction, to convince someone how good their new painting is, or to exaggerate how experienced they are during a job interview.

So Anthony Weiner certainly seems dishonest. But is he the exception or the rule?

Lying Behavior

Fortunately we have some clues to guide us, thanks to decades of research by the leading psychologist studying lying, Bella DePaulo.[6] DePaulo, who taught for much of her career at the University of Virginia, asked volunteers living in the Charlottesville area to record all of their social interactions and all of their lies each day for a week. A "social interaction" had to last at least ten minutes (unless a lie was told earlier than ten minutes). In addition, these volunteers were asked to keep a record of how intimate the interaction was, how much planning went into the lie, what their feelings were before, during, and after the lie, and how seriously they rated the lie. The results were startling.

What DePaulo and her colleagues found was that there seemed to be a real difference between what they called "everyday" lies versus "serious" ones. Let's start with the everyday lies, which were rated a 3.08 out of 9 in seriousness.[7] Actual examples included people saying things like:

> Told her her muffins were the best ever.
> Exaggerated how sorry I was to be late.
> Told customer it was her color.

When it came to everyday lies, here is what DePaulo found when she compiled the data from 70 participants during the course of the week:[8]

Number of lies in each social interaction	0.2
Percentage of people to whom they lied	30%
Number of participants who said they told zero lies	6

Thus, if this data is representative of our culture more generally, then during an ordinary week I should safely assume that people are lying to me about a third of the time. Yikes.

One problem with this data is that it is self-reported. Clearly this reporting could be biased. For example, perhaps some people did not accurately report how often they lied because they did not want to come across as bad people, or because they thought it was too small a lie to mention. I think these are fair points. Still, it is remarkable how much lying was reported *in spite of* these biases.

Here are some more results. The volunteers reported that on average they were moderately distressed when they lied (on a scale with 1 being very comfortable and 9 being very uncomfortable):

70 participants	
Distress before	4.09
Distress during	4.65
Distress after	4.54

It is interesting that distress tended to increase while the lie was actually told, and did not go back down after it was finished.[9]

One more thing. After the week was up, the volunteers noted whether they were caught lying or not. It turned out that 57% of their everyday lies went undetected. Would they be willing to tell them again? Here 82% said yes![10]

These were some of the findings for everyday lies. In order to focus on what DePaulo called "serious lies," she ran a separate study where community volunteers had to use a written form that was mailed to them to record the most serious lie they had ever told.[11] These lies got a 6.97 out of 9 on seriousness; 47% were either an 8 or 9.[12]

Stop and think for a moment what your most serious lie was about. Here were the most popular categories:

Misdeeds (23%)
Affairs (22%)
Money, job (21%)
Personal facts, feelings (16%)[13]

Not surprisingly, distress was much higher too when telling these serious lies (5.05 out of 9).[14]

DePaulo went on to make an additional discovery when she compared her results for serious and everyday lies. She noticed that these volunteers would tend to tell everyday lies primarily to acquaintances and strangers.[15] Why might that be? Perhaps it is because of the increased risk of getting caught by someone who knows us well? Or perhaps it is because we care more about the people close to us and don't see the benefits of a minor lie outweighing any damage to the relationship.

For serious lies, DePaulo found it works in the exact opposite way. We tend to use them more often with those who are closest to us.[16] It is not hard to see why. Revealing the truth about an affair or the source of the money could destroy a relationship. Trying to preserve the relationship is worth more, in many people's eyes, than telling the truth.[17]

As an amusing aside, one striking anomaly to the trend of telling everyday lies primarily to strangers had to do with college students talking to their mother. They told everyday lies *in one out of every two interactions with their mother*.[18] Amusing, yes, but as a parent myself a bit alarming too.

Lying and Motivation

So it seems that lying is an ordinary occurrence for most people, with everyday lies happening all the time (thereby living up to their name!). We also believe that some lies are more serious and distressful to tell than others, and we tend to use them more on those close to us rather than on mere acquaintances.

Why do we lie in the first place? What motivates us to do it? In Weiner's case the answer seems clear. He lied in order to try to protect himself from embarrassment, and to save his marriage and his job. He had done awful things and now did not want to pay the price for them. What are most people like?

Fortunately DePaulo was interested in this question as well. She asked people to not just report their lying behavior, but their reasons for why they lied too.[19] She discovered that the reasons people gave for their lies were very different, but they could be organized into self-oriented and other-oriented reasons.[20]

One self-oriented reason for lying that naturally comes to mind has to do with getting or keeping things like money.[21] Here is an example from one of the volunteers:

"Lady on phone asked if a number was my current phone number. I said yes when it fact it isn't."

Why did you lie?

"I want to make it hard for her to find me; they are after me for money."[22]

This is not the only kind of self-centered reason for lying. Indeed, it is not even the most common.

That title belongs to reasons having to do with what psychologists call "impression management."[23] For instance, we might want to make ourselves look good—so we lie about what we accomplished in our younger years, or last night at the club, or on the weekends. Equally familiar is the need to protect ourselves from embarrassment, shame, or other damage to our image. Here is an example:

"I told her Ted and I still liked each other when really I don't know if he likes me at all."

Why did you lie?

"Because I'm ashamed of the fact that he doesn't like me anymore."[24]

Still other reasons to lie involve gaining power for ourselves or avoiding punishment or blame.[25]

"Other-oriented" reasons to lie are pretty common too. Their focus is ultimately on another person, rather than on oneself. Here are two examples:

> "Told her she looked well, voice sounded good when she looks less well than a few weeks ago."
>
> Why did you lie?
> "Not to add worry as she undergoes chemotherapy treatments."[26]

This person's heart was focused on her friend. The lie was meant to protect her from further worry. Or consider this response:

> "Lied about cost per square foot."
>
> Why did you lie?
> "To make money for the company."[27]

This is an other-oriented reason also, with the focus being the well-being of the company. If the reason for lying is to protect someone from punishment, blame, embarrassment, shame, or material loss, or to increase his positive image or financial well-being, then these would all count as other-oriented reasons as well.

So our reasons for lying can be very diverse. Which kind of reason tends to dominate? In other words, are the majority of reasons people give for lying self-oriented or other-oriented? Here is what DePaulo discovered for everyday lies:

> 57% self-oriented reasons versus 24% other-oriented reasons.[28]

Probably not too surprising there.

How about for serious lies? What would your estimate be? I bet you would expect the percentages to be even more one-sided. We are talking about affairs, money, and jobs, after all. That is indeed what happened. DePaulo found 94.4% self-oriented reasons versus 5.6% other-oriented reasons for serious lies.[29]

Let's end with a disturbing wrinkle. When I first heard about these "other-oriented" reasons for lying, I thought they must be pretty admirable. Leopold Socha was willing to lie, for instance, to protect the Jews hiding in the sewers of Lvov.

However, "other-oriented" means just what it says. The focus is on another person. That doesn't tell us whether the focus is a positive or a negative one. Indeed, other-oriented reasons can be quite nasty. They can motivate a lie whose sole purpose is to hurt someone else. Here is an example of what one of the volunteers said:

Her sister told her that her biological father was not the man who raised her.[30]

Imagine a girl saying this in order to hurt her sister. Remember that it is also a lie. So not only is she saying this to her sister, knowing that it is not true. She is also doing it out of malice and spite. That is truly morally atrocious.

How often do other-oriented *hurtful* lies occur? DePaulo put the number around 4% of all the serious lies recorded in her study.[31] Of course, we should take this and all the other data about reasons for lying with a grain of salt. Again, DePaulo just gathered self-reported data. What people told her was likely being influenced by biases that painted a rosier picture of their motives to lie than was indeed the case. In addition, there could be unconscious motives for lying that they were not even aware of at the moment.[32]

Nevertheless, DePaulo's work is eye-opening. It provides strong evidence that we lie for a whole variety of different reasons. More often than not, these reasons have to do with ourselves, but sometimes they have to do with helping or hurting other people.

Lying and Character

So it appears that most of us have a lot of different inclinations when it comes to lying and telling the truth. Here are some of them:

Sometimes we want to lie to avoid feeling embarrassed.

Sometimes we want to lie to avoid being shamed.

Sometimes we want to lie to avoid losing money or other material possessions.

Sometimes we want to lie to help other people feel better.

Sometimes we want to lie to hurt other people.

I might want to lie at a party with people I don't know, in order to make a good impression. Or someone has embarrassed me in public and I might lie in order to hurt him and deflect the attention away from me. Or, like Wiener, I might lie to protect my job, my family, and my image.

In other words, as people who possess all these different desires, whether we tell the truth is going to be highly *fragmented* from one situation to another. In certain circumstances, it is very likely that I will tell the truth, but in others I will often lie. There are plenty of both situations.

To help visualize this idea, see figure 5.1 for our imaginary friend Frank. This is what psychologists call a "profile" of his lying behavior. To keep things simple, let's just pick four situations and see how often he lied in them in a particular year.

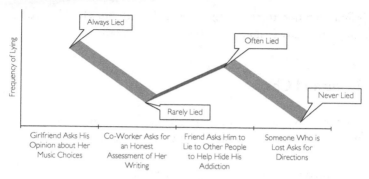

Figure 5.1 How Often Frank Lied in Four Different Situations during a Year

As we can see, Frank is fragmented in his lying and truth-telling. He always displays honest behavior in some situations (e.g., when giving directions) and dishonest behavior in other situations (e.g., when his girlfriend asks his opinion about her awful music choices). In still other situations he is sometimes honest and sometimes dishonest.

Indeed, this could be what happened with Anthony Weiner. There are probably many situations where he could be counted on to always tell the truth. Being caught sending out sexually provocative pictures of himself on Twitter was not one of them. He knew the truth about these pictures, and recognized that if this truth came out it would result in enormous embarrassment for him (as well as the potential loss of his job, divorce, etc.). Thus, we might understand some of what was happening in his mind using figure 5.2. This psychological story about Weiner is surely oversimplified, but it is good enough for our purposes.

We can expand this picture of how lying and truth-telling work by considering a longer period of time. For our friend Frank, we said that he showed fragmented behavior over the course of a year. But

I have gotten myself in a potentially embarrassing situation!
↓
I really don't want to embarrass myself.
+
I believe there are some ways to try to cover up what I did by lying.
↓
I want to lie to cover up what I did and avoid embarrassing myself.
↓
I tell the relevant lies.

Figure 5.2 A Partial Representation of Anthony Weiner's Thoughts about Lying

what happens if we were to compare one year to the next? Would we expect him to have changed much, or would we expect him to stay pretty much the same?

Of course, it depends on what has been going on in his life. Suppose he has had a transformative experience which has really changed his life in a fundamental way (think of a profound spiritual conversion, for instance). Then we might see him behaving in a radically different way a year later. Most of us, however, tend to stay roughly the same from year to year. In other words, if I had to guess, I would expect something like figure 5.3.

Frank's character (at least in this part of his moral life) is remarkably stable over time. We can predict fairly accurately what he will do next year in the same situations based upon what he has done this year. While it might seem paradoxical to say this, here Frank shows a high degree of *stability in his variability*.

Such a pattern of behavior accurately describes Frank. But not everyone is going to behave in exactly the same way in these situations. As DePaulo discovered, "Lies are [more likely] told by people who care deeply about what other people think of them. They are also told by people who are extraverted? and manipulative.

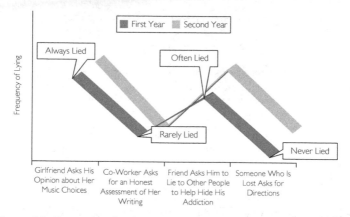

Figure 5.3 Comparing Frank's Lying over Two Years in the Same Four Situations

Lies are less likely to be told by people who are responsible and who experience gratifying . . . relationships."[33] Jones, for instance, might be honest for the most part with people, and unlike Frank, he is willing to tell his girlfriend that he does not share her taste in music.

So the lesson is that everyone's character is going to be different, and in particular people are going to have different profiles when it comes to lying. We need to take the time to learn what each person's character is like before assuming that everyone will generally tell the same lies in the same situations. Once we do know what someone is like, we can have a pretty good idea of what she will do in the future, whether that is a week, a month, or a year from now.

Despite this observation about how everyone's character is different, one thing does seem to be consistently missing from most of us—the virtue of honesty.

Lying, Virtue, and Vice

The virtue of honesty is very broad. It has to do with truth-telling and lying, to be sure, but also a whole lot more, such as stealing and cheating. With respect to truth-telling, we used to call the virtue "veracity,"[34] but we don't hear that word much anymore. So I will stick with *honesty*, because it is more familiar to our ears today. In the next chapter we will turn to cheating, but here the only focus is on honesty with respect to truth-telling.

As we proceed, we should be careful. We can't simply conclude that just because people tend to tell a fair number of lies, they are therefore not honest. Most philosophers think that certain lies are morally okay and so would not detract from being an honest person.[35]

Indeed, perhaps sometimes telling a lie is even morally *obligatory or required*. Immanuel Kant gave us a famous example where you can protect the life of an innocent person in your basement by lying to the murderer who is searching the neighborhood for him. When I poll my students in my ethics class about what to do in that situation, overwhelmingly they argue that not only is it okay to lie to the murderer, but that lying is precisely what you should do.[36]

So let us go slowly, and begin with serious lies. It seems clear to me that an honest person would not regularly tell lies about serious matters if those lies are not morally allowed. For example, he would not repeatedly lie to a spouse about an extramarital affair or lie on his resume in order to get a job.

Unfortunately the research by DePaulo and her colleagues on serious lies asked people to mention the single most serious lie they had ever told. It did not look at *how many* serious lies they had told and in what situations. Still, the results do provide some reason to doubt our honesty. Remember in the beginning of this chapter when we were discussing lying behavior, we found that 22% of serious lies were about affairs and 21% were about money or jobs. Three-quarters of serious lies total were trying to cover up bad behavior.[37] Were many of *those* lies morally okay? I doubt it. I suspect that—if we are honest with ourselves—we will discover that we too have told at least one serious lie in the past year that was morally wrong.

Still, even if this is true, that doesn't show we are not honest. There is a difference between being deeply honest and being weakly honest. Since virtues come in degrees of more or less, perhaps you can still be weakly honest while telling a serious lie from time to time.

But that is not the end of the story. For combine our tendency to tell serious lies with our strong tendency to tell everyday lies too. Would you expect an honest person, someone like Abraham Lincoln, to frequently tell everyday lies which are not morally okay?[38] I doubt it. Examples of such lies are the more mundane ones we have already seen, such as telling a friend how nice she looks or coming up with an excuse for why you don't have your homework. DePaulo's data suggests that we tell these everyday lies all the time—habitually, without even giving them much thought, experiencing only a moderate level of distress, and being fine with telling them again. Does this sound like you? We can all relate to this description to some extent, I would guess.

But again, we shouldn't jump right to the conclusion that we fail at honesty. It gets tricky here, too, since sometimes I tell everyday lies which might be okay. If I know someone is emotionally fragile, it might be okay to tell her that her new clothes look nice, even if they don't. White lies are a controversial matter, and readers can take reasonable opposing positions.

Regardless, I think we can all agree about this. Even if we say that *sometimes* everyday lies are morally allowed, the lies we usually tell do *not* fall into this category. When I lie, I am trying to manipulate someone for my own purposes. Or I end up hurting myself or other people. Or I violate the other person's autonomy. Or I undermine the trust that other people have in me. Or in some other way I do something that causes moral damage.

Furthermore, there is often a big difference between how serious I think a lie is (no big deal!) and how serious the other person takes it to be (a big deal!). Miami University psychologists Anne Gordon and Arthur Miller showed this by constructing the following example. Imagine a person seeing his or her significant other "leaving a restaurant with a former love interest after having stated that no such meeting would occur. The deception was furthered when this person did not acknowledge the meeting when given an opportunity to do so."[39]

Now imagine if it was you in the role of the lie-teller, the lie-receiver, or a neutral observer. If you can keep track of all that in your head, then ask yourself in which of these three roles you would most likely

1. Have a high impression of yourself
2. View your actions as justified
3. Claim that your actions are being misunderstood
4. Come up with a variety of reasons for lying to try to excuse yourself (i.e., "you are just overreacting again") or to try to explain what happened in some morally selfless way (i.e., "I just didn't want your feelings to get hurt")

Well, in this study the answer was clear—the lie-teller.[40] As Gordon and Miller wrote, "Lie-tellers' accounts seemed to focus on minimizing the importance of the event, whereas lie-receivers' accounts seemed to focus on damage done to the relationship. Observers tended to describe the situation more evenhandedly than did lie tellers or lie receivers."[41] While we might think an everyday lie is not a big deal, we could be badly mistaken.

To sum up, there is good evidence that everyday lies are widespread and unjustified. A person who is honest would not repeatedly tell them.

We have evidence for serious lying and everyday lying going on that is not morally acceptable. Furthermore, we saw some of the motives for why people tell lies, and a number of them do not seem very virtuous either, like fear of embarrassment. Now add to this that we tell lies for hurtful reasons. How could someone be honest and lie like *that*? Yet that's what we do. I think we all have examples from our own lives. DePaulo discovered that 4% of the *most serious lies* people told were lies with a hurtful purpose behind them. I bet that there were also many other hurtful lies that could have been reported too if she had asked for more than just the most serious lie.

Frankly, though, we probably already assumed that most people are not honest when it comes to telling the truth. We can just consult our own personal stories, how other people have treated us, what politicians and celebrities are doing, and the testimony of history to find plenty of evidence of a virtue that has gone missing. I see no reason to think that we are misinformed here.

In fact, the natural impression we might have of people today is the exact opposite. It can seem that most of the people around us have the *vice* of dishonesty (or what used to be called "mendacity," although again like "veracity" we don't hear that word anymore).

A few years ago, newspapers reported on a high school student in New York City who earned $72 million investing in the stock market. He became an immediate celebrity. Later we come to find out that it was all a hoax.[42] Does this really surprise us anymore? Not very much, I think. It is almost as if we expect lies from people in the public, rather than the truth.

But again, I recommend caution. I don't think we should jump right to the conclusion that most of us are dishonest people. Three reasons stand out for me. First, as we saw in the last chapter, a vicious person is not conflicted or torn while doing something vicious. He does it wholeheartedly. When it comes to dishonesty more specifically, you wouldn't normally find a dishonest person feeling distress during (and after) the telling of a lie. This is especially true if these are everyday lies with little risk of being caught.

Yet we saw that many people *are* distressed while lying. Recall that for everyday lies, the reported level of distress was 4.09 (out of 9) beforehand, 4.65 during, and 4.54 afterward. With serious lies, it increased to 5.05 while lying.[43]

So distress is the first reason to doubt widespread dishonesty—we feel bad about telling lies. Helpful lies are the second reason. In other words, sometimes we lie to help other people out for very good reasons. Here is an example.[44] Suppose Frank's close friend shares a deep secret with him. Let's say that he is a Christian living in a country where being a Christian is punishable by death. Unfortunately, suspicion is soon aroused about Frank's friend. His faith is about to be exposed, but at the last minute Frank lies on his behalf, successfully diverting public attention and keeping the secret safe. I think we could make a case that this lie was morally acceptable. And suppose Frank told the lie for altruistic reasons, out of genuine care and concern for his friend. Such an action does not seem to be something a vicious person would do.

Now the example is a fictional one. But earlier we saw that "other-oriented" reasons were behind 24% of everyday lies.[45] When close friends and family members were involved, people used other-oriented lies more often than self-oriented lies.[46] And when it came to the one most serious lie you have ever told in your life, even then 5.6% were other-oriented lies for the sake of another person, and not for what would benefit the liar.[47] That's not a terribly high percentage, I admit, but I still find it remarkable that for these people it was the most serious lie they ever told. None of this fits my mental picture of what a dishonest person looks like.

Finally, the third reason is that people do seem to be remarkably honest some of the time. Here is one last example. In 1996, DePaulo and Kathy Bell published the results of a study involving judging works of art. Our intrepid Frank is looking at several paintings. He is told that he must pick which two he likes the most and which two he likes the least.

Next, he gets a chance to talk about painting with an art student (who is really an actor). As you might have guessed, the art student knows which paintings are on Frank's lists. So she says, "This is one that I did. What do you think of it?" If she is pointing to a painting that Frank liked, then Frank says it is great. Not very surprising, really. In fact, none of the participants in the study lied in that case.

But how about when the art student points to one of the paintings that Frank *disliked* the most? What would you have done in this awkward situation?

Now we find something surprising: 40% participants told the truth and said that they disliked the painting. This number went up even more in a variation of the study where explicit instructions were given beforehand to be very honest. Then 62% told the truth. On the flip side, only 3% could muster the strength to say they "really did" like the painting.[48] These are examples of truth-telling that I would not expect from a dishonest person.

Hence at this point in my reading of the psychology literature—as well as in my examination of my own heart and my experience of the world—I have come to this conclusion:

> Most of us are not honest people. We are also not dishonest either when it comes to lying and telling the truth.

Clearly, though, this is an area where we need to gather a lot more data.

Conclusion

We have looked at helping. We have looked at harming. We have now looked at lying. These are rather different sides of morality. But the pattern remains the same. Our character appears to be very complex, and given the available evidence, it does not lend itself to being labeled as either virtuous or vicious. Instead, we seem to have powerful capacities for good, sitting side by side with powerful capacities for bad. In this chapter we have seen our ability to help others with our lies—or tear them apart.

The next chapter will consider one more moral domain before we step back and attempt to make sense of this complex emerging picture.

Notes

1. http://www.dailymail.co.uk/news/article-1393503/Anthony-Weiner-admits-Twitter-photo-taken-context.html. Accessed on September 29, 2015.

2. http://www.nbcnewyork.com/news/local/Weiner-Admits-Confesses-Photo-Twitter-Relationships-123268493.html. Accessed on September 29, 2015.

3. http://www.usatoday.com/story/news/politics/2013/07/23/weiner-more-lewd-messages/2579631/. Accessed on September 29, 2015.

4. http://nypost.com/2016/08/28/anthony-weiner-sexted-busty-brunette-while-his-son-was-in-bed-with-him/. Accessed on February 10, 2017.

5. They probably do not capture all there is to lying, but they are good enough for our purposes. For philosophical discussions that go much deeper, see Sorensen 2007 and Carson 2010: chapter 1.

6. See DePaulo et al. 1996, 2004; DePaulo and Bell 1996; Kashy and DePaulo 1996; DePaulo and Kashy 1998; and DePaulo 2004.

7. DePaulo et al. 1996: 989.

8. DePaulo 2004: 306. See also DePaulo et al. 1996: 984.

9. DePaulo et al. 1996: 989. Keep in mind that these are averages and so do not reflect a lot of the diversity in each individual's distress about lying. For instance, certain individuals could have felt very different levels of distress about lying during that particular week. Also, the same individual could have felt more or less uncomfortable depending on what a given lie was about. One of the participants, we can imagine, might have said that his everyday lie on Tuesday was not nearly as uncomfortable for him as his everyday lie on Friday.

10. DePaulo et al. 1996: 989.

11. DePaulo et al. 2004: 150–151.

12. DePaulo et al. 2004: 151.

13. DePaulo et al. 2004: 156.

14. DePaulo et al. 2004: 159.

15. Specifically, the volunteers averaged less than one lie in every ten social interactions with their spouses and children (DePaulo and Kashy 1998: 72).

16. DePaulo et al. 2004: 160.

17. See DePaulo et al. 2004: 148–149 and DePaulo 2004: 317–318, 324–325.

18. DePaulo and Kashy 1998: 72.

19. See also the brief review of different motives in Millar and Tesser 1988: 263–264.

20. See DePaulo et al. 1996: 983 and DePaulo 2004: 309–311. For a more extensive set of categories, see DePaulo et al. 2004: 152.

21. See also Rick and Loewenstein 2008: 645.

22. DePaulo et al. 1996: 983.

23. See DePaulo et al. 1996: 991, 2004: 148–149, 157, and DePaulo and Kashy 1998: 63.

24. DePaulo et al. 1996: 983.

25. For power and achievement motives for lying, see Gillath et al. 2010. For punishment and blame see DePaulo et al. 1996: 983; 2004: 152.

26. DePaulo et al. 1996: 983.

27. DePaulo et al. 1996: 983.

28. DePaulo et al. 1996: 987. See the footnote to table 5 in their paper for the reasons why these percentages do not equal 100.

29. DePaulo et al. 2004: 157.

30. DePaulo et al. 2004: 152. See also DePaulo et al. 1996: 983, note b.

31. DePaulo et al. 2004: 163.

32. For more, see Gordon and Miller 2000: 46–47.

33. Kashy and DePaulo 1996: 1050.

34. See, e.g., Baier 1990. Another candidate would be "truthfulness" (Adams 2006: 190).

35. For a thorough and careful discussion, see Carson 2010.

36. Kant 1996. Of course, Kant himself said it was wrong!

37. DePaulo et al. 2004: 156.

38. As Aristotle noted long ago, a person should be "truthful both in what he says and in how he lives, when nothing about justice is at stake, simply because that is his state of character" (1127b1–2).

39. Gordon and Miller 2000: 49.

40. Gordon and Miller 2000: 50.

41. Gordon and Miller 2000: 51.

42. http://time.com/money/3633433/72-million-high-school-stock-trader/. Accessed on 9/24/2015.

43. DePaulo et al. 1996: 989 and 2004: 159.

44. This is a version of an example I used in Miller 2013: 304.

45. DePaulo et al. 1996: 987.

46. DePaulo and Kashy 1998: 71.

47. DePaulo et al. 2004: 157. Of course, we need to remember that all this data is self-reported and could be biased.

48. For more, see DePaulo and Bell 1996 and DePaulo 2004: 319–323.

6 | CHEATING

If there is one crystal-clear example of a cheater, it has to be Tiger Woods. Of course, it wasn't for anything on the golf course that the dark side of his character was exposed. It was for how he routinely cheated on his wife and family.

The details of Woods's affairs remain murky, and we may never have a final count of all the women he was sexually involved with while married. Conservative estimates put the number at ten women, who were mostly cocktail waitresses and porn stars, but the real number is likely higher. From what has been reported, these were not one-time rendezvouses, but repeated encounters over months and even years.

Woods, then, looks like he had the vice of unfaithfulness. He cheated on his wife over and over again, both with the same woman and with different women, consistently and reliably over time, in a cunning and devious way. And, it goes without saying, for morally awful reasons. It was always about pleasure for himself.

Our Cheating Hearts?

As far as celebrities are concerned Woods is, of course, not alone. Extramarital affairs are widespread—Bill Clinton, John F. Kennedy, Eliot Spitzer, John Edwards, Elizabeth Taylor, Prince Charles,

Hugh Grant, Kobe Bryant, and Jude Law are just the beginning of a long list.

It is not just the celebrities who are cheating in this way either. After the Ashley Madison website was hacked (it caters to married users—"Life is short. Have an affair."), we learned quite a bit more about how common extramarital affairs are. The site supposedly had thirty-seven million users worldwide at the time, although to be fair it is not clear how many of those accounts were fake.[1] Today its website boasts fifty-one million members since 2002. A competing website, Gleeden.com, reports over three million current members.

Of course, extramarital affairs are only one kind of cheating, albeit an extremely important one. But we also know about Charles Rangel, Bernard Madoff, and Kenneth Lay being found guilty of various forms of financial cheating. In athletics, icons like Lance Armstrong and Alex Rodriguez have let us down by using banned substances.

Then there is academic cheating. As a professor I am constantly worried about whether cheating is going on in my classes. Just recently, I discovered that two students in my introduction to philosophy course were using old copies of my tests to prepare for a midterm exam (which is a violation of our honor code). Ironically, the class for which I have had the most trouble with cheating is Ethics. The first assigned paper for that class has had more instances of plagiarism than all the other papers in my classes combined. No, I am not making that up.

I am not the only teacher who has had to deal with cheating, of course. Every teacher does, and it is a burden. The formal process involved in prosecuting cheating at a university is often long and time consuming. It can get to the point where many faculty members prefer to just overlook a transgression or handle the punishment themselves without bothering to go through official channels.

However, sometimes academic cheating happens at such a large scale that it is impossible to ignore. Take an introductory psychology course at the University of Southern Mississippi, as vividly documented by the professor, Patricia Faulkender, and her colleagues.[2] It turned out that the second test of the semester had been removed from the department printer and distributed widely. Faulkender figured this out since, in comparison to the first test, students completed this one much faster with much better grades (no surprise). Faulkender launched a formal investigation, and all the students had to take a retest. In the process, she surveyed the 633 students enrolled in the class. It turned out that 22% anonymously reported having been helped by a copy of the test. An additional 35% reported that they would have done this too if they had gotten the chance. Hence 57% either did or would have cheated on this test if they could get away with it. In addition, Faulkender asked students in a math course that semester (where this time there was no evidence of cheating) whether they would have cheated using a stolen copy of a test if it had been possible. The result was 49% said yes.[3]

In general, research on academic cheating among North American and European students suggests it is rampant today. Average cheating rates of students in college have been found in recent studies to be as high as 60%, 70%, and even 86%.[4] According to sociologist Valerie Haines from the University of Calgary, there is an epidemic of cheating on college campuses.[5] I suspect most researchers in the field would agree. Nor is *academic* cheating special. Rather, most people seem to be willing to cheat in a variety of situations, whether academic, athletic, financial, or some other.

Yet by now you know that I want to be cautious. We can't just assume that the examples above speak for all of us. Celebrities are a very small group of people and can be rather unusual too. They may not reflect what most of us are like when it comes to cheating. Same

for those students at Southern Mississippi. While I have caught a
few students cheating in my classes, the vast majority of them seem
to be following the honor code. So in order to discover a more accurate and comprehensive picture of our character in this area, we
need to probe deeper using carefully controlled experiments.

Some forms of cheating lend themselves to experiments better
than others. Extramarital affairs—not so much. But breaking the
rules of a game or an assignment—that is a different story. This will
be the main form of cheating we examine in what follows.

Many studies of rule following have been conducted, and it turns
out, on the surface at least, that they have also found extensive evidence of cheating. For instance, in an older study the psychologists
Edward Diener and Mark Wallbom (1976) had people take a test
involving anagrams. They designed it so that only half of the test
could be finished before the five-minute time limit was up. As each
participant was about to take the test, the experimenter in charge
said that he had to leave to assist other participants. So he set a timer
bell for five minutes and issued a clear warning: "Remember not to
go any further after the bell rings."[6]

What do you guess happened? Did most people follow the
instructions, or did they keep going even after the bell rang?

Fortunately there was a two-way mirror off to one side of the
room, so Diener and Wallbom could find out the answer. It turned
out that 71% of participants continued after the timer went off (and
not just for a little bit longer, either).[7]

So, unlike in the previous chapters, it looks as if we might be able
to show how a vice is widespread throughout our culture. Perhaps
people are downright dishonest when it comes to cheating, or at
least this kind of cheating. We typically want to cheat and will try
to do so when it is worth the risk and we can avoid getting caught.
That, clearly, is vicious.

Complicating the Picture

Not so fast. Researchers have just recently developed a clever strategy to examine cheating. The results, so far at least, have been quite puzzling.

The new strategy is demonstrated well in a study published in 2011 by Lisa Shu of the London Business School and her colleagues. Imagine you are about to take a test with a bunch of people. You receive $10 and a worksheet with twenty problems. You are told that you only have four minutes to do the problems (which the experimenters made sure is not long enough), but you have an incentive to do well since you know you can keep 50 cents of the $10 for each right answer. When the four minutes are up, you grade the test, the experimenter checks the answers to make sure you graded everything correctly, and then he pays you accordingly. Given the difficulty of the questions and the time limit, if you do an average job you would get about 8 problems right:[8]

> No opportunity to cheat = 7.97 problems answered correctly on average

Now, that is not so interesting in its own right. But here comes the twist.

It turns out that your best friend, who happens to be Frank again, has also signed up for the experiment, and he is taking this very same test in the next room. As before, when the time is up, Frank and everyone else with him are told the answers. But they are also told to shred their worksheet and then pay themselves accordingly. The experimenter in the room does not check any of this. In other words, participants in this "shredder condition" can decide for themselves how many of their answers were correct, pay themselves based upon what they decide, and walk out of the room. So how well do you think Frank and his group did on the test?

Well, apparently they did much better than the people in the first group:[9]

Opportunity to cheat = 13.22 problems answered correctly on average

Or did they? It could be that Frank and his cohorts were just that much better at problem-solving than your group was. Let's be honest with ourselves, however. Clearly what *really* happened is that they took advantage of an opportunity to cheat and get away with it. They wanted to get paid more than they deserved.

Once again this looks like evidence of widespread dishonesty. After all, there was nothing special about this second group—they were just a random collection of people. Plus, there have been many additional studies done with the same setup that have found similar results.[10]

Like the participants in these studies, many of us would have done the same thing if we were in the "shredder condition." Still, there is something puzzling here. For while on average they put down roughly thirteen problems as answered correctly, why didn't they say they got all twenty correct? If you are going to cheat anyway and you know for sure you can get away with it, why not earn the extra $3.50? That seems irrational. In fact, when we look at the results of six different experiments involving 791 participants, researchers found that only 5 (!) people were willing to cheat all the way.[11] I can understand full-blown cheating (even if I don't endorse it). What is puzzling is what the remaining participants who cheated to some degree were thinking, since they were already willing to cheat in the first place. Let us call this the *puzzle of limited cheating*.

Now, you might think that fear of detection had some role to play. Perhaps participants were worried that the experimenters would somehow figure out that they were cheating if they claimed to have solved all the problems. So they limited their cheating to try to minimize detection.

But apparently that's not the case. In another study Nina Mazar at Toronto's Rotman School of Management and her colleagues lied to participants, saying that the average problem-solver gets 8 problems right within the time limit. Even so, the shredder condition only produced 4.8 correct answers. That was higher than controls at 3.4 problems, which is what you'd expect by now. However, it is still much less than what cheating participants could have gotten away with without looking suspicious at all.[12]

The puzzle of limited cheating is not the only puzzle that has emerged. As I mentioned earlier, this kind of experiment has really taken off in recent years. Another version, published in 2008 by Mazar, had a control or baseline group of college students with no opportunity to cheat. As before, there was also a group of students who shredded their worksheets and so could cheat as much as they wanted and get paid accordingly. But the interesting new wrinkle was a third group of students. Before they started the test, they saw the message "I understand that this short survey falls under [name of your school] honor system," and they had to print and sign their name to continue. Here were the results:[13]

	Correct answers ($0.50 per correct answer)
Control condition	3.4
Shedder condition	6.1
Shredder + honor code condition	3.1

Even though nothing changed in the third condition in terms of their ability to get away with cheating, participants on average performed slightly worse even than those in the control group.

Interestingly, we see the same pattern even if we increase the reward per correct answer to $2, which is a significant increase:

	Correct answers **($2 per correct answer)**
Control condition	3.2
Shedder condition	5.0
Shredder + honor code condition	3.0

The honor code seems to be doing a great job of keeping cheating in check.

This fascinating data supports the belief that researchers have had for a long time—that honor codes can reduce cheating at schools that take their codes very seriously. For instance, two of the leading researchers on honor codes, Donald McCabe from Rutgers Business School and Linda Treviño from Penn State's Smeal College of Business, found that 28% of college students at schools without an honor code reported helping another person on a test, whereas only 9% did at schools with an honor code. Similar trends were found with plagiarism (18% versus 7%), unauthorized crib notes (21% versus 9%), and unpermitted collaboration (39% versus 21%), among other forms of cheating.[14] In particular, they found that to be effective an honor code cannot be, in their words, mere "window dressing," but rather "a truly effective code must be well implemented and strongly embedded in the student culture."[15]

This is puzzling too. For if we are so willing to cheat in an environment where we can get away with it, then why would the honor code change things so dramatically? In other words, if people will cheat when there is no honor code, then why wouldn't they just go ahead and sign the honor code as a formality, and then proceed to cheat as before without fear of punishment? The cheating opportunity itself is completely unchanged. This is what we might call the *puzzle of the honor code*.

A mirror on the wall may show us the answer to these puzzles.

The Psychology of Cheating

Our friend Frank has just signed up to take an anagram test. The experimenter has to leave during the test, but tells Frank very clearly to stop the test when the five-minute timer goes off. Then Frank goes to work. He is seated at a desk, and directly in front of him is a mirror (a two-way one, in fact, but he does not know that). So every time he glances up he sees himself in the mirror. After five minutes, the timer goes off. What does he do? He stops, just as he was told to do.

Frank is not alone. One person after another stopped at five minutes. In fact, only 7% of all the participants cheated by continuing after the timer had gone off.

This study should sound familiar. It is, in fact, just what the psychologists Diener and Wallbom did in a version of their 1976 experiment that we saw at the beginning of the chapter. Remember that in the first version 71% of the participants cheated by not stopping when the timer went off. Now it is only 7%.[16] What a dramatic difference!

What did they change in the second version? Only the bit about being seated in front of the mirror. That's it.

Why did it make this difference? That's a really important question, I think. I also think we know at least part of the answer. But it will require telling a bit of a story about how our minds work. The story has three basic parts.

First of all, most of us seem to really believe that cheating is wrong, both in the abstract and in particular instances like copying off another person's test or having an affair. So the correct moral beliefs seem to be right there in our mind, and they can keep us in check when an opportunity to cheat arises. Indeed, when studies are run with a "shredder" opportunity to cheat, researchers find no evidence of cheating if the participants are first asked to recall the Ten Commandments, for instance.[17] The implication should be clear enough—a moral reminder serves to call our attention to our moral commitments, and so makes it much more difficult in our own mind to justify doing the wrong thing by cheating.

At the same time, even though the beliefs against cheating appear to be somewhere in our mind, we still need a moral reminder like the Ten Commandments to make us more mindful of how wrong cheating is. Hence we have seen that when these moral reminders are not present, cheating can become commonplace. Why? I think the answer is that we also have a deep desire to do things that will benefit us—things that are in our self-interest. We calculate (often unconsciously) what the costs and benefits of cheating would be, and if the calculation comes out in our favor, we tend to go for it. As we know all too well, there are many different kinds of benefits that can come from cheating, such as avoiding failure (and, relatedly, embarrassment or shame), succeeding at a project or achieving a competitive advantage, or just enjoying the rush of excitement that comes from breaking the rules and risking getting caught. That is the second part of the psychological story.

So far this is nothing very complicated. We all know what it feels like to be reminded of the right thing. We also know what it feels like to not pay any attention to the right thing and just go ahead and cheat. Thus, if these two parts were all there was to the psychological story, it would be seriously incomplete and our puzzles would remain. We should expect people who are going to cheat to go ahead and cheat as much as they can so long as they can get away with it. And why would the mirror make such a big difference?

The third and most interesting part of the psychological story, I believe, is that most of us want to cheat when it would be overall beneficial, but we *also* want to seem moral to other people and—crucially—to our own selves. We care a lot about being honest people in our own eyes.[18] This matters to us.

Now try to think of yourself as an honest person while also aggressively cheating when an opportunity arises. That is going to be a tough one to pull off—those two things do not go hand in hand. More moderate cheating, though, is a different story. There a bit of self-deception can help us out. When I cheat just a bit, I can deceive myself by not giving much thought to whether this action is morally right or wrong. I can just forget about that question for a while and enjoy the fruits of my cheating. When I blatantly cheat, that is another matter. Then it is a lot harder to just pretend like it is no big deal morally speaking, and so a lot harder to still think of myself as honest. This, then, is the answer to the *puzzle of limited cheating*.

That is why something so trivial, like where a mirror is positioned, can make such a big difference in what we do. With the mirror in front of me, I don't have much room to hide. A mirror forces me to confront what I am doing, whether I want to or not. As a result, I either cheat and abandon thinking of myself as honest, or (like most people in the mirror study) I preserve my positive self-image of honesty and stop when the timer goes off.

We can now see why being reminded of the Ten Commandments or signing an honor code has such a dramatic effect. They make our moral beliefs more visible to ourselves, and we really do want to live up to them. But these moral reminders also reinforce how hard it is to cheat and still think of ourselves as honest. So we have an answer to the *puzzle of the honor code*.

Of course, we shouldn't take this idea too far. There are people like Tiger Woods out there who have cheated aggressively. If they think the benefits from cheating will be great enough—the sexual pleasure, say, or passing a course needed for graduation—then their selfish desires can simply overpower any motivation to do what they believe is right. Swept aside is also the motivation to think of themselves as honest. Such a person might concede that he is being dishonest, but just not care enough about that.

So when we put our characters to the test in this area of our moral lives, we find the makings of a very complex story about honesty and cheating.

Why We Are Not Dishonest After All

To my mind, anyone with the pattern of behavior and motivation described in this chapter is clearly not an honest person. Maybe this is obvious. If so, then just skip ahead a few paragraphs. If not, let me expand a bit before turning to the much more interesting and controversial question of whether we are therefore dishonest people.

When I think of an honest person, I think of someone who will regularly avoid cheating when the relevant rules are fair and appropriate. This is true *even if* by cheating she is assured of benefiting herself somehow.[19] Such a person won't cheat on her taxes, won't cheat on her take-home exams, and won't cheat on her husband.

Now, I have to admit there might be exceptions. For instance, cheating might be okay if it is the only way to help your friends or loved ones in desperate need. Or it might be okay for a spy to hack a company's computer system, thereby stopping a terrorist attack. That's cheating the company, but it might not go against the virtue of honesty. Same thing with cheating in some cases where no one gets harmed, such as when playing a game of solitaire by yourself. But I am not too worried about cases like these. The key point is that all the examples we have talked about in this chapter—adultery, doping, cheating on exams, etc.—are not going to be morally justified. What we have seen from the experiments in particular is that most of us would cheat—at least in the situations they examined—so long as we thought we could get away with it. And we would cheat for reasons that are hardly morally good ones.

Here is another way in which most of us seem to fall short of honesty. Our motives are simply not good enough much of the time. I tend to think of the honest person as not cheating (or cheating) for good (admirable, praiseworthy) reasons. The honest person refrains from cheating, for instance, out of a sense of fairness to his teammates, or because he does not want to hurt other people by damaging the company, or because he loves his spouse. Instead, like Tiger Woods, our self-interested motives for pleasure, or avoiding failure, or gaining an advantage over our enemies, play a far bigger role than they should. Even the subtle influence of thinking of yourself as an honest person is *not* a factor that should matter to someone who in fact *is* an honest person. Yet we already said that it matters a lot to most of us, whether we realize it or not.

One more expectation I have of an honest person is that she would not cheat *regardless* of whether she has been reminded of her moral commitments or not. Wouldn't you expect that too? In other words, she would naturally not want to cheat; it is just second nature for her to refrain. She does not have to first be reminded about what the right thing to do is before she does it. But that is exactly what we saw happen in the studies. Cheating was high in the regular "shredder conditions," but disappeared when the Ten Commandments or the honor code served as moral reminders.

To sum up, then, I think the best experimental evidence backs up our initial hunch from watching the nightly news. Most people today, at least in the places where the studies have been conducted, do not qualify as honest when it comes to cheating.

This picture of character can look rather bleak from a moral perspective. No surprise at this point, though, if you find me saying that this is not the lesson I take away from the research. Indeed, there seem to be at least four quite positive aspects to our characters here. The first just builds on the previous point. While it is true that an honest person would not show remarkable differences in behavior depending on whether her moral beliefs are fresh in her mind, a dishonest person would not have those particular beliefs in the first place! A dishonest person does not think that cheating is wrong in general, nor that cheating on a test or a spouse is wrong in particular. Or, if he *does* happen to have such beliefs, he would not care much about them and they would not play a significant role in his psychology. Yet when it is as simple as recalling the Ten Commandments, people no longer exhibit any signs of dishonesty. That is quite an astounding testament to the strength of our moral convictions, in my opinion.

Another positive sign is revealed by the role of honor codes. In one study, Shu found that only one out of twenty-two participants cheated in the shredder condition when first signing an honor code. I cannot see how a dishonest person would genuinely commit himself to behaving honestly—and follow through on that commitment later—when he has a chance to cheat for financial gain in a way that is completely undetectable. A dishonest person instead would sign the honor code as a mere formality, and then go right ahead and cheat.

Here is a third thought I have about dishonesty. Dishonest people do not tend to cheat just a little bit. Rather, they try to maximize their rewards from cheating when they think it would be worthwhile and they can get away with it. Someone like Tiger Woods does not stop with just one sexual escapade. Or with just one woman. He keeps going and going. But not most people. This was our first puzzle, the puzzle of limited cheating. Most cheated, to be sure, but they only did it to a moderate extent.

We tried to explain why that was the case. And that explanation serves as the final point here. Cheating was restrained by the desire to think of ourselves as honest people. But I do not see a dishonest person caring about *that*.

This is just an opinion I have about dishonesty. Perhaps you disagree. You might say that a dishonest person could still think of himself as honest without really being so. I don't have a really strong argument to give you to change your mind. I can only note that this picture seems to imply that the dishonest person has a lot of psychological tension in his life. He has some desires that push him to cheat more, along with other desires keeping his cheating in check so he can still think of himself as honest. That tells me that he faces a continual battle between two sides of his mind struggling with each other. I do not think of dishonest people as conflicted like *that*. They seem to me to be pretty wholehearted—committed and confident—in what they are doing. Don't they?

But even if you are doubtful about this last point, the overall conclusion from all four of these observations is hard to resist. Most of us are simply not dishonest people.

Conclusion

As we have seen in this chapter, the story emerging from research on cheating closely resembles what we have already seen for helping, harming, and lying. Here too there is good reason to believe we have a powerful capacity to follow the rules and not cheat in certain situations. Yet right alongside is a powerful capacity *to* cheat for our own benefit in other situations. "Honesty" seems too simple a label. But so does "dishonesty." A different way of thinking about our characters is needed.

Enough already, then, with introducing more experiments. Let's step back from the details and, using the studies we have already seen, try to paint a bigger picture of what most of us are really like deep down.

What we find is that our characters are, to put it bluntly, pretty mixed up.

Notes

1. http://www.bbc.com/news/magazine-33738020. Accessed on August 8, 2016.
2. Faulkender et al. 1994.
3. Faulkender et al. 1994: 212.
4. See Klein et al. 2007; McCabe et al. 2006; and Rokovski and Levy 2007.
5. Haines et al. 1986: 342.
6. Diener and Wallbom 1976: 109.
7. Diener and Wallbom 1976: 110. Hence they were not just finishing up the problem on which they were working. The average number of additional responses after the timer went off was 2.71 (110).
8. Shu et al. 2011: 339.
9. Shu et al. 2011: 339.
10. See Miller 2014: chapter 3 for a review.
11. Mazar et al. 2008: 643. For similar results, see also Vohs and Schooler 2008: 52; Gino et al. 2009, 2011; Mead et al. 2009: 595–596; Zhong et al. 2010: 312; Gino and Margolis 2011; and Shu et al. 2011.

12. Mazar et al. 2008: 640.

13. Mazar et al. 2008: 637. Even more interesting, the school did not have an honor code at that time! So there was no threat of actually getting punished for an honor code violation if the cheating was discovered. To be thorough, Mazar also ran the study at another school with a "strict" honor code. The results were similar (Mazar et al. 2008: 637).

14. See McCabe et al. 2001: 224.

15. McCabe et al. 2001: 224. For more on honor codes and cheating, see McCabe and Treviño 1993; McCabe et al. 2001; and Thorkildsen et al. 2007: 191. The paragraph above is derived from Miller 2014: 66–67.

16. Diener and Wallbom 1976: 110.

17. Here are some more details if you are interested. Control participants either got a nonmoral reminder (write down ten books you read in high school) or a moral reminder (write down as many of the Ten Commandments as you can). This didn't make a difference in how they answered the 20 problems—they averaged 3.1 problems solved. Remember that there was no opportunity to cheat in this setup.

   But it did make a difference for the participants in the shredder condition. With the nonmoral reminder, 4.2 problems were "solved" on average (indicating some cheating). But with the moral reminder in the shredder condition, only 2.8 problems were solved on average (Mazar et al. 2008: 636).

18. For more, see Gordon and Miller 2000: 47.

19. For recent philosophers saying the same thing, see Hursthouse 1999: 10 and Adams 2006: 121. I developed this idea in Miller 2014: 77.

7 | PUTTING THE PIECES TOGETHER

Thanks to the hard work of psychologists over the past sixty years, our character has been put to the test and we have learned a great deal about what people tend to do in different situations. The past few chapters, indeed, have only begun to scratch the surface of what we now know.

My goal here in this chapter is to step back and try to piece together a more general story about what has been discovered up to this point. This story will be incomplete in a couple of important ways. First, since it draws on studies in our recent history, we do not know whether it applies to our distant ancestors (my hunch, for what it is worth, is that it does). Also, the vast majority of studies on moral behavior have been done using participants from North America and Europe, and so I want to be careful in not overgeneralizing to everyone. Finally, the story is not complete because there are many future studies that need to be done. For instance, there have been almost no carefully controlled experiments testing people's inclinations to steal from others.

Nevertheless, despite these caveats, the story we can now tell is rich, novel, and very important.

What Is the Story about Our Behavior?

We all remember Frank. He has demonstrated such a kind heart in wanting to help out researchers with their studies. What a ride it has been for him! From shocking strangers, to cheating on tests, to helping a fellow student, Frank has been through an awful lot. In the process he has learned a great deal about himself and his character, too.

Frank, of course, is not a real person. But he has served a very important role in illustrating how the typical person—you and I, perhaps—would act if *we* had faced the same situations he did. What can we learn from his many adventures?

First of all, most people have a tremendous capacity for good in their hearts. This lesson is worth putting front and center, as we are bombarded with so many negative stories.

With respect to the psychological studies, the clearest illustration of this capacity for good comes from research on empathy. We saw that 76% of people like Frank volunteered to help someone they had never met before due to their empathy for her situation. They stepped up to the plate, even though it would come at a significant cost to them. We have also seen the good side of our character in other places, such as our willingness to not cheat when we are reminded of our values—even though no one would catch us if we did.

This capacity for goodness often carries over into real life. The Norwegian government wanted to make a film to encourage people to help children in need. So they had a child actor, around ten years old, wait by himself at a bus stop in the harsh winter weather of Oslo, Norway. He only had a shirt on, with no gloves or hat, and was clearly freezing. The filmmakers then secretly recorded what real people would do when they saw him.

Whenever someone joined the boy at the bus stop to wait for the bus, a beautiful thing happened. Time and time again, complete strangers gave him their gloves, their hat, or even their jacket. They did not ignore his suffering, and in the process they acted compassionately. His suffering sparked something inside of them, and they did the right thing.[1]

So here is the first lesson I have learned in my research on moral character:

Lesson 1: There are many situations in life where most people will demonstrate the finest forms of moral behavior.

I know this to be true in my own life too. When my wife and I were leaving Yellowstone National Park late one summer day in 2009, it was dark and foggy outside. There was hardly anyone on the road, and we were tired and eager to return to our hotel. Suddenly a tire on our rental car made a loud noise and we had to pull over. This was not going well, I thought. Then it got worse. When I looked in the trunk for the spare, I found a tire all right, but on top of it was a large skull! I was, needless to say, shocked (alarmed, freaked out), and only later realized that it was a deer skull that must have been left by a previous driver of this rental car. Clearly the rental company had not done a good job cleaning up the car.

So here we were on the side of the road, with a large skull keeping us company, as I tried to change the tire in the pitch dark. Along comes another car, pulling up behind us. To make a long story short, twenty minutes later we were back on the road, thanks to two complete strangers from the UK who like us were visiting the park. I will never see them again in my life, but I know one thing for sure. That night they exhibited tremendous character.

If only Lesson 1 were the end of the story about how we act morally. Of course, we know it is not. Milgram's experiments provide us with a clear example of the opposite tendencies that reside in our hearts as well. In the standard Milgram situation, Frank was willing to shock all the way to the XXX level, thereby killing an innocent person (or so it seemed). But I find the "bystander effect" studies in some ways even more troubling. For in those situations, there is a clear emergency going on, and there is no authority figure like an experimenter telling Frank what to do. When joined by an unresponsive bystander, Frank just sits there doing nothing, leaving the person to suffer. We saw other data collected from studies on hurtful lies and blatant cheating on tests that is not so flattering either.

These results are not confined to the lab, either. I began the book with the story of Black Friday in South Charleston, where people ignored Walter Vance as he lay dying on the floor of the local Target. There is also the story of Hugo Alfredo Tale-Yax, who was stabbed in New York City after trying to help a woman who was being attacked. He bled to death after lying on the sidewalk for more than an hour and after more than twenty people walked by without doing anything to help.[2] Or Wang Yue, a two-year-old girl from China who was hit by a van and then, because no one helped her, was run over by a truck. Eighteen people ended up ignoring her, even walking around her blood on the ground, before anyone intervened.[3] These are just anecdotes and not the basis of the argument of the preceding chapters. But they are very much in line with what that argument predicts will happen.

Consequently here is a second lesson I have learned from my research on moral character:

Lesson 2: There are many other situations where most people will exhibit the worst forms of ethical behavior.

Now, you might be thinking: there is nothing new here. We did not need psychologists to teach us these two lessons. They are obvious from our ordinary lives, from the nightly news, and from human history.

Maybe so, but there is more going on here than it might seem at first. We need to keep in mind that Lessons 1 and 2 apply to the *very same people*. In other words, it isn't just that there are a bunch of "good people" who usually act well, and then a different bunch of "bad people" who usually act poorly. Rather, the upshot is this:

> **Lesson 3**: For most of us, we will behave admirably in some situations and then turn around and behave deplorably in other situations.

Frank can be so selfless when he is feeling empathy. Then, a week later, he can do nothing in an emergency when he is in a group of people watching a stranger cry out in pain. To help illustrate this idea visually, figure 7.1 shows how Frank might have acted in four different situations related to helping people over the course of a year.

Bringing more situations into the picture, figure 7.2 captures how Frank might act in *all* the helping situations he encountered in a year. Note how his helping fluctuates remarkably from situation to situation over the course of this year. He is all over the map.

This pattern of behavior is not limited to helping, as we have seen in the previous chapters. Figure 7.3 is an illustration for Frank and his aggressive behaviors. As we can see, Frank was rarely very violent

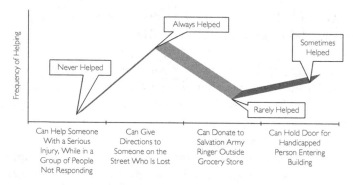

Figure 7.1 How Helpful Frank Was in Four Situations during a Year

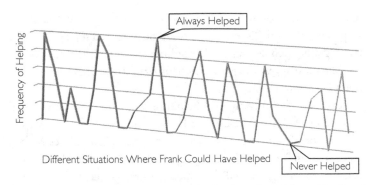

Figure 7.2 How Helpful Frank Was in All the Situations Where He Could Help during a Year

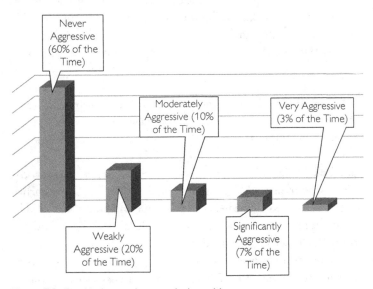

Figure 7.3 Frank's Aggressiveness during a Year

or hurtful. Much of the time he was a pretty decent fellow. That is not surprising, after all, given how he could be punished if he got caught hurting other people. But the key point is that, over the course of the year, Frank displays the *entire range* of aggressive behaviors at some point in time or other.

These are all illustrations of helping and harming. What we need to appreciate about Frank is that his behavior is all over the map in *all* areas of his moral life. Sometimes he cheats, sometimes he lies, and sometimes he hurts other people. Other times he plays by the rules (even though he will lose money in the process), he tells the truth (even though it would be painful to do so), and he does not behave aggressively (even though he could get away with it). How well he behaves in any hour does not predict very accurately how well he will behave in a new situation the next hour. He is a complex person, morally speaking. And the same is true about ourselves. We are complex people, morally speaking.

This leads to the next lesson, perhaps the most surprising of the four:

> **Lesson 4**: Our changing moral behavior is extremely sensitive to features of our environment, and often we do not even realize what those features are.

Sure, Frank does not help everyone he comes across. No surprise there—who of us could last long doing that? We would get burned out and exhausted. So he helps some people and not others. And he lies sometimes and not others. And he cheats sometimes and not others. Really, what is the big deal?

The big deal is *when* those things happen. A fascinating experiment illustrates the point. Robert Baron at Rensselaer Polytechnic Institute wanted to see whether people would help in a simple way—make change for a dollar bill—in a shopping mall.[4] He had actors approach shoppers and ask for help in two different locations in the mall. Before I tell you what the difference was between the two locations, here were the results:[5]

	First location	Second location
Males helping	22%	45%
Females helping	17%	61%

So there must have been a big difference between the people he came across in those locations, right? Maybe the shoppers in one group had more college education? Higher socioeconomic status? Better moral upbringing? Nope. The only relevant difference was whether the shoppers had just passed a clothing store (first location), as opposed to Cinnabon or Mrs. Field's Cookies (second location). It was the smell of cookies and cinnamon rolls, in other words, that had a significant impact on helping. Who would have thought that!

This is not the first time we have seen this kind of result. Recall the difference that coming out of a bathroom made to helping. Or breaking someone's camera. Or being with an unresponsive stranger. Or the temperature of the room. Or sitting in front of a mirror. Or reciting the Ten Commandments. Or signing an honor code.

Did some of these results surprise you? They surprised me when I first learned about them. Ordinarily, we would *not* expect those factors to make such a large difference in how we behave. Surely, I used to think, I would not cheat regardless of whether I signed an honor code or not. Surely I would help someone in terrible pain, even if no one else was doing anything. Surely I would not be influenced by what the temperature was (within reason, of course), or what the smells were in a shopping mall. Surely the presence of a mirror was completely irrelevant.

But apparently I was wrong.

What Is the Story about Our Motivation?

This is not the end of the story, though. We really care, not only about what people do (or fail to do), but also about what the *motives* are behind their behavior. When a friend visits me in the hospital, it matters an awful lot whether she is there to see me because she cares about me. Imagine how you would feel if you were on the receiving end of an act of "charity," and then came to find out that the person did it only to improve her resume for the job market!

Here too I believe we are now in a position, thanks to the work of psychologists, to say several important things about character and motivation in ordinary life. The first is this:

Lesson 5: We are not always motivated just by self-interest, but have the capacity to be motivated in several different ways.

Psychological egoism, which we said in chapter 3 is the idea that we are only out to promote our self-interest, can be put to rest. We are complicated creatures who care about other things at the end of the day besides just our self-interest.

Specifically, we are able to care for others in a selfless and altruistic way. This is truly an awesome capacity. Even when it comes to complete strangers, like the boy freezing at the bus stop, we can care about him for his own sake, and not primarily about what is best for ourselves. We know this thanks to the research on empathy and helping that was mentioned in chapter 3.

That is not all. Suppose your friend visits you in the hospital, and when pressed to explain why she is there, she says, honestly and directly, "Because it is the right thing to do." It is her duty. This is a third, distinct kind of moral motivation. It appeals to what is right in general for us to do. It is not primarily aimed at benefiting oneself or benefiting the other person. Its focus is on what morality says to do. These three categories are summarized below.[6]

Kind of motive

Egoistic	Concerned ultimately with what is good for myself
Dutiful	Concerned ultimately with what is right or required to do
Altruistic	Concerned ultimately with what is good for another person

So not only is psychological egoism false. There is more than one alternative to self-interested motivation.

It also turns out that we can shift between these motives fairly quickly from one situation to the next. Indeed, this can happen *even in the same situation*. My friend initially may have visited me in the hospital out of a sense of obligation ("It's the right thing to do"). Then she was moved by my suffering and continued to keep me company out of compassionate concern. Our motives are complicated, and they can change rapidly.

Hence, during the course of a week or a year, Frank can be behaving quite well in lots of situations, and yet deep down have different motives for what he is doing in many of them. Despite the uniform excellence of his behavior, the quality of his motives could resemble a roller coaster.

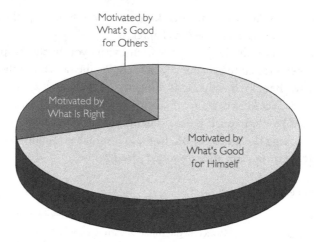

Figure 7.4 Frank's Type of Motivation in All Morally Relevant Situations during a Year

To illustrate this idea, figure 7.4 adopts a broader perspective on Frank and considers how often he was motivated in each of the three different ways (egoistic, dutiful, and altruistic) over the course of an entire year of his life. As we can see, egoistic motivation was the front-runner. But dutiful and altruistic motivation also played a significant role at various points during the year.

Even with Lesson 5 and this idea of a plurality of different kinds of motives, the emerging picture is still much too simple. Here is another part of the story:

Lesson 6: Many of our moral actions are not driven by just one motive, but rather have mixed motives behind them.

My friend's primary motivation for visiting me in the hospital might be because she cares about me and is concerned about how I am doing.

But she is also trying to avoid feeling guilty if she does not come to see me. So overall there is a combination of altruistic and egoistic motivation present here, with the former taking the lead role. In other situations, the lead role might be reversed. Conceivably we could even be motivated by self-interest, by duty, and by altruistic concerns all at the same time—and only think that one of them is present. For what we are *actually* motivated by can be different from what we *think* is motivating us. Indeed, there are times when we do not have an accurate picture of *any* of our motives. This takes us to the next lesson:

> **Lesson 7**: Sometimes we are not aware of an unconscious motive behind an action, and we might be completely wrong in our understanding of our own motives.

We have already seen this happen in some earlier helping studies, whether it was emerging from the bathroom or being influenced by the smell from Cinnabon in the shopping mall.

Even more noteworthy is what people said in the bystander-effect studies. For instance, when participants were asked why they did nothing to help someone who was screaming in pain in the next room, all sorts of different answers were given. But typically none of the answers mentioned the role of the unresponsive stranger who was in the room with participants.[7] So these participants seemed to completely miss the heart of the matter and not understand their fear of embarrassment. Nor are they unusual in that regard. The rest of us would have likely missed what was going on in our own mind too if we had been in their shoes.

A lot more could be said here in filling in the details. But this much is clear. The part of the story we are telling about moral motivation is going to be surprising and complex in all kinds of ways—just as it was for moral behavior.

What Is the Story about Our Character?

All this complexity reminds me again why most of us are not fundamentally good and virtuous people. Just ask yourself the following question: is what we have said in this chapter about behavior and motivation really what you would expect from a virtuous person? What I would expect is a relatively consistent pattern of good behavior. It does not have to be perfect or flawless behavior to count as virtuous, but it had better not be fragmented either, where unjustified cheating, lying, aggressing, and failing to help are regularly taking place. Furthermore, it had better not be sensitive to morally irrelevant factors like the temperature in the room or the smells in the air.

The same thing applies to motivation. It does not have to be perfectly altruistic or dutiful motivation, but it had better not be highly fragmented either, where many morally important situations lead to thoughts mainly about ourselves. There had better not be a lot of sensitivity to morally irrelevant factors, either.

To put this a different way, I would expect a virtuous character to lead to a relatively consistent pattern of praiseworthy motives, followed by a relatively consistent pattern of good behavior. This motivation and behavior should be responsive to the most important moral factors in our environment, rather than the trivial ones. Unfortunately, as we have seen, the evidence emerging from psychology does not paint such a picture for most of us.

Now let's flip to the vices and consider whether the evidence takes us in that direction instead. Is the lesson of the previous four chapters that most of us are callous, cruel, and dishonest people?

Let's spend a moment thinking about what that would mean. First, a vicious person would have to be relatively consistent in his bad behavior. Not while he is in public, since he might pretend to be good when other people are watching. What matters, though, is how he behaves when he can do whatever he wants and get away with it. Does he cheat in the "shredder condition"? Does he tell hurtful lies? Does he ignore the freezing child at the bus stop on purpose? Does he kick a defenseless dog? Not every time, perhaps, but fairly reliably over time? That is what I would expect of a vicious person.

Similarly his motives would rarely be altruistic. That seems obvious. Do you think a vicious person is concerned with doing his duty or doing the morally right thing? I do not. Rather, I would expect his motives to be self-centered—focused on his own pleasure or fame, status, wealth, and so on.

This is a rather abstract way to talk about a vicious person. Jeffrey Dahmer was someone who was surely vicious in reality. Dahmer murdered at least seventeen people from 1978 to 1991, and his treatment of their bodies, both alive and dead, was horrifying. Here is a brief description of what he did to his first victim, Steven Mark Hicks, an eighteen-year-old whom Dahmer picked up as a hitchhiker:

> Dahmer bludgeoned him with a 10 lb. dumbbell. Dahmer later stated he struck Hicks twice from behind with the dumbbell as he (Hicks) sat upon a chair. When Hicks fell unconscious, Dahmer strangled him to death with the bar of the dumbbell, then stripped the clothes from Hicks' body before masturbating as he stood above the corpse. The following day, Dahmer dissected Hicks' body in his crawl space; he later buried the remains in a shallow grave in his backyard before, several weeks later, unearthing the remains and paring the flesh from the bones. He dissolved the flesh in acid before flushing the solution down the toilet; he crushed the bones

with a sledgehammer and scattered them in the woodland behind the family home.[8]

This is an extreme example. Plenty of people can be vicious—or in this specific case cruel—without being *that* vicious. And Dahmer was likely mentally ill. But he does serve to illustrate my general point.

To sum up, a vicious person should have a relatively consistent pattern of morally problematic motives, leading to a relatively consistent pattern of morally problematic behavior. At least when he thinks no one is looking. Does the emerging evidence from psychology lead us to think that most people are vicious? You know by now what I am going to say. I think the answer is no.

Ask yourself if the pattern of behavior and motivation we documented over the past few chapters is what you would expect from a vicious person. We saw people who were deeply empathetic at times, doing costly and selfless things for others. We saw people refrain from inflicting electric shocks, even when they could shock as much as they liked. We saw people help in emergencies when they were by themselves. And we saw people not cheat when signing an honor code, even when they could have cheated as much as they liked to make more money. This is not what I would expect if most of us were vicious people.

Thus, it seems to me that most people have characters which are *neither* virtuous nor vicious. They instead fall in a middle space *between* virtue and vice. We can see this in figure 7.5.

Of course, you are probably asking what counts as "most people." I do not have any precise way to answer that question. But I can say this—if I am right, whenever you meet someone for the first time, your assumption should be that he or she belongs in this middle space. You should assume, in other words, that a person's character is

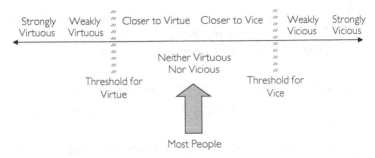

Figure 7.5 Where Most of Our Characters Reside

very much a mixed bag, with some good features but some bad ones too. We will see why this matters later in the chapter.

Now, please don't misunderstand me. I stress "most" people—not "all" people. Perhaps a few people *do* qualify on both sides of the spectrum. I think Mother Teresa, Leopold Socha, and Paul Farmer qualified when it came to the virtue of compassion, for instance. And I think it is safe to assume that Robert Harris and Jeffrey Dahmer did when it came to cruelty. Perhaps at certain times in the past, there have been more people on the virtue end than there are today. Perhaps today some countries do a better job of nurturing virtue in their citizens than others do. Nevertheless, it seems to me that, as far as the relevant evidence can tell us, virtuous people are very much in the minority.

So much for what most people's characters are *not* like. What more can be said about this vast middle space of mixed character? In particular, why is it that most of us seem to have such piecemeal characters that vary so much from situation to situation?

The answer, unfortunately, is a messy one. Rather than having the virtues or vices, most of us have a whole bunch of different likes and dislikes, feelings and emotions, beliefs and values, convictions and commitments, some of which are morally admirable and some of which are not. For example, here are some of the desires we saw earlier when it comes to helping others:

> I want to help when doing so will make me feel less guilty.
>
> I want to help when doing so will keep me in a good mood.
>
> I want to not help when it would potentially earn the disapproval of those watching me.
>
> I want to help so as to relieve someone else's distress (in cases of empathy).

Collectively these hardly look like they belong in the mind of a compassionate person.

Similarly, rather than the virtue of honesty when it comes to telling the truth, it is more common to find desires like these:

> I want to lie in order to avoid feeling embarrassed.
>
> I want to lie in order to avoid being shamed in front of others.
>
> I want to lie in order to hurt another person in certain situations.

But we also find evidence for the following desires:

> I want to lie in order to help another person avoid feeling embarrassed.
>
> I want to lie in order to prevent another person from getting hurt.

While the first group is nothing to write home about, morally speaking, the second group is. Together, they are quite a mixed bag.

When it comes to cheating, at least in cases involving tests and games, we also saw that the typical person is like this:

> I want to cheat in order to avoid personal failure and embarrassment.
>
> I want to cheat in order to avoid getting caught or punished for my wrongdoing.
>
> I believe that it is morally wrong to cheat (at least in most cases).
>
> I want to do the right thing and not cheat (at least in most cases).

Again, the good is mixed together with the bad.

To summarize, then, our characters are piecemeal and fragmented because we have so many different things going on in our mind that we bring with us to ethically charged situations. Depending on how we engage with those situations, the more positive side of our minds might be activated—or the more negative side.

Now we can see better why Frank is all over the map when it comes to helping other people, for instance. Today he comes across the Salvation Army ringer and donates five dollars. Why? He had been experiencing a lot of guilt, so he helps primarily to make himself feel better. The next day, he has a chance to help by standing up in front of a crowd, but he doesn't do it because he is worried about embarrassing himself. Then, the following week, he reads a story about a child hit by a drunk driver, feels a lot of empathy for her, and altruistically writes a check to help with the medical expenses. And so on.

Hence, we can expect lots of variation in a person's ethical behavior, which stems from lots of variation in her motives, which stems from lots of different mental "stuff" in her mind that could come into play in any given situation. Not everyone's mixed character is going to be mixed in exactly the same way, though. Larry might care a lot more about getting revenge on other people than Sam does, leading him to behave more aggressively in certain situations by comparison. So even if most people have a mixed character, we still have to take the time to get to know them and learn exactly how their particular character is put together.

In general, then, we are a lot better than we could be, but we are also a lot worse than we should be.

Why We Should Care about This Story

While it might be interesting to learn that most people are this way, what difference does any of this make at the end of the day? I can think of at least five ways in which it makes a whole lot of difference.

We Have False Beliefs

If what I have said is correct, then we are seriously mistaken about many of the people in our lives. I suspect you think that your friends are honest, for instance. Some of them might be—virtue is not impossible to attain—but I am betting that many of your friends really are not honest people. The sooner you learn this, the better.

But wait, you might protest. I have known John Smith for ten years and he's a great guy. If he were dishonest, surely I would have found out by now.

Not so fast. Yes, he might have been honest *around you*. But that does not make him honest, *period*. Again, what matters is what his heart is really like and what it leads him to do when he thinks no one is looking or he cannot get caught. And that may not be quite so easy for you to figure out.

Don't Be So Quick to Judge

We should be very hesitant to call anyone honest or dishonest, compassionate or callous, or any of the other virtues or vices. We will often be wrong in our assessment, unless we have unusually good insight into what is going on in the person.

In the case of Tiger Woods, we did. Given his pattern of behavior and motivation, it was not a stretch to call him dishonest and sexually intemperate. Other examples, like Robert Harris, Jeffrey Dahmer, Adolf Hitler, Joseph Stalin, Pol Pot, and Mao Zedong, are ones where we have plenty of evidence about their poor character at our disposal.

Now consider someone whom you just read about online. She is featured in the article because she has given $50,000 to start a clinic for Ebola victims in Africa. Our natural temptation is to go from the action—which is certainly wonderful—to a conclusion about her character. I think this is a big mistake. We know nothing about her motivation. Nor do we know anything about how she would be motivated and behave in other situations of need. For all we know, she could actually be a callous person, with selfish motives for starting the clinic. This is why we should not put people on a pedestal as being moral saints too quickly. They can just as quickly disappoint us. Caution and reserved judgment are needed.

We Can Understand and Predict People Better

If we think people are purely virtuous or vicious, we will be misunderstanding them. If we take the time to wade into the messy world of their actual psychology, we can understand better where they are coming from. For instance, we can comprehend some of what happened with the abusive behavior by American soldiers of prisoners at Abu Ghraib, Iraq.[9] Similarly we can understand better why Walter Vance was left to die on the floor of Target on Black Friday.[10]

Plus, we can *predict* the future better too. Here is an example. While it is true that some people are more empathetic than others, most of us are capable of experiencing empathy for the suffering of others. Knowing this fact can be important for getting people to help in the future. I would bet that if you can get people to feel empathy for the children captured by sex traffickers in India, you would find them volunteering for a greater number of hours to help than would a control group not made to feel empathy. Additionally, I would predict that if people felt empathy for these children in India and volunteered to help them today, then that will be a stable part of their characters which would show up again next month or even next year.

The same is true for morally problematic behavior. Frank might typically be very mellow and calm at the bar where he goes for a drink after work. In contrast, when he is cut off by someone on the road, he might tailgate the person aggressively. This is a stable feature of his character. He does the same thing next week when it happens again. Hence, his level of aggressiveness in this situation at one time can be used to predict his level of aggressiveness in the same situation at other times.

This point generalizes to the various situations Frank is in and how aggressive he ends up being in them, as we can see in figure 7.6. Here each dot represents one of twenty different situations that Frank has been in where he could have been aggressive. We can see that in some of them he was not aggressive at all, in others he was slightly aggressive, and in a few he was very aggressive (like when he got cut off in traffic).

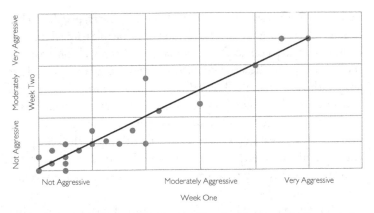

Figure 7.6 How Aggressive Frank Was in Twenty Situations during Two Weeks

The key point of figure 7.6 is that how aggressive Frank is when he is in one of these situations (for instance, the bar) is very similar to how aggressive he is the next time he is in the same situation (the bar a week later). This is true *despite* the fact that Frank behaves so differently from one situation (the bar) to the next (when he is cut off in traffic). His aggression fluctuates significantly *from* situation to situation, but it does not do so over time in the *same* situations.[11]

Frank is one of us. Once someone understands *my* character well, he can predict when my good moments will be and also when my bad moments will be. Past results are a reliable guide to future success and failure—at least when it comes to our characters.

We Should Lower Our Expectations . . . and Raise Them Too

Given the lack of virtue in our character, we should lower our expectations about how well people are going to behave. I do not just mean the politicians or celebrities that I have already mentioned (we already have low expectations there, perhaps), but coworkers, people in chat rooms, volunteers on the weekends, and other people with whom you come into regular contact. We should expect that not all, but many of them would try to cheat their company if they thought they could get away with it, or would tell harmful lies online, or would betray you and hurt you when under pressure from a boss or authority figure.

On the flip side, given the right conditions—moral reminders, inducements to feel empathy, or even minor things such as the presence of a mirror or a delicious smell—we should raise our expectations. Good behavior is to be expected here; it becomes the rule, not the exception.

It all depends on which side of our mixed characters is being activated.

We Fall Short

If most of us do not have the virtues, then most of us (myself included, no doubt!) are not currently the people it would be good to be. As we saw in chapter 2, being virtuous is very important and worthwhile.

For instance, we saw that a virtuous character is related to many good things in life, like increased life satisfaction, better health, and decreased anxiety. If we do not have a good character, then we could be missing out.

Also, the consequences of not being virtuous can be terrible. If the wrong kind of situation comes along, we could neglect the suffering of someone in an emergency. Even worse, we could ourselves willingly abuse and even kill innocent people out of a misguided sense of obedience.

Finally there is the possibility of God and the afterlife. Having a mixed character could land us in a lot of trouble in the next life, if there is one.

Conclusion

It matters that most of us have mixed characters that are neither virtuous nor vicious. It also matters whether we do something about this fact and try to become virtuous people. Given that most of us are not virtuous, what can we do to bridge the gap between our actual selves and the moral people we should become?

The remaining chapters will see if there is anything that can give us a helping hand.

Notes

1. See http://sfglobe.com/?id=13336. Accessed on February 2, 2017.
2. http://nypost.com/2010/04/24/stabbed-hero-dies-as-more-than-20-people-stroll-past-him/. Accessed on August 5, 2016.
3. http://www.telegraph.co.uk/news/worldnews/asia/china/8830790/Chinese-toddler-run-over-twice-after-being-left-on-street.html. Accessed on August 5, 2016.
4. Baron 1997.
5. Baron 1997: 501.
6. There may even be more kinds than these. See Batson 2011 for the most comprehensive discussion in psychology of these issues that I am aware of.
7. Latané and Darley 1970.
8. https://en.wikipedia.org/wiki/Jeffrey_Dahmer. Accessed March 7, 2016.
9. See chapter 4 and the discussion of obedience to authority figures.
10. See chapter 3 and the discussion of bystander effects.
11. To use fancy language from psychology, Frank's aggressiveness displays a great deal of within-person variability *across* these various situations. But *within* any one situation, it is also remarkably stable! Here and in figure 7.6 I have been helped by Fleeson 2001: 1018.

PART III

What Can We Do to Improve Our Characters?

8 | SOME LESS PROMISING STRATEGIES

Here is the predicament that most of us seem to be in. We are not virtuous people. We simply do not have characters that are good enough to qualify as honest, compassionate, wise, courageous, and the like. We are not vicious people either—dishonest, callous, foolish, cowardly, and so forth. Rather, we have a mixed character with some good sides and some bad sides. This, I have claimed, is the most plausible interpretation of what psychology tells us. It is also true to our lived experience in the world.

Those are the facts as I see them. Now comes the value judgment—*this is a real shame*. It is very unfortunate that our characters are this way. For reasons outlined in chapter 2, it is a good thing—indeed, a very good thing—to be a good person. Excellence of character, or being virtuous, is what we should all strive for.

Admittedly, the news is not all bad. It would be a lot worse if most of us were vicious people. Imagine what it would be like to live in a world full of mostly cruel, self-centered, dishonest, and hateful people. It would be hell on earth.

Nevertheless, at this point we are confronted with a significant gap:

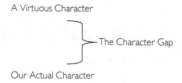

A Virtuous Character

The Character Gap

Our Actual Character

In the final part of this book, we will take up the question of how to bridge this *character gap*. In other words, what strategies are there to try to develop a better character, and which of these strategies show substantial promise? Here in this chapter, we will see three strategies that have some serious limitations. Chapter 9 provides us with several more promising alternatives. Finally, in chapter 10 we will end by looking at the character gap from a religious perspective.

Of course, you may not agree with my assessment of these strategies. Some might seem more promising to you than I think they are, or vice versa. That's okay with me—I am perfectly fine with being corrected about any of this. But I should at least be transparent about the criteria I will be using to judge the different approaches:

1. Is the strategy supported by empirical studies?
2. Would the strategy, if used successfully, actually improve our behavior? Would it do more than that, such as improve motivation as well, which is also necessary to becoming virtuous?
3. Would the effects of the strategy be long-lasting or quickly fade away?
4. Is the strategy realistic for most of us to adopt given our busy lives?
5. Does the strategy seem morally questionable in certain ways— say, by requiring that people be deceived?

We could think of more criteria than these five, and perhaps some of them are more important than others. For now, though, they give us plenty to work with.

One final note before we get to the strategies. If you are reading this, you have already experienced many years of character formation, whether you realize it or not. So these are strategies aimed, not at people whose characters are a blank slate, but rather at people like you and me who are already saddled with a character that is somewhere on the spectrum between being fully virtuous and being fully vicious. Given our rich and complex moral characters, the question for us becomes what we can do to make gradual progress toward being virtuous.

Having said this, going all the way back to Plato and Aristotle, many writers on character have held that childhood is the single most important period for character development. So I encourage you to think not only about how these strategies might be helpful (or not) for you personally, but also about how they might be important in aiding the character development of your own children, students, or other young people.

Don't expect any miracles here. None of these strategies will deliver quick results in terms of transforming someone's character. Character change is real, fortunately, but it is also very slow. These are our moral habits, and as we know from other areas of life (such as eating, exercising, and checking our phone), habits can be very hard to change. Slow, gradual progress is all we should reasonably expect, over the course of months or even years.

Now, on to the strategies.

Do Nothing

Here is the easiest one of the lot. In fact, it is so simple that you do not have to give it any effort. The strategy for bridging the character gap is to . . . simply do nothing and hope that over time you will just naturally become a better person.

Now, on the face of it, this strategy seems like a dead end. How is doing nothing going to make me better? When do we ever become better at *anything* without putting some effort into it?

But there might actually be more to this thought than meets the eye, for two reasons. First, as we get older, the demands of life change and can mature us in the process. Here is a much-studied example from the psychology literature. Conscientiousness, which includes traits like being self-disciplined, orderly, and deliberate, has been found to change over a life span. College students are notoriously low on this dimension, but it does gradually rise on average during our forties and fifties.[1] Why? Is it because by then we start putting a lot of time into developing a higher level of conscientiousness?

No, of course not. It is because our jobs and family situations often necessitate being a lot more conscientious. We have to show up on time to work or risk the consequences. That report had better not be late. The meeting is happening in five minutes. The kids need to be picked up from school. I must get the shopping done or we won't have anything to eat for dinner. If I don't change the diaper trash, the room is going to smell bad. And so on.

The second reason that doing nothing might still be a good strategy for promoting character development is that it gives us time to realize and learn from our mistakes. If we get caught cheating on our taxes or our resume, the ensuing punishment may teach us a lesson. If we are called out for telling lies at parties, the ensuing embarrassment may teach us a lesson. If we have a heart attack in our forties due to overeating, the ensuing fear may teach us a lesson. These lessons, and many more, can make us better people.[2]

So this "do nothing" strategy has more to recommend it than you may have originally thought,[3] but I do not think we should rest content with it. After all, we also know that the more time passes, the more we get set in our ways. Our habits, in other words, become more ingrained. This is especially true if there are no immediate repercussions for our bad habits.

Plus, it *is* a good question to ask how often in life it happens that we become excellent at something by doing nothing to work at it. I cannot think of many examples. Maybe some people are just genetically lucky or have some God-given talent for doing a difficult task well. But it rarely works out that way. Consider chess masters. They spend thousands and thousands of hours honing their skills to achieve genuine excellence. They were not born that way, and they would not have become chess masters on their own by doing nothing. No, they had to work at it.

The same, I submit, is true of moral character. We are not born honest or compassionate. Some people might be more predisposed in those directions than others, but still, character development takes both time and work to make a lot of progress. The morally best were helped along in their journey to becoming that way, either by themselves or others (or both).

These are valuable lessons to keep in mind in developing a strategy for character development. Virtues are acquired habits, which means that we don't have them to start with, and they will take time to cultivate. Repetition and practice are important, just as they are with becoming a chess master or NFL quarterback or champion diver. Promising strategies for character development, therefore, need to outline how they will help us become habituated in the right direction.

Let's see what else is out there that might assist us on the path to moral excellence.

Virtue Labeling

Here is a strategy for bridging the character gap that I bet you never thought of. Suppose you are convinced by what I have said up to this point, and have come to really believe that most people you know do not have any of the virtues. So your friend, your boss, your neighbor . . . you need to change your opinion of all of them.

Now, here is the interesting idea—even with this new outlook firmly in mind, you should still go ahead and call them honest people next time you see them. You should still praise them for being compassionate. You should go out of your way to comment on their courage.

Why would you do such a thing? Isn't that just wrong?

Let's wait and see. The idea is to attach a label to people you know. Labels make a big difference. For with that label attached to them, there is a good chance that they will try to live up to it. And perhaps the more they care about living up to the label, such as *honest person*, the more they will actually *become* that honest person.[4]

Thanks to some clever experiments, we know that this kind of thing works quite well, at least in some contexts. Here are examples:

The tidy study. The most famous experiment was published back in 1975 by the University of Nebraska psychologist Richard Miller and his colleagues. One group of fifth graders was labeled "tidy." The researchers tried to persuade a second group of kids to be tidier. A third group functioned as the controls. The results? It was the "tidy" group that actually was the tidiest.[5]

The tower-building study. Another study with children, this time conducted by Roger Jensen and Shirley Moore in the 1970s at the University of Minnesota, had one group receive "cooperative" labels, while a second received "competitive" labels. Later in the same day, the kids played a tower-building game. It turned out that by the time they played the game, many of the children forgot their labels, but still the ones in the "cooperative" group placed double the number of blocks in the game![6]

The environmental study. To take a more recent study from 2007, consider what happened when the economist Gert Cornelissen at the Pompeu Fabra University in Italy used the label "very concerned with the environment and ecologically conscious" for some customers looking for TVs. These labeled customers turned out to be more environmentally responsible in their shopping than (1) shoppers in a control group, and even (2) shoppers who had been urged to be more environmentally mindful in their spending.[7]

What is going on here? What explains these results?

One thing we know is that the label does not need to work its magic at the conscious level; indeed, many participants did not even recall the earlier labeling. Yet it still made a difference. Furthermore, we know that when we get labeled a certain way, other people will expect us to act that way in the future. If the label is a positive one, we don't want to let them down. We like being thought highly of and want that to continue.[8] Beyond these preliminary observations, though, there does not seem to be a well-developed and widely accepted model in the psychology literature to explain how character labeling makes such a difference. For instance, do people actually come to *believe* that they are honest, and integrate that belief into how they think and act? Or is it just that they know that *others* believe this about them, regardless of whether they share this perspective too?

Leaving aside this unfortunate lack of clarity, you might have noticed that the studies above did not involve clear examples of moral traits—the examples were tidiness, competitiveness, and ecological consciousness. So do we have any reason to think that this labeling effect happens in the moral realm too? Yes we do. For the same pattern of results shows up in studies involving what are obviously morally relevant labels. In an early study, for instance, Robert Kraut at Carnegie Mellon had his assistants knock on doors during the day and ask people at home to make a donation to a heart association. For those who did donate, half were told, "You are a generous person. I wish more of the people I met were as charitable as you," and half were not.[9] For nondonors, half were labeled "uncharitable" and half were not.

What difference did these labels make? Well, a week later the same people were this time asked to donate to a local funding-raising campaign for multiple sclerosis. Here are the results:[10]

	Average amount of donation to MS research
Donor, charitable label	$0.70
Donor, no label	$0.41
Nondonor, uncharitable label	$0.23
Nondonor, no label	$0.33

Note the significant difference in donation amount in the first two lines, a difference that seems to be influenced by the difference in label.

Or consider how Angelo Strenta at Dartmouth College and William DeJong at Boston University gave the label "kind, thoughtful person" to some participants, and a few minutes later an actor dropped a stack of 500 computer punch cards. These labeled folks helped to pick up an average of 163.5 cards and spent 30.1 seconds doing so. By comparison, the results were 84.4 cards and 21.6 seconds for those in the control group who never got the label![11]

So indeed, labeling people with moral virtue terms does seem to make a difference, at least as far as the preliminary evidence suggests. Given this, let's think for a moment about how we might take these findings and use them in developing a strategy for bridging the character gap. One idea goes something like this. Start praising your spouse or your children for their compassion, even if you have reason to doubt it. Extoll the honesty of your friends, even if you have to bite your tongue in doing so. Whenever anyone does something nice to you, thank him or her for being a gracious or loving or kind person, rather than just showing appreciation for a particular kind act.

Suppose you are a middle-school teacher. You have reason to suspect that some of your students might have cheated on a recent homework assignment. Soon you have to give them an important test, and the classroom is crowded. You worry that there might be some temptation to glance at other exams or trade answers under the desks. You could ask them to not cheat. You could remind them of the possibility of suspension or expulsion. Yet what comes to mind is the psychology research on the power of labeling. So instead you go out of your way to convey the message in the days leading up to the test that you think they are *honest people*. Then, on the big day, you say something like, "Given that this is such a trustworthy class, I'm not worried about copying and I'm not going to separate you." Or perhaps "Because I know that you all care about honesty, I'm sure that you'll do the right thing."

The hope, in all these examples mentioned above, is that you will see a change over time as these folks—your family members, friends, and students—actually improve their behavior, even if gradually, in the direction of living up to the expectations of the label.

That is the hope, at least. But how realistic of a hope is it, really? It is certainly a clever idea. But I think we should be hesitant to adopt it, for three important reasons. First, *we really have no idea if virtue labeling actually works.*

Wait, didn't I just mention a bunch of studies where it does? But we need to be careful. For one thing, there have actually not been that many studies done on this phenomenon, especially when it comes to using virtue labels, which is our main interest here. Of course, that doesn't by itself show that the strategy is unpromising. It could still end up working really well. It just means that we need to do a lot of work in testing it out first.

We also do not know whether a virtue label encourages more virtuous behavior only in the short run, or whether the effect persists.[12] For that kind of discovery, we would need longitudinal studies that follow the same people over time and regularly assess the impact of these labels on their behavior—say, over the course of months or even years.

In addition—and this is the third reason for hesitation—even if someone's behavior *does* gradually improve over the long run due to the labeling effect, we know that this alone would *not* automatically make someone a virtuous person. As we said all the way back in chapter 1, motivation matters to virtue too. So do people labeled as compassionate or honest come to cultivate the right kinds of motives over time?

You might think not. As noted above, people who receive the virtue label seem to behave better. Is that because, for instance, they genuinely care about others (compassionate motivation) or they genuinely care about telling the truth (honest motivation)? Or is it because they want to live up to the label they have been given? If it is the latter, then that is hardly a virtuous kind of motive. It is self-interested, with the focus on making a good impression or not disappointing someone, which is not where it needs to be for virtue.[13]

So on the basis of three of my criteria, I can't get very excited about this strategy just yet, given our limited understanding of it. But suppose that in the next hundred years, the stars align. Lots more research is done on the effects of virtue labeling, it probes motivation as well as action, *and* the results are surprisingly positive in showing long-term virtuous effects. *Even still*, there is a reason to be nervous.

How can that be? Yes, I admit that people becoming more virtuous would be great. But what about the means of getting there? Isn't there something downright disturbing about labeling people with virtue terms when you know that they don't have any of those virtues?[14]

Now for some people the outcome is all that matters. The ends justify the means. Since this strategy would—if the stars aligned in the way I just described—give us a great outcome, then it is perfectly fine.

However, many of us are not prepared to go that far in general and say that the ends always justify the means. I am one of those people. To my mind, this way of thinking could be used to try to excuse terrible atrocities along the way to achieving something worthwhile.

When it comes to virtue labeling, we are not talking about terrible atrocities, of course. Yet there still might be something morally questionable about praising someone for being an honest person while all along believing she is not in fact honest. My goal is supposed to be the noble one of contributing to her becoming a better person in the long run. To achieve that goal, though, I am supposed to get her to believe something about herself that I know is not true, and do this in a way that sounds genuine and heartfelt. In other words, I am to come across as sincere in thinking she is honest, thereby enabling her to trust me and believe it herself. A clever ruse on my part that can sound morally repugnant—hypocritical, deceptive, manipulative, and a violation of someone's autonomy. To many people, it is all of these things.

Indeed, if you were really committed to this strategy for bridging the character gap, you would *not* want to tell people about it. You would even be annoyed at someone like me spilling the beans. For the more word gets out, the less effective the labeling will become as people grow suspicious about whether the praise of their characters is genuine or manipulative. So there is another level of deception involved here—in order to effectively implement this strategy you would need to take steps to *suppress* other people knowing about the strategy!

None of this sounds very good, does it? Do you really want to adopt a strategy—for promoting virtue, after all—that has to rely on multiple layers of deception to be successful?

By now you might be fed up with this strategy and are ready to see what else is out there. Before we do, I think we should be fair to both sides. I always tell my students that this is one of the things they need to do to become good philosophers. So here is one parting thought in defense of virtue labeling.

Consider placebos. Doctors have been using them on patients for decades, and there is some evidence that they are effective. They are not legally banned, nor are they morally condemned by the American medical profession for use in clinical trials (although there is more resistance to using placebos in clinical practice).[15]

Now think for a moment about what administering placebos often involves. The organizers of a trial might decide that certain participants will receive a sugar pill. If it is a double-blind trial, then the actual doctor who meets with the participants does not know whether the treatment she is prescribing is a placebo or not. She will simply come across as medically authoritative and confident. The participants, meanwhile, might have been notified that there is a chance they could receive a placebo, but will likely believe that in fact they are receiving a promising drug treatment. Naturally the organizers of the trial do not want word about placebos to get out to the general public, as otherwise their participants might start becoming suspicious, which would undercut the effectiveness of the placebo in the first place.

The parallels to virtue labels should be obvious. Indeed, these labels can be viewed as a kind of placebo. Where does this leave us, then? We might try to think of important differences between the virtue-labeling case and the medical case. If there are none, then if you are okay with placebos, you should be okay with virtue labeling. Or if you are not okay with virtue labeling, then you should not be okay with placebos. Where do you end up?

I personally still think the deception involved with using this virtue-labeling strategy is a major problem. But as I said at the beginning of the chapter, I know that others might assess things differently, and I am open to being wrong.

Nudging toward Virtue

Let's shift gears here, and turn our attention to the bathroom (again!). Consider the following from a recent book:

> *Fly in the Urinal.* A wonderful example ["of nudging people towards change"] comes from, of all places, the men's rooms at Schiphol Airport in Amsterdam. There the authorities have etched the image of a black housefly into each urinal. It seems that men usually do not pay much attention to where they aim,

which can create a bit of a mess, but if they see a target, attention and therefore accuracy are much increased.[16]

Most male readers have probably come across such a fly at one point or another in a public bathroom. The surprising thing is—they really work! According to one study at this airport in Amsterdam, spilling decreased by 80%.[17]

The fly in the urinal is an example of a nudge offered by the behavioral economist Richard Thaler and the law scholar Cass Sunstein. In their bestselling book *Nudge: Improving Decisions about Health, Wealth, and Happiness*, they introduced the idea of nudges to a general audience. It struck a chord with readers and generated a huge amount of discussion, some of which has found its way into influential public policy decisions in the United States, the United Kingdom, and elsewhere.[18]

What are nudges? Thaler and Sunstein provide the following definition:

> A nudge, as we will use the term, is any aspect of the choice architecture that alters people's behavior in a predictable way without forbidding any options or significantly changing their economic incentives. To count as a mere nudge, the intervention must be easy and cheap to avoid. Nudges are not mandates.[19]

What they mean by "choice architecture" is just the context or situation in which a decision is being made.

The fly in the urinal counts as a nudge on this definition. It is an aspect of the situation of going to the bathroom at a urinal. It does not forbid any options—you can still aim in any direction you like. Not much has changed with the economic incentives, as far as I can see, by adding the fly to the urinal. It is easy to avoid when going to the bathroom. There is no mandate to try to hit the fly. And yet it does alter people's behavior in a predictable way.

You might be thinking that this is a pretty trivial example. Here are some other examples of nudges:

> *Retirement enrollment.* When eligible, employees are automatically enrolled in their company's retirement plan. They have to complete a form to opt out of it. "Automatic enrollment has proven to be an extremely effective way to increase enrollment in U.S. defined-contribution plans."[20]

> *Organ donor.* Currently in the United States you do not have to give any thought to organ donation when you renew your driver's license. But this could be changed, so that now before renewing, the driver has to complete a form indicating whether he would like to participate in the program or not.[21]

> *Quit smoking.* As a way to nudge smokers, someone who is trying to quit could start a bank account with a dollar in it at the start. Then, "For six months, she deposits the amount of money she would otherwise spend on cigarettes into the account. After six months, the client takes a urine test to confirm that she has not smoked recently. If she passes the test, she gets her money back. If she fails the test, the account is closed and the money is donated to charity."[22]

Now that we are talking about organ donations and quitting smoking, no one is going to deny that a lot is at stake in this discussion.

Here is something worth noting about nudges. As defined by Thaler and Sunstein, there does not actually have to be a person or group of people who does the nudging on purpose. Nudging can happen by accident—say, by walking up to a group of people and seeing that they are doing nothing to stop an emergency, which nudges you to do nothing as well.

Harmless environmental influences can also serve as nudges. Recall the effect of good smells in a shopping mall that was discussed in chapter 7, and how those smells subsequently led certain shoppers to help much more than controls. The smell was a by-product of baking the cookies, and yet the smell happened to nudge shoppers in the direction of helping.

While these count as cases of nudging, what has generated a lot of interest are cases where nudging is done *on purpose*, particularly by larger entities like schools, companies, and governments. We can see this in the examples above. A company nudges its employees to save better, or the government nudges drivers to become organ donors.

Here is another thing that Thaler and Sunstein emphasize. Nudging is meant to take advantage of our psychological irrationalities and limitations. If we were perfectly rational people, we would have no need for nudges. We would just choose the option that is most rational, such as joining the retirement plan, quitting smoking (or even better, never starting in the first place), and, for males, aiming well in the urinal.

Clearly we are anything but perfectly rational. As Thaler and Sunstein document at length, we fall prey to all kinds of fallacies, irrationalities, biases, and the like.[23] Nudges are specifically designed to take advantage of these issues.[24] We are susceptible to inertia, for instance, and so often don't rock the boat by changing whatever the default setting is on something. For example, every semester my students inevitably sit in the same seats in the classroom, even though I don't have assigned seating. Similarly, magazines love it when customers sign up for automatic renewal, since they know that many of them will never bother to call and cancel their subscriptions even long after they have stopped reading the publication.[25]

Inertia is fine when the default setting is for something good, but not so fine when it isn't. So given this tendency, the fan of nudging might say:

> Let's have a company or the government try to compensate for people's inertia by making the default setting something that is good for the employees or citizens. That way they still have the choice to get out of the deal if they want to (opt out of the retirement plan, for instance), but given that most people won't do this due to inertia, these folks will still benefit in the long run thanks to this nudge.

If instead the default was to not be enrolled in the retirement program, or to not be asked about organ donation, the long-term effects of inertia would be much worse.

This highlights one last point—nudges can be toward what is good for people or toward what is bad. By itself a nudge does not have to be toward one or the other. Hence people could be nudged toward healthy eating, or toward junk food. Nudging can happen toward smoking, rather than away from it. The fly is placed in the center of the urinal and has a good result. But it could be placed in another spot instead. Imagine what would happen then.

There is much more to Thaler and Sunstein's position, including the development of an entire philosophy of using nudges, which they call "libertarian paternalism."[26] Rather than getting bogged down in the details, I want to keep the focus squarely on character development.

What really *is* the connection to character development, though? In some cases, the connection is far from obvious. Donating organs is clearly morally relevant—lives could be saved by this medical intervention. Yet suppose the only change is that now you have to choose, when renewing your driver's license, between joining the program or not. It is hard to see how this would really have any impact on shaping your character for the better in a significant way, even if you decide to enroll. You simply check a box and then move on with life.

There are other examples from Thaler and Sunstein, though, that are both rich in their moral implications and that could help to bridge the character gap:

> *Give more tomorrow.* Oftentimes we know we ought to help someone in need, but we get distracted and then the opportunity is gone. With the Give More Tomorrow program, people would be asked "whether they would like to give a small amount to their favorite charities starting sometime soon, then commit to increasing their donations every year."[27]
>
> *The civility check*: A computer program would scan an email you just wrote to make sure it is not angry or uncivil. If it is, then before the email is sent you would get a message like: "WARN-ING: THIS APPEARS TO BE AN UNCIVIL EMAIL. DO YOU REALLY AND TRULY WANT TO SEND IT?"[28]
>
> *Dollar a day.* This program has been tried in several cities as a way to reduce teenage pregnancies. If a teenage girl already has a child, then for every day she is not pregnant she receives a dollar from the government that, depending on the details of the program, could be designated toward paying for college.[29]

Yet here too, despite these examples, I think we need to be cautious.

First of all, we simply have no idea what the long-term effects of these nudges will be. Both *Give more tomorrow* and *The civility check* are merely hypothetical programs at this point. No one is actually being nudged in this way. Other nudges that are in fact being used, such as *Dollar a day*, have not yet been studied over the long run with a control group and a group of people being nudged, to see what differences in their character emerge. So the first caution is simply that we do not yet have the data.

Without the data, we have to speculate a bit. My speculation is that many of these nudges pertaining to moral behavior will not have a significant lasting impact on character. Take *Give more tomorrow*. It could make the world a better place, but all it involves is signing up for a donation arrangement that handles your donations, in progressively increasing amounts, far into the future. That doesn't seem to me like it would move the needle very much in strengthening our compassionate character. It remains to be seen whether other nudges will do better. That is my second caution.[30]

No surprise—I also worry about what happens to motivation with nudges. Take *The civility check*. Here I could see this having some lasting effects on my email behavior. After a while, I would get tired of these warning messages and could imagine regulating my civility in my emails so that I avoid this annoyance. As hoped, I just might become a calmer and nicer person over email.

Notice, though, that I wouldn't be changing for a virtuous reason. It isn't because I have come to appreciate the harm I might be causing with my angry words, the hurt feelings or damaged relationships. It is because I don't want to have to be warned again. The reason is egoistic, not virtuous. So whether nudging improves motivation, and not just behavior, is my third caution.[31]

Finally, I worry about who is doing the nudging. Let's think about this some more. Someone or some group of people is trying to arrange the situations of our lives so that we are nudged into having better characters. As parents we do this with children all the time, and they have no idea what we are up to. But it's a different story when we are talking about companies or governments nudging adults in one way or another.

After all, since virtue is rare, that would apply to companies and governments as well. I am a bit nervous about their taking on the job of nudging the rest of us. Even if they do have good intentions, how does it make you feel to know that the government is aware of your faults, foibles, and fallacies, and is using them in order to nudge you toward virtue?

I suspect that many of us would be quite uncomfortable if the government were to adopt a secretive program of nudging. It makes sense, after all, that some nudges won't be nearly as effectively if we are told about them and how they worked. For them to be most effective, we need to be paying attention to something else. So the government (or your company, your school, etc.) could have reason to want to keep those nudges a secret. But I doubt most of us would stand for this.

In light of this fourth caution, then, the most morally respectable character nudges would be ones where we are informed about what is going on, and we are okay with it. *Give more tomorrow, The civility check,* and *Dollar a day* would come out okay. However, a secret program to improve character that relied upon subliminal advertising messages about giving more to charity would not. Nor would a company using smaller plates in the cafeteria in order to nudge its employees to eat less, without telling them that this is what they are doing.[32]

Let me be very clear. Nothing I have said is meant to close the door on using the nudging strategy to improve character. Rather, it is meant to help emphasize the difficult task that awaits those who want to go down this road. For I hope we can see more clearly that a successful character nudge will have to pass a number of tests:

1. Does it have lasting positive effects in promoting virtuous behavior?
2. Does it have lasting positive effects in promoting virtuous motivation too?
3. Have these effects been demonstrated in experimental studies that follow people over the course of months and even years?
4. Will the nudges come from a good or trustworthy source?
5. Is the nudge transparent to everyone involved, rather than being secretive or deceptive?

These tests should remind you of the criteria from the start of the chapter for assessing character improvement strategies. I remain skeptical that many nudges will survive this gauntlet. But I would be happy to stand corrected.

To make this all a bit more concrete, consider a very clever nudge study that we funded through the Character Project. The researcher, a psychologist at Indiana University named Sara Hope, wanted to find a way to increase empathy in college students. Recall from chapter 3 that empathy is an extremely promising starting point for developing the virtue of compassion, given that it can increase helping for altruistic motives.

Knowing how savvy students are with their phones these days, Hope had an experimental group of students receive text messages relevant to empathy six times a day for fourteen days. A control group of students did not receive such messages. Here is an example of one of these texts: "Think about your last social interaction. What obstacles or challenges does the person face? See these problems from their point of view."[33]

Hope used all kinds of measures to see what impact, if any, these texts had on the students in comparison to the control group. Let me mention just two. Four days after the texts stopped coming, the students went back to her lab and, among other things, "were asked to watch a short video depicting Karen Klein, a school bus monitor who was bullied by adolescent males on her school bus. This was a real video that was recorded by the actual bullies and then later posted on YouTube."[34] Then they were given an opportunity to volunteer for an antibullying organization.

In addition, six months later, students received the following text from what, to their eyes, would appear to be a random number: "stop txting me u jerk!"[35] The texts back from the students, which actually came to Hope's lab, were then coded for their level of aggressiveness.

What did Hope find? Compared to the control group, the students who had been through the empathy text nudges signed up to work more with the antibullying organization, and six months later, responded less aggressively to the rude text message.

Sara Hope's study is very promising. The students were nudged by the empathy texts, and the nudges seemed to make a difference to their character both in the short run and in the long run. The source of the nudges is trustworthy, and there was no deception behind the messages. The students could easily recognize the purpose of the texts.

Alas even here, not all the tests were passed. For we don't know about the motivation behind the student's behavior, both in the short run with the antibully campaign and in the long run with the rude text message. And I would add that how students respond to one rude text is a very weak indicator of how compassionate they are. It is hard to know from their response whether the empathy nudges six months earlier had any significant impact or not. Much more of a test is needed.

Again, though, I don't want to come across as overly negative about nudges and character. My hope is that, at some point in the future, we can come up with some useful ones that pass the tests.[36]

Conclusion

As we start to think about ways to try to shrink the character gap in each of our lives, we have considered three different strategies—do nothing, use virtue labels, and nudge toward virtue. In each case I have tried to be as fair as I can in assessing the strategy, and they all do have some good features.

But we need more help than this. In the next chapter, let's turn to some more promising approaches.

Notes

1. Roberts 2009.
2. Note that even here, we are moving beyond the "do nothing" strategy. Responding in a positive and character-building way to our mistakes is not "doing nothing."
3. This is especially true in the case of someone who is brought up in a virtuous society with a stable family, good moral upbringing, plentiful role models, and so forth. All of this can be deeply formative, even if the person herself does not consciously take any steps to work toward becoming a better person (and so "does nothing" in this respect). This theme is prevalent in the writings of ancient Greek philosophers like Plato and Aristotle. And I find it very persuasive, *if* one happens to be so fortunate growing up. Of course, most of us are not.
4. How about in the other direction—can using a vice label lead to people acting worse? The answer, based on some preliminary research, seems to

be yes, although as we know acting worse does not automatically mean becoming vicious. For the research, see Kraut 1973 and Strenta and DeJong 1981: 146.

5. Miller et al. 1975.

6. Jensen and Moore 1977.

7. Cornelissen et al. 2007: 281.

8. For relevant discussion, see Jensen and Moore 1977: 307 and Cornelissen et al. 2007: 279.

9. Kraut 1973: 554.

10. Kraut 1973: 556.

11. Strenta and DeJong 1981: 145. For additional studies using moral trait labels, see Grusec et al. 1978; Grusec and Redler 1980; and Mills and Grusec 1989. For additional discussion, see Alfano 2013.

12. For studies that found the effects lasting at least one to two weeks, see Kraut 1973 and Grusec and Redler 1980. For speculation that the effects may only be short-lived, see Strenta and DeJong 1981: 146.

13. To be fair, it might be better in many cases to try to live up to someone's impression that you are honest, than it is to not care about whether you are thought of by others as honest. Similarly, it might be better to feel bad that others think you are dishonest, than it is to not care. Nevertheless, even despite these positives, the focus is still in the wrong place. It is on what others think of you, rather than on what is true and false (in the case of the virtue of honesty).

14. This is different from just being generous in calling someone a virtuous person when you don't have much evidence one way or the other about her. I have much less reservation about doing that. But here the idea is that you should use the virtue label, *even when* it is clear that the person does not qualify as virtuous in the first place.

15. See "Opinion 8.083—Placebo Use in Clinical Practice," American Medical Association Code of Medical Ethics. Adopted November 2006.

16. Thaler and Sunstein 2008: 4.

17. Thaler and Sunstein 2008: 4.

18. For a brief review, see Hansen and Jespersen 2013: 4.

19. Thaler and Sunstein 2008: 6. There are problems with this definition, as pointed out by Hausman and Welch 2010 and Hansen 2016, but we don't need to get into those issues here.

20. Thaler and Sunstein 2008: 111.

21. Thaler and Sunstein 2008: 182. Although as Walter Sinnott-Armstrong pointed out to me, it is not completely clear how this would be a mere nudge if checking a box is now required of each person. Which box to check, though, would still not be mandated at least.

22. Thaler and Sunstein 2008: 234.

23. They mention errors that arise in association with anchoring, availability, representativeness, overconfidence, framing, and conformity, among others. For what these terms mean and why the errors are thought to be widespread, see Thaler and Sunstein 2008: part 1.

24. Thaler and Sunstein 2008: 8. See also Hausman and Welch 2010: 126 and especially Hansen 2016.

25. These two examples are used in Thaler and Sunstein 2008: 34–35.

26. Thaler and Sunstein 2008: 5.

27. Thaler and Sunstein 2008: 231.

28. Thaler and Sunstein 2008: 237.

29. Thaler and Sunstein 2008: 236.

30. In an interesting study of treatment methods for cocaine dependence over the course of twenty-four weeks of counseling, Stephen Higgins and his colleagues at the University of Vermont offered participants a nudge in the form of either vouchers or lottery tickets for each cocaine-negative urine specimen. Compared to controls which just received the counseling, cocaine abstinence in the voucher group was significantly higher both during the twenty-four-week treatment period *and* even eighteen months posttreatment. See Higgins et al. 2000. Thanks to Walter Sinnott-Armstrong for pointing this study out to me.

31. To be fair, even if it doesn't improve motivation in the short run, it might do so in the long run. Perhaps after a while of using the civility check I could, for instance, come to appreciate how frequently I am being uncivil over email, and commit to becoming a more civil person. Not because of the

annoyance created by the warning messages, but because I come to see how important civility is.

32. For further discussion of this issue, see Thaler and Sunstein 2008: 247–248 and especially the very careful analysis in Hausman and Welch 2010 and Hansen and Jespersen 2013. For highly critical discussion of nudging as violating core liberal values, see Grüne-Yanoff 2012. In particular he notes that even a program like *Give more tomorrow* might backfire if people were made aware of the reasons donations are being structured this way. Finally, for more on the specific nudge of using smaller plates, see Kallbekken 2013.

33. Hope 2015: 419.

34. Hope 2015: 423.

35. Hope 2015: 423.

36. This includes self-nudges, or nudges that you self-consciously give to yourself in an effort to improve your future behavior (and character). We will see some examples of these self-nudges in the next chapter.

9 | SOME STRATEGIES WITH MORE PROMISE

There are three strategies for bridging the character gap that I think we should put into practice this very day—looking to role models, selecting our situations, and getting the word out. For each of them, I will suggest that they are on the right track, but I will also be a bit guarded: first, because the experimental evidence supporting these strategies continues to be limited, and second, because each strategy can only do so much to help improve character. This will prepare the way for the final chapter, where we will look to see if any additional help can be provided by religious communities, and ultimately by the divine.[1]

Moral Role Models

Who have been your moral role models in life? It is worth spending a moment thinking about this. They may be one of the keys to making progress in developing your character going forward.

For me it starts with my parents. My mother, for instance, has battled a debilitating and terribly painful nerve condition in her legs for over twenty years now. Despite constant pain and cramping that will sometimes keep her awake for three or four nights in a row, she hardly ever complains and manages to handle her situation with uncommon grace, fortitude, and faith. Whenever I am going through a difficult time, I am reminded that my situation is nothing like what she faces on a daily basis. That serves as a source of strength and resolve for me.

As a boy growing up in South Florida, I was inspired by my father to help protect the endangered sea turtles where we lived. Every day for at least six months of the year, we would patrol our three-mile stretch of beach and rescue baby hatchlings that would not have survived on their own. There were times when I couldn't join him (or was just too lazy). Yet there he was out on the burning sand for three hours each day without fail. After a number of years working with the sea turtles, I started to receive some media attention and recognition. My father had done the majority of the work and was the one who deserved to be recognized. But he was always content to stay on the sidelines. I didn't realize it at the time, but he was a great example to me of what dedication, sacrifice, commitment, and humility really mean.

There are other examples from my life. My middle-school English teacher, Mr. Greco. My college roommate and best man at my wedding, Dr. Andy Chu. My wife and young children, who teach me to see the world in such a joyful and loving way.

Then there are the people I have never met. Jesus forgiving his enemies. Mother Teresa ministering to lepers in India. The courage of William Wilberforce to work toward abolishing the slave trade in England. And naturally the three examples of virtue we saw earlier: Leopold Socha, Abraham Lincoln, and Paul Farmer.

Add to this list literary examples. I think about the power of the parable of the Good Samaritan and how many times throughout history it has inspired acts of charity:

Jesus said: "A man was going down from Jerusalem to Jericho, when he was attacked by robbers. They stripped him of his clothes, beat him and went away, leaving him half dead. A priest happened to be going down the same road, and when he saw the man, he passed by on the other side. So too, a Levite, when he came to the place and saw him, passed by on the other side. But a Samaritan, as he traveled, came where the man was; and when he saw him, he took pity on him. He went to him and bandaged his wounds, pouring on oil and wine. Then he put the man on his own donkey, brought him to an inn and took care of him. The next day he took out two denarii and gave them to the innkeeper. "Look after him," he said, "and when I return, I will reimburse you for any extra expense you may have."

"Which of these three do you think was a neighbor to the man who fell into the hands of robbers?"

The expert in the law replied, "The one who had mercy on him."

Jesus told him, "Go and do likewise."[2]

The sacrifice of Sydney Carton at the end of *A Tale of Two Cities* is also incredibly powerful, but I don't want to ruin the story for you if you have not read it. Instead, let me take another moving example from literature, this time of deep forgiveness. It is the famous scene from *Les Misérables* by Victor Hugo, where the main character, Jean Valjean, has just been released from prison. In a moment of desperation he steals some silver from a bishop who has welcomed him into his church, and then flees the scene:

The door opened. A singular and violent group made its appearance on the threshold. Three men were holding a fourth man by the collar. The three men were gendarmes; the other was Jean Valjean...

"Ah! here you are!" he exclaimed, looking at Jean Valjean. "I am glad to see you. Well, but how is this? I gave you the candlesticks too, which are of silver like the rest, and for which you can certainly get two hundred francs. Why did you not carry them away with your forks and spoons?"

Jean Valjean opened his eyes wide, and stared at the venerable Bishop with an expression which no human tongue can render any account of.

"Monseigneur," said the brigadier of gendarmes, "so what this man said is true, then? We came across him. He was walking like a man who is running away. We stopped him to look into the matter. He had this silver—"

"And he told you," interposed the Bishop with a smile, "that it had been given to him by a kind old fellow of a priest with whom he had passed the night? I see how the matter stands. And you have brought him back here? It is a mistake."

"In that case," replied the brigadier, "we can let him go?"

"Certainly," replied the Bishop...

"My friend," resumed the Bishop, "before you go, here are your candlesticks. Take them."

He stepped to the chimney-piece, took the two silver candlesticks, and brought them to Jean Valjean. The two women looked on without uttering a word, without a gesture, without a look which could disconcert the Bishop.

Jean Valjean was trembling in every limb. He took the two candlesticks mechanically, and with a bewildered air.

"Now," said the Bishop, "go in peace. By the way, when you return, my friend, it is not necessary to pass through the garden. You can always enter and depart through the street door. It is never fastened with anything but a latch, either by day or by night." ...

The Bishop drew near to him, and said in a low voice:

"Do not forget, never forget, that you have promised to use this money in becoming an honest man."

Jean Valjean, who had no recollection of ever having promised anything, remained speechless. The Bishop had emphasized the words when he uttered them. He resumed with solemnity:

"Jean Valjean, my brother, you no longer belong to evil, but to good. It is your soul that I buy from you; I withdraw it from black thoughts and the spirit of perdition, and I give it to God."[3]

It is hard not to deeply admire what the Bishop did, and I hope I would feel a powerful call to forgive if I am ever placed in a similar situation.

We can draw out several themes from these examples. First, our moral role models can be actual people living today, or they can be people from the past who are no longer with us. Furthermore, they may be role models because of one single action they performed, as in the case of Sydney Carton or the Bishop. Or they may be role models because of the kind of life they lived in general, as in the case of Jesus, Abraham Lincoln, Paul Farmer, or closer to home for me, my mother, father, and wife.

Third, role models can be important not only because of what they *actually* did or the lives they *actually* lived, but also because of what they *would have done* in a situation. This point was noted thousands of years ago by the ancient Stoic Epictetus: "When you are about to meet someone, especially someone who seems to be distinguished, put to yourself the question, 'What would Socrates or Zeno have done in these circumstances?' and you will not be at a loss as to how to deal with the occasion."[4] Today we would be at a loss if we asked ourselves what Zeno would have done in a difficult moral situation, but the same underlying idea is still familiar. For instance, "WWJD" wristbands were extremely common for a time among Christians ("What Would Jesus Do?"), and they served the same function that Epictetus had in mind.

Finally, we can see that role models do not even have to be real people to have a powerful effect on our moral lives. Narratives, works of fiction, stories, plays, poetry, movies, television programs, and the like, all have models of morally inspirational behavior and lives. Again, the parable of the Good Samaritan and *Les Misérables* are two clear examples.[5]

How exactly do moral role models have an effect on us? No one has come up with a detailed account of how they function, as far as I am aware. We did see one idea in our discussion in chapter 2 of how moral exemplars help us care about becoming better people. That element had to do with the emotion of *admiration*. I admire the Bishop's action, and the self-sacrifice of the Good Samaritan. I admire Mother Teresa's virtue of compassion in helping the poor, and Leopold Socha's virtue of courage in repeatedly risking all that he had to protect the Jews in the sewer. I admire the lives of Jesus and Abraham Lincoln. These actions, character traits, and lives appear deeply admirable or *worthy of* admiration to me. Plus there are distinctive feelings that come along with my admiration of them. These include feelings of being uplifted and inspired in which my heart is moved and energized. Back in chapter 2 we called them feelings of elevation.

Importantly, one of the feelings that typically come with admiration is *emulation*. I want to *be like* Lincoln; I want to *do* what the Bishop did. So it is not just that I have positive feelings about these people and their behavior. It is that admiration works on me too, inspiring me to change myself to become more like them, at least in the ways in which I admire them.

That's the key part, as far as the character gap is concerned. My admiration for Paul Farmer can hopefully lead to my emulation of his character, which can in turn help me to become more compassionate toward others in need myself. I don't try to bring him down to my level, but rather try to raise myself up to his.

Moral role models can improve our characters in other ways as well. For instance, they can reshape our moral imagination. I can see a situation in a different way thanks to the new frame of mind that the role model has provided me with. When I see how Mother Teresa treats a leper, I don't just admire her and try to be like her (though I hope that happens too). She also *gives me a whole new way of seeing lepers*—they look different to me through the lens of her example.[6] Literature and film can have this effect on our imaginations as well. As Iris Murdoch once wrote, "The most essential and fundamental aspect of culture is the study of literature, since this is an education in how to picture and understand human situations."[7] All of this can be character building as well.

One benefit of real-life role models, though, is that you can also live alongside them. It is as if we were apprentices to them, whether we ever think that way or not. Often without realizing it, we can pick up their mannerisms, patterns of thinking and caring, and ways of seeing the world. In the long run, this can include picking up their character.[8]

So far I have shared some of my experiences of admiration for different people and their behavior. I have also suggested that, in a variety of ways, admirable role models can make a significant difference in improving our behavior and our characters too. This all might sound great, but is there any concrete *evidence* that moral role models actually have this impact, at least in terms of improving people's behavior?

There is indeed. In fact, there is a rich tradition in psychology going back at least sixty years of studying models, especially those who are lending a helping hand.[9] Here are two representative studies:

The broken foot. John Wilson and Richard Petruska from Cleveland State University had an actor scream in pain from the next room that he had broken his foot. Did the participant in the study do anything to help? The participant's behavior was rated on a scale from 1 to 10, with 1 being staying in the seat and saying nothing, and 10 being actively walking to the other room and offering aid. We have seen this kind of situation before in chapter 3 when we looked at studies of the powerful effects on helping of being in a group.

When in the room with someone who is passive (who "remained in his seat and essentially ignored the crash"),[10] participants helped at a mean level of 6.21. But with an active role model (who "looked up from his work and said, 'Jesus, what was that?' and walked into the control room and asked, 'What happened? Are you okay? Let me help you!'"),[11] the mean level of helping jumped all the way to 9.05 out of 10.[12]

Blood donations. The psychologists J. Philippe Rushton from the University of Western Ontario and Anne Campbell from Oxford University looked at role models and blood donations. They found that when they saw a model go first and sign up for a blood donation, eighteen out of the twenty-seven participants signed up too. Plus, nine of them carried through with their pledge and really gave blood. Strikingly, without a model, not one of the participants in the control condition gave any blood.[13]

So these studies, and plenty of others besides them, provide good initial support for the idea that moral role models can significantly improve our behavior.[14]

Let me end with a caution, as I said I would. Despite these positive words about the model strategy, we really do not know very much about how it works. For example, how long does the effect of admiration last? When I am inspired by the Bishop's powerful act of forgiveness and want to emulate him, will this desire stay with me for months? Or is the effect fleeting? We again need longitudinal studies. Right now we simply do not have them.[15]

In addition, does the effect of admiring what someone did have an impact beyond just that particular type of action? In other words, will I be more inclined to forgive people in general after being inspired by the Bishop's action, or will its impact be more narrowly restricted to cases where someone steals from me first? Indeed, there is some evidence that modeling effects do not generalize beyond the situation or environment in which the modeling occurred.[16] That would be bad news for developing the virtues, since a virtue like forgiveness is supposed to be expressed across a wide variety of different situations, many of which may have little resemblance to that of the Bishop and Jean Valjean.[17]

Finally, what is the motivational impact of admiration? When, after being moved by the compassion of the Good Samaritan, I go out and work at a homeless shelter, what drives me to do this? Unfortunately, as far as I can tell we are in the dark about this too when we look to the psychological research.

We could try to imagine some answers. They might be self-interested, such as these:

> I see the recognition and rewards that this other person got for herself when she helped others, and I want them for myself too.

I see these helpful things she is doing, and want to do them too so as to relieve my feelings of guilt from my past.

Instead, they might be more morally praiseworthy, such as these:

I want to be a better person, just like she is, and to act better toward others.[18]

I want there to be more charity, more love, and more kindness promoted in the world, just like she did.[19]

I want to help people more, just like she did.[20]

These seem to be much more in keeping with my own experience of admiring Mother Teresa or Leopold Socha. But it would be nice to have the psychological research to back them up too.

So the moral modeling strategy has much to recommend it. Using our criteria from the previous chapter, it fares better in my opinion than do any of the previous strategies we have seen up to this point. Yet even so, it is still in need of much further study.

These are early days.

Selecting Our Situations

Here is another approach to bridging the character gap, one that probably came to mind earlier in the book and has a lot of common sense behind it.[21] The thought is that we should actively *seek out* those situations which are going to inspire us to act well, while actively *avoiding* those situations that are fraught with temptation and other pitfalls. Consider a well-known example by the philosopher John Doris, where you have been invited to a secluded dinner with a flirtatious colleague while your spouse is out of town.[22]

Should you trust your strength of character to keep you out of trouble? Isn't it far better to never get into such a precarious situation in the first place? The answer to these questions is clear.

Part of selecting our situations includes actively seeking out people whose character is better than ours. They can serve as moral role models, as we already discussed (which helps to illustrate that the strategies can nicely complement rather than compete against each other). In addition, being around better people helps to shield us from temptation. Our friends with high moral character can encourage us to make good choices and not exert pressure to go along with the group in doing things that we will live to regret. Over time, the hope is, our characters will be molded so that we just naturally want to make these good choices and seek out positive situations. Even when the role models are not around to encourage us, we will no longer find the problematic situations tempting anymore.

Of course, in the meantime you can't always avoid difficult situations. The flirtatious colleague is, after all, still a colleague. Rather than meeting with that person alone, however, you can form a habit of only meeting with him or her when you are with your spouse or another colleague. This is an example of what economists call a "precommitment strategy." With these kinds of strategies, you take steps now to make it harder for your future self to get into bad situations and easier for your future self to get into good situations. As Thomas Schelling, the Nobel Prize–winning economist who coined this term, writes:

> Many of us have little tricks we play on ourselves to make us do the things we ought to do or to keep us from the things we ought to foreswear. Sometimes we put things out of reach for the moment of temptation, sometimes we promise ourselves small rewards, and sometimes we surrender authority to a trustworthy

friend who will police our calories or our cigarettes. We place the alarm clock across the room so we cannot turn it off without getting out of bed. People who are chronically late set their watches a few minutes ahead to deceive themselves.[23]

The thought is that we can do similar things when it comes to moral challenges too. Such precommitments thereby help to avoid situations where we are prone to fall into temptation.

As with moral role models, I think we should say about this strategy—of course! Surely if we care about becoming better people, we should try to put ourselves in positive situations with good influences. Who would argue otherwise?

The worry I have, though, is that this "selecting the situations" strategy is only going to be of limited value. Unfortunately, many of the influences that sway us are not things to which we pay a lot of attention. So it is hard to make good choices about our situation if we are ignorant of a lot of the variables that will make a difference to how we end up behaving.

That is rather abstract. To illustrate what I have in mind, recall some of the environmental influences we saw in earlier chapters that made a difference to how people behaved. One was coming out of a bathroom and helping carry papers. Another was the smell of Mrs. Fields cookies in a mall and helping to make change. A third was being under an authority figure and hurting an innocent person. There are many other factors from additional studies, such as hot weather, touching something warm, using hand wipes, being in a room cleaned with Windex, lawn mower noise, and so forth.[24] Clearly we are not even aware of many of these environmental variables, or if we are aware of them, we usually assume they do not make any difference. At least in cases like the flirtatious colleague, the moral dangers are obvious to most of us. But using hand wipes?

There are really two concerns here. One has to do with information. We are simply not aware of all the influences on our moral behavior that could arise in a given situation. So, despite our best intentions, our choices will still often go wrong. I might have given a lot of thought to going to the mall, only to fall prey to the influence of the smells when I get there. Plus, the more we learn about these influences, the harder it will be to keep track of them all accurately. I foresee major problems with information overload.

Then there is a big practical concern too, since many of these influences are simply unavoidable during our ordinary lives. There will be times when you can't do anything about the hot weather or the loud noises or the pleasant smells. Are you going to walk out of a room when you smell Windex? Hide when the neighbor turns on his loud lawn mower? Run for the car when the temperature gets above ninety degrees? You don't have any control over a lot of these factors, and there isn't much point to talking about selecting our situations with them in mind.

Hence, this is why I am positive about our second strategy in this chapter—of course we should seek out positive situations, and we can do a good job of that when it is clear what the moral pitfalls are in front of us. But I am also concerned about its limitations. Before moving on, though, there is an interesting variation of it that I think we should consider for a moment. As the CUNY psychologist Paul Wachtel noted long ago, we often don't get to stand apart from the situations of life so that we can inspect them ahead of time. We are *in* our situations, and we have an impact on them with our very *presence*:

> . . . the understanding of any one person's behavior in an interpersonal situation solely in terms of the stimuli presented to him gives only a partial and misleading picture. For to a very large

extent, these stimuli are created by him. They are responses to his own behavior, events he has played a role in bringing about, rather than occurrences independent of who he is and over which he has no control.[25]

So, for example, the dynamics of a conversation at a party will be very much influenced by my contributions to that conversation. Any understanding of that situation has to factor in what I am bringing to it myself.

If this is right, then we should pay attention to the role we have in *creating* which situations to be in, at least to some extent. How? By choosing how we are going to shape our environment through our behavior. We might, for instance, ask ourselves questions such as these: How am I going to shake hands? What is my posture going to be? What about eye contact? Should I try to be outgoing or introverted? Should I lead or follow? And so forth. As the CUNY philosopher Hagop Sarkissian writes, "We hardly notice it, but oftentimes a kind smile from a friend, a playful wink from a stranger, or a meaningful handshake from a supportive colleague can completely change our attitudes. Such minor acts can have great effects. If we mind them, we can . . . prompt or lift one another toward our joint moral ends."[26] Therefore intentionally selecting morally positive cues might help call forth positive responses in others (thereby, in a sense, "nudging" them along in a way that harkens back to the previous chapter). That in turn can be reflected back in a good way onto ourselves, leading to each of us reinforcing the other. I have even found this works well with my young kids, where a quick tickle or high-five can diffuse a difficult situation and reinforce positive behavior.

The hope is that this focus on our own role in shaping our situations will mold better character in the long run. I do not know of any studies, though, that have tested this claim. Such studies are certainly worth doing. In the meantime, we will need to remain cautious about this particular version of the selecting situations strategy until the empirical results come in.

As with role modeling, the selecting situations strategy doesn't satisfy all of our criteria from the start of the last chapter. Yet so long as it does not promise to be the *only* way to help make people virtuous, I think we can all agree that it has something helpful to offer in bridging the character gap.

Getting the Word Out

Long ago, one of the most influential Western philosophers writing on character development had this to say:

> We must also examine what we ourselves drift into easily. For different people have different natural tendencies toward different goals, and we shall come to know our own tendencies from the pleasure or pain that arises in us. We must drag ourselves off in the contrary direction; for if we pull far away from error, as they do in straightening bent wood, we shall reach the intermediate condition.[27]

These words by Aristotle go to the heart of what we might call the "getting the word out" strategy. The idea is that it is important to get to know our own "tendencies," or what I would call our desires. As we saw in previous chapters, desires are sometimes unconscious and so can be a great surprise to us when we learn about them and what they are doing. Examples of both conscious and unconscious desires from earlier in the book include these:

> I want to help when doing so will make me feel less guilty.

> I want to help when doing so will keep me in a good mood.

I want to not help when it would potentially earn the disapproval of those watching me.

I want to lie in order to avoid being shamed in front of others.

I want to lie in order to hurt another person in certain situations.

I want to cheat in order to avoid personal failure and embarrassment.

I want to cheat in order to avoid getting caught or punished for my wrongdoing.

Since these desires can make a big difference to our behavior, we should first familiarize ourselves with them as we try to become better people. Once we recognize their presence, the thought is that we can then be more mindful about whether they are influencing us in a given situation, and do our best to compensate for, correct, or counterbalance them.

Here is an example of how this might go in practice. We hear someone crying out for help in the next room. But we notice that no one else is responding. So we find ourselves holding back too. But then something clicks in our mind. We remember that we learned about the psychology of the bystander effect, and how fear of embarrassment might be very influential in group settings. So we try hard to think about what the right thing to do is, and quickly realize that helping someone in need is more important than whether we embarrass ourselves. This thought takes the lead in our mind, we overcome our initial hesitancy, and we try to help after all.[28]

The hope is that we could get to the point where this kind of thing happens a lot. Through educating ourselves better about our desires—especially the largely unconscious ones—we can correct for them when they try to take us in troublesome directions. Over time we could make real progress toward becoming virtuous.

Is there any data backing this up? There are only a few relevant studies that I am aware of:

Educating about the bystander effect. In two studies from the 1970s, University of Montana psychologist Arthur Beaman and his colleagues first taught a bunch of college students about the effect being in a group has on inhibiting helping (the bystander effect). Later that day these students individually witnessed a (staged) emergency. In one case it was someone in a bicycle accident; in the other case it was a man lying against a wall. When there was an indifferent stranger as part of the situation who was doing nothing to help, these college students still helped 67% of the time. Compare this to another group of students who had not attended the lecture on the bystander effect; only 27% of them helped. This is a large difference. Also interesting is that Beaman did the study over again and changed the emergency so that it happened two weeks after the lecture. Still, 42.5% who had been to the bystander effect lecture helped, versus 25% of students who had not.[29]

Learning about helping. In a less significant but still interesting study from the 2000s, Steven Samuels and William Casebeer at the Air Force Academy got in touch with their students from a social psychology class two years after they completed the course. When asked, "Did learning about helping behaviour lead you to help in any situation in which you believe you would not have otherwise helped?," 72% said that it did.[30]

Obviously it would be nice to see more work done than this.

In the meantime, let's try to develop this "getting the word out" strategy a bit further. Unlike the previous "selecting situations" strategy, the goal here is *not* to try to avoid all the problematic situations and their influences. Instead the goal of the current strategy is to become more cognizant about *when we are already in those situations*, and more thoughtful about how we should respond as a result. So when you are out for a walk and hear what sounds like a bicycle crash, you will not be sidetracked by someone else being too embarrassed or timid to respond. Instead you will know to ignore the bystander and check on the bicyclist.

Or someone drops some papers on the floor at the office. You do nothing right away, but now you can ask yourself: do I have any good reason for not helping? Perhaps what is holding you back is something unconscious, such as a desire to not embarrass yourself. In that case, you recognize what happened and chastise yourself for not doing better. The next time this happens, you can remember the earlier event and quickly overcome any hesitation. Even better, this can set you on a path of getting used to overriding unconscious influences that are leading you to not help.

Here is one more example where something significant is at stake. Suppose your boss or landlord or elected representative puts a lot of pressure on you to do something that directly conflicts with your personal morality. The results of Milgram's experiments might come to mind, and you might pause and try to discern very carefully whether doing what this person demands is justified or not.

Stepping back, what should we say about this strategy for bridging the character gap? In theory it sounds great to me. After all, what person interested in becoming virtuous would really object to knowing more about the problematic desires he or she has, so as to be on guard against their influence?[31]

Before we end this chapter, though, here are three cautions. First, as I already pointed out, there is very little research that tests these ideas. This surprises me, and I am not sure why this topic has been neglected. Obviously lots more needs to be done in examining how well "getting the word out" works for a wide variety of different desires in lots of different situations. Again, these are early days.

There is more. For the second caution takes us back to something we saw in the previous section. Here again we are faced with the question of whether ordinary human beings are being asked to do too much. Keep in mind that there are many different areas of the moral life, such as helping, harming, lying, cheating, stealing, and so forth. In order to cover all these bases with the "getting the word out" strategy, I had better have a smartphone with me at all times. There will be an *enormous amount of information* to keep track of! To begin with, I need to learn about the hundreds of unconscious desires in my mind and how they might lead me to act poorly (or well!), depending on my surroundings. Then, when I take a test, or am ordered to hurt someone, or see a child cry, I need to be paying attention to whether any of my desires might be influencing me away from what morality requires. I had better not be too slow about any of this, either. If it is an emergency, or even if it is just an opportunity to stand up for the right thing at a homeowner's association or PTA meeting, if I delay too long, the moment will pass. So I need reliable information about myself, a good way to store that information, the ability to recall it accurately and apply it correctly in a real-life situation, and the skill to do all of this quickly. The question is whether this is realistic for most of us, or whether it is simply asking too much.

To be fair, though, maybe this is the wrong way to think about the "getting the word out" strategy. Maybe we should just take baby steps, learning something about the bystander effect, and trying to implement that knowledge. Then learning something about cheating and our desire to think of ourselves as honest people and trying to implement that knowledge. Then learning . . . so on and so forth over the course of many decades of our lives. Again, baby steps.

This does seem like a more manageable (and sane!) way to go. I am left with one final concern, however. I wonder what this strategy would do to our quality of life. What if we were always monitoring ourselves and our situations to make sure we do not fall prey to the negative influence of our unconscious desires? Would that take the enjoyment out of life? Would trying to be a virtuous person become such a heavy burden that we would rather cast off that burden altogether? I do not have an answer to these questions at the current time.

Final Thoughts

I want to share two final thoughts. The first is to correct any misleading impression that there can only be *one* promising strategy for cultivating the virtues and bridging the character gap. If I did create this impression, it needs to be fixed right away.

Surely there is something of value to *all* the strategies from both chapters. The best approach, in other words, will likely be a sophisticated, multifaceted one where all of the following matter—getting the word out, *and* selecting our situations, *and* admiring moral role models, *and* nudging, *and* judiciously using virtue labels as needed, *and* doing nothing while letting the ordinary flow of life do its work. Also there are other that which I haven't mentioned at all but that are no doubt very important. A secure family, a morally supportive school environment, and a safe community come to mind. A sophisticated approach to character development will have to take into account all of these factors, and more besides.

In addition, it will have to take all these strategies into account, while not overwhelming people who just want to become better. We already noted the danger of information overload that can come with just *one* of these strategies. Adding other strategies to the mix seems like it could make the problem even worse.

Leave that aside. Let's assume for now that we can arrive at a compelling, sophisticated approach to character development. By itself, it will be useless. We can develop all the strategies we want, and package them in fancy workbooks, fun self-help guides, and free podcasts. Unless we are either starting with highly motivated adults, or we are trying to train the next generation of young children, all this hard work will be for naught. No one is going to bother with the difficult endeavor of character building without being significantly motivated to do so.

So how do we get people to *care enough* about becoming virtuous, so that they are willing to give these strategies a try?[32] Not just in the short run either, but care in a way that is long-lasting and sustained?

In chapter 2 I tried to give some reasons for why it is important to become a virtuous person. Those reasons are compelling ones, I believe. But note that they mostly appealed to our heads, rather than to our hearts. The exception was the portrait I gave of several virtuous lives, lives that have the power to trigger something emotionally powerful inside of us.

We need the tug of our emotions. The head alone will not motivate us enough to keep working at becoming a better person. We need our hearts to care deeply about virtue as well. Yet how does this happen? That question is extremely urgent. Unfortunately, as far as the psychological research is concerned, it remains largely unexplored.

Notes

1. I also want to be very clear that chapters 8 and 9 are *not* intended to outline *all* the strategies there are for bridging the character gap, or even all the promising ones. This is a huge topic that needs an entire book of its own. For instance, we should also consider approaches having to do with behavioral conditioning, with therapy, and with the contemplative study of the virtues and vices. I fully acknowledge that a lot more needs to be said.
2. Luke 10:30–37, NIV translation.
3. http://www.online-literature.com/victor_hugo/les_miserables/26/. Accessed August 19, 2016.
4. Epictetus 1983: 33.12–13.
5. For an interesting discussion by a psychologist of stories and moral development, see Vitz 1990. According to Vitz, "A very effective way to introduce children to the moral life, short of actually placing them in morally challenging situations, is to have them hear, read, or watch morally challenging narratives" (1990: 716). See also Coles 1986 for the role of biblical stories during desegregation in the 1960s.
6. For more on Mother Teresa and how her work can help us see people in a new way, see Muggeridge 1971.
7. Murdoch 1971: 34.
8. I am grateful to Ryan West for the ideas in the last two paragraphs. For more on role models and apprenticeship, see Willard 1998.
9. For a review of early studies with a focus on helping, see Krebs 1970: 267–277.
10. Wilson and Petruska 1984: 462.
11. Wilson and Petruska 1984: 461.
12. Wilson and Petruska 1984: 464.

13. Rushton and Campbell 1977: 303. Admittedly in both studies these were "role models" in a loose sense. They modeled the right thing to do, which had a positive effect on many participants. But otherwise they were complete strangers to these participants.

14. See also Bryan and Test 1967; Rosenhan and White 1967; White 1972; Mischel and Mischel 1976: 188, 191–192, 202–203; and Rushton and Campbell 1977: 298.

15. However, even if the desire to emulate the Bishop may not be long-lasting, some other effects might persist. The Bishop has, for instance, shaped my moral imagination by revealing a dramatically new (forgiving) way of conceiving of offenders. That hopefully "sticks" with me. Thanks again to Ryan West for this suggestion.

16. See, e.g., Grusec, Saas-Kortsaak, and Simutis 1978 and Grusec and Redler 1980: 529.

17. This is where the apprenticeship idea can help. By learning from the actual role models in our lives and implicitly picking up on their moral character, we can hopefully apply what we acquire to new situations.

18. For some psychologists who propose this option, see Haidt 2000: 2–3; 2003a: 282; Aquino and Freeman 2009: 385; Algoe and Haidt 2009: 108, 116, 119, 123; and Aquino et al. 2011: 704.

19. See Haidt 2003a: 284.

20. For some psychologists who propose this option, see Haidt 2000: 2–3; 2003a: 282, 285; Aquino and Freeman 2009: 385; Algoe and Haidt 2009: 116, 119, 123; and Aquino et al. 2011: 704, 709. As one participant said, "I felt the desire to be like my grandma, and have the same goodwill and huge heart—I wanted to help!" (Algoe and Haidt 2009: 112).

21. Material in the second, third, and fourth sections of this chapter is adapted from Miller 2016a.

22. Doris 2002: 147. For discussion of selecting situations, whether in the service of developing virtue or not, see Doris 1998: 517; 2002; Merritt 2000; Merritt et al. 2010: 389–391; and Slingerland 2011: 414–415.

23. Schelling 1978: 290. Some of these tricks seem like forms of nudging, where now it's me doing the nudging to myself.

24. For these specific influences, see Miller 2013: chapters 2 through 6.

25. Wachtel 1973: 330, emphasis removed. See also Bowers 1973: 329 and Funder 2008: 575.

26. Sarkissian 2010: 12. As he also writes, "Influencing how situations unfold begins with minding the cues arising from one's person" (9). Whether this promotes better moral character, though, remains to be seen.

27. Aristotle 1985: 1109b2–8.

28. For a similar example, see Mele and Shepherd 2013: 80.

29. Beaman et al. 1978: 407–408, 410.

30. Samuels and Casebeer 2005: 80.

31. For related discussion of this strategy, see especially Samuels and Casebeer 2005 and Mele and Shepherd 2013.

32. The ones, at least, that require some initiative on our part. The "do nothing" strategy doesn't require us to care about becoming virtuous. But "getting the word out" does, for instance.

10 | IMPROVING OUR CHARACTERS WITH DIVINE ASSISTANCE

As we have seen, there do appear to be some promising strategies for helping us bridge the gap between the character we actually have and the virtuous people we should become. But *how* promising are they really? We simply do not know, or at least psychologists have not done nearly enough to tell us. And we shouldn't forget that the obstacles to virtue are many. Sometimes they can be very subtle, too, such as the influence of food smells in the air or the number of people in a room.

In this final chapter, I think we would be wise to consider whether there are other, complementary approaches to character improvement that might lend a hand as well. In particular, up to this point we have looked only to secular strategies. But the majority of people in the world today are religious in some way. It is worth taking a brief look at some of the resources to be found within religious traditions for addressing the wide character gap most of us face.

Or, more precisely, one religious tradition. For in a short chapter like this one, it would be hopeless to try to examine Buddhism and Confucianism, Daoism and Judaism, Hinduism and Islam, and all the rest of the major world religions. Instead, I will just pick one of them—Christianity—and go into a bit more detail about what Christians have traditionally done to improve their characters.

Let me be very clear from the start. In focusing on Christianity, I am *not* claiming that it is any more plausible than any other religion, nor am I trying to convert people to Christianity. Rather, I focus on Christianity because:

1. It is the world's largest religion.
2. It is likely going to be a familiar religion to readers of this book, whether they are Christians themselves or not.
3. It puts great emphasis on virtue and character development, and has a long history of important teachings and practices aimed at bettering character.
4. Many of the ideas in Christianity about character development have clear parallels in other major world religions, so we can readily adapt the discussion that follows to those religions too. Hence I hope that followers of these religions will still find this chapter rewarding.

Three points in particular will be emphasized in discussing Christianity: the importance of Christian rituals and practices, the social dimension to Christian character development, and the help of the Holy Spirit.

For readers who are not religious at all, there is still good reason to keep reading. For one thing, I think it's important to try to step into other worldviews and better understand how people who follow them see the world. That's invaluable for promoting understanding, respect, and tolerance. In addition, while I won't have space to investigate this here, it is definitely worth thinking about what secular versions of Christian practices like fasting and confession might look like, and whether they are worth encouraging apart from a religious foundation.

Having said this, let's begin with some background about Christianity and character that will be useful to set the stage.

Christianity and Character

From a Christian perspective, it is clear that God cares about virtue, and it is extremely important to him that we become virtuous people. Hence we see biblical passages such as the following:

> For this very reason, make every effort to add to your faith goodness; and to goodness, knowledge; and to knowledge, self-control; and to self-control, perseverance; and to perseverance, godliness; and to godliness, brotherly kindness; and to brotherly kindness, love.[1]

> Therefore, as God's chosen people, holy and dearly loved, clothe yourselves with compassion, kindness, humility, gentleness and patience. Bear with each other and forgive whatever grievances you may have against one another. Forgive as the Lord forgave you. And over all these virtues put on love, which binds them all together in perfect unity.[2]

> ... whatever is true, whatever is noble, whatever is right, whatever is pure, whatever is lovely, whatever is admirable—if anything is excellent or praiseworthy—think about such things.[3]

But at the same time, the New Testament is also clear that we do a pretty bad job of being good people:

> There is no one righteous, not even one.[4]

> For what I do is not the good I want to do; no, the evil I do not want to do—this I keep on doing.[5]

When I want to do good, evil is right there with me. For in my inner being I delight in God's law; but I see another law at work in the members of my body, waging war against the law of my mind and making me a prisoner of the law of sin at work within my members.[6]

The spirit is willing, but the body is weak.[7]

In fact, the picture of our character outlined by the New Testament seems to fit quite comfortably with the research findings from psychology we have seen in this book.[8]

Hence Christianity affirms the character gap too. Indeed, it takes on special significance within Christianity in a way that it would not from a secular perspective. God is all-knowing, and so is very familiar with our characters, indeed even more familiar with them than we are ourselves:

[T]he word of God . . . judges the thoughts and attitudes of the heart. Nothing in all creation is hidden from God's sight. Everything is uncovered and laid bare before the eyes of him to whom we must give account.[9]

He [the Lord] will bring to light what is hidden in darkness and will expose the motives of men's hearts. At that time each will receive his praise from God.[10]

So one day, according to Christianity, our characters will be revealed before God, and we will be held accountable for them.

This creates additional self-interested motivation for Christians to try to become better people. Presumably most people do not want to be judged and punished because of their character faults. Nor do we want to experience the shame, embarrassment, and guilt that will come from confronting our faults face-to-face, and especially in front of the perfect being who is said to have created us.

However that is not the only source of motivation for becoming better people from a Christian perspective. Indeed it is not even a particularly good or admirable kind of motivation. After all, it is purely egoistic just to worry about ourselves and to try to make sure we avoid punishment, guilt, or embarrassment.[11]

There is a more complicated story to be told, however, about motivation in the Christian life. As part of that story, here are three additional reasons for becoming better people, reasons that do not have to do primarily with ourselves:

1) God has the qualities of being perfectly loving, perfectly just, and perfectly honest. Christians are to love, trust, and worship God for who he is. So that means, in part, loving his perfect character. In loving his perfect character, Christians are to strive to embody that character in their own lives, while recognizing that this is impossible without divine assistance. So God's character provides Christians with motivation to try to become better people, regardless of whether they benefit in the process.

2) From a Christian perspective, Jesus was a perfect person with a perfectly virtuous character. Christians are to model their lives after Jesus. So this provides them with motivation to try to become better people, regardless of whether they benefit in the process.[12]

3) Gratitude can be a powerful motivator as well. As Christians see the world, there is much to be grateful for, e.g., the creation of this universe, their own existence, and being loved by God. There is also immense gratitude for forgiveness—that

God would become one of us, die, and rise again for the forgiveness of human sin and wrongdoing. This can supply Christians with motivation to try to become better, regardless of whether they benefit in the process.

These three reasons are closely related. From a Christian perspective Jesus was both fully human and fully divine. His perfectly virtuous character was also God's perfectly virtuous character, and as divine he was able to bring about forgiveness for human sin.

Therefore collectively there are powerful reasons, both self-interested and not, for Christians to care about the fact that their character falls far short of what it is supposed to be. This is another way of saying that there are powerful reasons for Christians to care about their character falling far short of Jesus's character. What is to be done about this? What steps should Christians take to try to bridge the character gap?

It is clear that mere "head knowledge," without any emotional support from a Christian's will, is not going to be enough. We might know all kinds of facts about Jesus's life and teachings, for instance, while intellectually acknowledging that this is how we should live our lives. But as Paul says:

I see another law at work in the members of my body, waging war against the law of my mind.[13]

Rather, *in addition to* knowing what we should be doing and what the story of Jesus says, Christians need to have their will reoriented in a new direction. In other words, both the head and the heart need to be habituated toward following Jesus. Then—to complete the metaphor—the feet will reliably carry out the actual doing.

Apparently this does not happen overnight in the Christian framework, barring rare exceptions like the transformation of Paul on the road to Damascus.[14] Rather, the journey for most Christians is a slow one, with many obstacles and setbacks. It is not a linear process either. Some years, rather than making progress toward becoming better, a Christian's character might regress. Nor, by the end of her life, is the Christian guaranteed to have become virtuous. She still might have a long way to go. Indeed, some non-Christians might have made more progress in developing an honest or compassionate character than a Christian did, especially if she started in a darker place.[15]

With this background in mind, let us turn to the first of the three ideas we will examine in this chapter for promoting character improvement from a Christian perspective.

Christian Rituals and Practices

From its birth, certain rituals and practices have been at the heart of the Christian life. Examples include prayer, reading scripture, contemplating the lives of the saints, fasting, confessing sins, giving to charity, tithing to the church, and helping those in need.

To be sure, the *main* purpose of these practices may not be to become better people. They may ultimately, for Christians, exist to better worship or bring glory to God. But in the process of engaging in them, Christians *also* take concrete steps that can have a beneficial impact on their character.

This is all very abstract. Let's see how it might work using particular examples. So consider prayer. Christians typically pray to one of two people—either God or Jesus (some would add Mary and the saints to the list, but we won't worry about that here). What do they pray about? Sometimes they use traditional prayers, the most famous of which is the Lord's Prayer:[16]

> Our Father, which art in heaven,
> Hallowed be thy Name.
> Thy Kingdom come.
> Thy will be done in earth,
> As it is in heaven.
> Give us this day our daily bread.
> And forgive us our trespasses,
> As we forgive them that trespass against us.
> And lead us not into temptation,
> But deliver us from evil.
> For thine is the kingdom,
> The power, and the glory,
> For ever and ever.
> Amen.

Other times they might craft a prayer on their own that reflects what is going on in their personal lives. For example, they may say things like:

> Thank you Lord for healing my son from disease. We thought he wasn't going to make it.

> I praise you God for bringing Sarah into my life. She is such an incredible blessing.

Note that these words are ways of expressing gratitude.

Or Christians might say things like this, even in the very same prayer:

We come before you in prayer tonight, Jesus, and ask that you help the people in North Carolina who have been affected by the forest fires. Lord, we cannot imagine what it is like to lose one's home in this way, but we pray that you will comfort these people and help them find a way to recover as quickly as possible.

Jesus, please help my neighbor who is going through such a difficult time right now financially. If it is your will, help him to find a job. Help to open doors for him and help potential employers see his many gifts.

We find something in common here as well. These are all expressions of compassion for the suffering of other people, and also of humility about our inability to solve the problems of the world ourselves.

Now for the connection to character building. Admittedly, the primary purpose of these prayers is not, on the face of it, to improve the Christian's own character. It is to thank God. Or to call upon God to help someone else in need. Things like that. Nevertheless, imagine the effect of saying prayers like these on a daily basis over the course of years or even decades. I think it is not hard to see how they could have a beneficial impact on one's character. Using the examples above, for instance, the Christian's own gratitude, compassion, and humility could all be strengthened. By praying every day, "And forgive us our trespasses, As we forgive them that trespass against us," the Christian can become a more forgiving person in general.[17]

Here is another example, confession. In confession the Christian reveals his sins, whether more formally to a priest in a confessional, or more informally to a fellow Christian, a spouse, or a small group of believers. Or he simply confesses sins to God directly. Here too the primary goal from a Christian perspective is not strictly to become virtuous, but it is again not hard to see how that might happen in the process. To admit a lie, or a theft, or an affair, can take a great deal of *courage*. We are often afraid of revealing our deepest secrets and wrong-doings to others, especially to those we want to like and admire us. Confession can also strengthen our *trust* in other people by sharing deeply personal information with them, which is another virtue. It takes a degree of *humility* to acknowledge where we have messed up. When others forgive us, and we experience God's forgiveness, it can make us more *forgiving* as well. Christians are *grateful* for being for-given. Not to mention that confessing wrongdoings will hopefully make Christians less likely to commit the same ones again in the future. By confronting a sin and confessing it, a Christian can dislike it even more and thereby strengthen his resolve to change his life. And part of becoming more virtuous is ceasing to do things that are not virtuous.[18]

Consider a third example of tithing. For Christians, that means setting aside a certain percentage of one's income for the church or charity. One traditional percentage is tithing 10%, but that's not important for the point here. What is important is that tith-ing is meant to be a difficult commitment to make initially, not just financially, of course, but also motivationally as the Christian's heart struggles with giving up such a significant amount of money every month. However over time, as with all these practices, the hope is that it can become more routine, more second nature, more auto-matic. Temptations and struggles weaken, and the virtue of *generos-ity* is strengthened. Not just toward the church, either, but toward those in need in general.

Hopefully the general point about the impact of Christian practices on character improvement is clear enough, and we can see how it would apply in other cases, like fasting (temperance and self-control), reading scripture (faith, understanding, wisdom, and self-control), and worship (humility, love, faith, and gratitude). What ends up happening from the Christian perspective is that, if all goes well, the Christian will be directing her attention in a better way (the head part) and reorienting her motives to respond accordingly (the heart part), whether she knows it or not. The head and the heart, in other words, are being aligned in a way that, Christians would say, is virtuous.[19]

Interestingly, these rituals and practices are not seen as replacements for the character-building strategies of the previous two chapters. Christians have embraced much of what they have to offer too, while adding to them a number of additional resources. An ordinary Christian church, for instance, is filled with nudges like crosses. For a time many Christians wore WWJD bracelets, to remind them of what their role model would do (and many today still wear crosses around their necks). Each Christian is even called a "saint" in the New Testament (not because Christians always act saintly, of course).[20] Hence the Bible attaches a virtue label to Christians that becomes part of their identity. So Christians, it seems to me, have no reason to dismiss these earlier strategies, and instead should continue to seek ways to enrich them.

Finally, the rituals and practices mentioned above are not restricted to Christianity but can be found in other major world religions as well. Obviously Christians are not the only ones who pray to a higher being, or confess their sins, or tithe. While Christianity has been the specific focus of this section, many of the points can be applied more generally.[21]

The Social Dimension of Christian Character Improvement

There is more to the Christian outlook on character improvement than just a bunch of different rituals and practices. In fact, the picture I have painted so far is badly skewed in an important way. I have made it sound like the individual Christian is on his own when it comes to bridging the character gap. He just needs to do some things in the right way, and over time (and with God's help) he will gradually become a better person.

Now, it *could* work like that, and indeed some of the most famous teachings about character in Christianity have come from people who lived very solitary lives. A particularly dramatic example is St. Simeon Stylites the Elder, who was born somewhere around A.D. 388. Here is a description of what he did:

> Simeon had a pillar erected with a small platform at the top, and upon this he determined to take up his abode until death released him. At first the pillar was little more than nine feet high, but it was subsequently replaced by others, the last in the series being apparently over fifty feet from the ground.[22]

No shelter. No bed. No comforts at all. Just a platform on a pillar, with local villagers and his disciples bringing him food to survive. Simeon remained there for thirty-six years. Unbelievable.

I don't want to disparage someone like Simeon at all. The self-control and discipline involved in doing what he did are almost inconceivable in our Western culture today, and are far greater than anything I will ever know in my own lifetime. But such isolation is the exception in the Christian tradition, rather than the rule. In fact, even Simeon recognized the importance of being with other people. Thus we learn that:

> even on the highest of his columns Simeon was not withdrawn from intercourse with his fellow men. By means of a ladder which could always be erected against the side, visitors were able to ascend; and we know that he wrote letters, the text of some of which we still possess, that he instructed disciples, and that he also delivered addresses to those assembled beneath.[23]

The norm, in other words, has always been to engage in Christian practices together with fellow Christians as part of one body, the church.

When Christians pray, they often do so with other people. Christian families say a blessing at the dinner table. Christians ask for prayer requests which are prayed for in church or in small groups. They recite the Lord's Prayer together.

When Christians confess sins, they do so to God. Often they also confess to fellow believers, whether a priest, minister, spouse, or trusted friend. Or they say a confessional in unison as part of a service.

When Christians tithe, or donate more generally, this can be as one body of believers in a public forum, such as when the collection plate is being passed around.

When Christians worship, they are in unity with dozens, or hundreds, or even thousands of other people, joining their own voice to these others in prayer, song, and laughter.

Why does this social dimension matter? For all kinds of reasons. Here are a few. The most important in my mind is *support*. The Christian knows that she is part of a community of millions of fellow believers who have said that they are committed to loving God and loving their neighbors as themselves. The Christian, in other words, is not on her own. When she needs advice, she has people to turn to. During difficult times, she does not have to face them alone. She has other people who can pray for her, share advice, provide meals, and perhaps even offer financial support. As she struggles with a deep sin, she can turn to a minister or priest or fellow Christian at church to work through that sin, ask God for forgiveness, and try to come up with a plan for eradicating it going forward with God's help.[24]

This serves to highlight another reason why according to Christianity the social dimension matters to character development—it can be a source of great *comfort*. For many

Christians, it is comforting to know that there are others on the same path, all working together to, among other things, become better people. Even more so, it can be comforting to see that it is not an easy road for any Christian, and everyone will have to struggle individually and collectively.

Amid this struggle, being in a Christian community provides many *role models* who serve as inspirational examples to follow in the Christian's daily life. This harkens back to the previous chapter and the importance of having examples of virtue in one's life. The Christian tradition is certainly rich with them, as are other religious traditions too. It starts with Jesus himself as the perfect role model. The early disciples and followers of Christ as well as figures from the Old Testament are exemplars too. They continue down throughout history in the form of saints and other spiritual leaders such as St. Francis of Assisi. Exemplars continue to this day with people like Mother Teresa, C. S. Lewis, and Pope John Paul II. Closer to home, the role model might be a particularly saintly member of the congregation or a spiritually profound relative or friend.

Given this last point, these role models for Christians need not be someone they only see on TV or read about on the Internet. They can be personal figures in the Christian's own life, ideally serving as religious mentors who are willing to *disciple* other Christians. This might take the form of praying together, reading the Bible together, holding each other accountable, and more generally sharing one's life together. In such a personal setting, sins are confessed and progress can be made in becoming better people.

All these social dimensions can make a real difference in closing the character gap, at least from a Christian perspective. There are many other social dimensions too, but let me mention only one more here before moving on. That is *church discipline*. This is a topic which some Christians are no doubt embarrassed to discuss, but all the way back to the New Testament itself, there are instructions for addressing wrongdoing among fellow Christians. Jesus said:

> If your brother sins against you, go and show him his fault, just between the two of you. If he listens to you, you have won your brother over. But if he will not listen, take one or two others along, so that "every matter may be established by the testimony of two or three witnesses." If he refuses to listen to them, tell it to the church; and if he refuses to listen even to the church, treat him as you would a pagan or a tax collector.[25]

From the Christian perspective such discipline, when carried out in a loving way, can help to open a person's eyes to how something has gone terribly wrong in his life. It can then serve as a badly needed wake-up call that God can use to bring the person back into better relationship with him. In the long run, the person's character might be much better off for having gone through this process of church discipline.[26]

Obviously this is just scratching the surface of a much larger discussion about how other people can play a role in shaping character from a Christian perspective. Here too we should note that many of the points in this section carry over to other major world religions as well. Worship in a community, role models, and discipline are not unique to Christianity, for instance.[27]

Is There Empirical Support for These Claims?

We have been considering a variety of ways in which religious rituals and practices, whether performed individually or collectively, can seem to have a significant impact on character improvement. At least, that is according to the way Christians see the world. But do such practices *actually* have this impact?

Most Christians would point to their own lives and those of people they know, and say that the answer is a definite yes! They might also point to the lives of Christian saints over the past two thousand years. But if the standard we are using is empirical measurement, then the answer is much murkier.

This is not surprising. To really test for the impact of Christian practices on character development, you would ideally want to have a control group of nonreligious people together with a group of, say, recently converted Christians. You could perform some initial baseline assessments of their characters—try to get a good read on the honesty, compassion, humility, and so forth of individual members of both groups. Then, over the course of the ensuing months and years, you could periodically repeat the same character assessments with the same participants. At the end of the study, you could then see how much progress was made by individuals in both groups.

But this really is idealistic. As noted in an earlier chapter, studies that follow people for years are very rare in psychology. They cost a lot of money, it is hard to track people for that long, as some participants drop out of the study or move to other parts of the world, the time frame is not helpful for the researcher's professional advancement via publications and presentations, and so forth. Furthermore the character assessment would need to be very sophisticated. Merely having participants fill out a few surveys with questions about their level of honesty or humility would not be nearly enough. And then there are all kinds of confounding variables. There are different branches and denominations of Christianity. Did some of the nonreligious participants receive a religious upbringing and then fall away from it? What about other major life changes, like getting fired from a job, married, or divorced? The complexity involved in this kind of research is staggering.

So I doubt we have much of an idea about the effectiveness of these religious practices using the best psychological measurement tools. We do have something, though.

In dozens of studies in recent years, psychologists, sociologists, economists, and other researchers have been looking at the relationship between different measures of religiosity—like the frequency of attending religious services, or the frequency of prayer—and various important social goods—like education and crime prevention. So rather than following the same people over time, they are asking people questions about their religious lives and also about some other behaviors of interest to the researcher. Here is a sampling of what they have found.[28]

Crime prevention. The sociologists Christopher Ellison at the University of Texas at San Antonio and Kristin Anderson from Western Washington University discovered that domestic violence is 60.7% higher among male survey participants who do not attend church, as opposed to men who attend religious services once a week or more. When the relationship partners themselves are directly asked, it turns out that the percentage of domestic violence is still 48.7% higher in the group of people who do not attend church.

For violence committed by women, the percentage is 44.2% higher in the nonattending group. It is 34.8% higher for the nonattending group when it is relationship partners who are the ones asked about domestic violence.[29]

More broadly, another study linked religious attendance with reductions in the rate of forty-three different crimes.[30] Economists have also linked various religiosity measures and decreases in local crime.[31]

Education. Another pair of sociologists, Mark Regnerus at the University of Texas at Austin and Glen Elder at UNC Chapel Hill, looked at the connection between various religiosity measures and whether students in grades 7 through 12 stayed on track.[32] Being academically "on track" has a specific definition as a composite of grade-point average, completion of homework, getting along with teachers, expulsions, suspensions, and unexcused absences. Using church attendance, they found a link with staying on track, and this link was especially pronounced in neighborhoods with high poverty rates. Thus they write, "As the extent of poverty rises in neighborhoods, the relationship between church attendance and change in on-track behavior becomes more positive."[33]

Another study reports that religious involvement is "associated with subsequent (two years later) higher parental educational expectations, more extensive communication with parents about schooling, advanced math course credits, time spent on homework, and successful degree completion, as well as avoiding cutting classes."[34] There are more studies showing similar results.[35]

Health benefits. We see religiosity measures significantly linked to reduced suicide rates,[36] lower drug use,[37] increased health care utilization,[38] reduced smoking,[39] reduced alcohol abuse,[40] healthier lifestyles,[41] the promotion of mental health,[42] and even mortality rates.[43]

To expand on just one of these trends, Maureen Reindl Benjamins at the Sinai Urban Health Institute and her colleagues found that out of 1,070 Presbyterian women, 75% had sought out a mammogram in the past two years. In comparison, the national average at the time was 56% for the same age group. Also, looking at weekly attendance at religious services as the variable, Benjamins discovered that regular attenders were nearly twice as likely to report having a mammogram as those who attended less often.[44]

Subjective well-being. Christopher Ellison also looked at religious certainty (one's degree of certainty in one's religious beliefs). He found that it directly correlated with higher self-reported life satisfaction. That in turn has a number of dimensions—how satisfied you are with your community life, with your nonworking activities or hobbies, with your family life, with your friendships, and with your health. Positive links were also found to self-reported personal happiness and to reduced stress.[45]

Other studies report that religion plays just as much of a role in how well we think our lives are going as do marital status, work status, and education.[46] Religiosity also predicts one's tendency to be satisfied with family life, finances, friendships, and health.[47] Other studies have found links to increased social support[48] and marriage satisfaction and adjustment.[49]

Charity. The former Syracuse University business professor Arthur Brooks reported some striking data about charitable giving.[50] Regular service attenders are more likely to give (91% to 66%). As for volunteering, they outperform rare and nonattenders (67% to 44%). Specifically in 2000, regular attenders would donate 3.5 times more money per year ($2,210 versus $642). And they would volunteer more than twice as frequently (12 times versus 5.8 times). The same pattern held when Brooks switched to other measures like prayer frequency, spiritual intensity, and merely belonging to a congregation regardless of attendance rate. The pattern also held for other types of charity: "In 2002, religious people were far more likely to donate blood than secularists, to give food or money to a homeless person, to return change mistakenly given them by a cashier, and to express empathy for less fortunate people . . . [R]eligious people were 57 percent more likely than secularists to help a homeless person at least once a month."[51]

One more finding here: 20% of fundamentalists, evangelicals, mainline, and liberal Protestants said that they gave away "a lot" of money at some point in the past two years to organizations which focus on the poor. Among nonreligious participants, by contrast, 9.5% said they did.[52]

The 2002 report of the National Study of Youth and Religion provides a nice way to sum all of this up into one wide-ranging set of results. The report looked at what 2,478 twelfth-grade students had to say about a host of issues they face, and among many other results it found the following:[53]

	Weekly religious attendance	No religion
Avoided smoking regularly	88.1%	73.2%
Avoided selling drugs in past 12 months	93.3	81.6
Avoided hard drugs in past 12 months	80.2	62.9
Avoided driving tickets	71.9	63.0
Avoided trouble with police in past 12 months	93.6	86.3
Never shoplifted in past 12 months	76.3	65.9
Never skipped school in past school year	47.8	31.0

	Weekly religious attendance	No religion
Never suspended or expelled	82.2	70.9
Never does community service or volunteers	13.1	37.8
Never participated in student government	71.6	84.5
No daily sports or exercise	51.4	66.4

If we switch to how important religion was to the students, or the number of years they had spent in a religious youth group, the same patterns persist.

I could go on and on—there are literally *hundreds* of studies that make similar connections.[54] Yet they all share the same limitation, and it is important to be up front about that. These are merely correlational studies, and we all know that correlation does not equal causation. So we don't know what is causing what—perhaps it is the people who already are low on criminal behavior, high on making donations, low on health problems, and so forth who gravitate toward religion. If so, then these studies are of little help to the concerns of this chapter.

I do not see a way to sort out the causal question using the existing empirical research that we have available today. So I can only register my own personal opinion that I would be shocked if religious practices didn't have *some* causal impact on these behaviors. And the other direction too—I would be shocked if the behaviors didn't some impact on the religious practices as well. I see the causal arrow going in *both* directions.

As an example, take the finding that regular service attenders are 25% more likely to give to charity.[55] Focusing again on the case of Christianity, it would be shocking to me if all the ways that a church stresses charity didn't have *some* impact in increasing giving. There are frequent sermons on the topic. The collection plate is passed every service. Numerous passages in the New Testament stress the importance of giving, such as this:

> In everything I did, I showed you that by this kind of hard work we must help the weak, remembering the words the Lord Jesus himself said: "It is more blessed to give than to receive."[56]

Role models are seen giving to charity. Churches usually have several fundraisers every year to raise money for worthy causes. And so on and so on.

Psychologically, it seems to me that these influences would have the effect of first reiterating what is morally expected of Christians in this area of their lives. Significant giving is supposed to be the norm, not the exception. Second, these influences can have the effect of making this moral expectation *salient* to Christians. Similar to what we saw in chapter 6 with how an honor code and the Ten Commandments can curb cheating, these tangible reminders of the importance of helping others can inspire Christians to actually follow through and make a contribution.

Similar psychological stories could be told about how religious practices can help to bring about the other good outcomes reviewed above. Many Christians would, I imagine, find such stories plausible. But whether they are accurate accounts of what *in fact* is going on and thereby explain the correlations we have noted, remains to be seen.

What, if anything, does all this have to do with *character*? Here we need to be even more careful. Finding a positive relationship—*even if* it were somehow shown to be a causal relationship—between being religious and lots of good things like health, donations, and reduced crime is one thing. But it is not the same as finding a positive relationship between being religious and being *virtuous*.

To stick with the same example of donating to charity, what is going on at the level of *motivation* when religious believers are writing a check or the offering plate is going around? It could be that (certain) religious practices are helping to foster feelings of genuine compassion for others, and this compassionate motivation in turn leads to increased donations. But it could be instead that the increased donations are due to some self-interested motivation linked to religion, such as a desire for rewards in the afterlife. In that case, there would not be much support for the idea that religious rituals and practices contribute significantly to compassionate character.

The truth, if I can be allowed to speculate, is likely somewhere in between. It is hard to make blanket statements about the motives of all people who report being religious. In some cases, when they act particularly well, that is likely to be because their religious practices have shaped them into being better people. In other cases, it may be because they were led by some self-interested concerns instead. But sadly we don't have nearly enough data about the motivational lives of religious believers to know where the truth lies.[57]

So, to echo a familiar refrain from the last few chapters, we have some interesting and suggestive preliminary results, but we should be cautious for now until a lot more data comes in. As far as the empirical research is concerned, the jury is still out on the effects of religious rituals and practices on character improvement.[58]

What about All the Harm Caused by Christianity (and Other Religions)?

Wait, you might say. Despite this last word of caution, the chapter overall has painted a far too rosy picture of religion and character. What about all the harm that has been done in the name of religion throughout the centuries? What about all the persecution, intolerance, and hate that have been fostered? How has religion helped to shape the characters of ISIS members for the better? How did it improve moral character during the Inquisition, the Crusades, or the Salem Witch Trials?

The worry here is that, overall, religious beliefs and practices may tend to do more harm than good. This is true both with respect to the harm done to others that is inspired by religion, and with respect to the damage done to the believer's own character.

This concern is a serious one, I think. But there is a response available too. In the process of developing it, I will be able to more carefully refine the approach developed in this chapter.

Focusing on Christianity once again, there is no denying that so-called "Christians" throughout the past two thousand years have committed terrible atrocities in the name of Jesus. Any Christian today has to acknowledge this sad fact, and the same is true for every other major world religion; they all have shameful moments in their histories.

But when it comes to committing atrocities, secular worldviews do not seem to have any better track record. We all know that some atheists have been influenced by their particular worldviews to commit tremendous atrocities too. Indeed, the twentieth century has arguably been the bloodiest and most horrific in human history, filled with mass graves, gulags, and concentration camps. In many instances, these can be traced back ideologically to secular worldviews like Nazism, Stalinism, and Maoism. Here, for instance, are rough estimates of the carnage wrought by some of these leaders:

Mao Zedong	45 million lives lost[59]
Stalin	20 million lives lost[60]
Hitler	18 million lives lost[61]
Pol Pot	1.7 million lives lost[62]

What should we make of these stunning figures?

As it relates to this section, the lesson is that everyone should agree there are secular worldviews which deserve our moral condemnation. Atheists should join forces with religious believers in working against anyone adopting or promoting them. Everyone should agree, for instance, that the secular ideologies which spawned the Gulag and the Nazi concentration camps are without merit.

Instead, the atheist can say, it is only *reasonable* versions of secular thinking that should be taken seriously. Those are the ones that should be examined to see what impact they might have on character. Stalinism, Nazism, and Maoism are simply not reasonable positions.

This seems like an entirely sensible thing to say. But notice what happens next—religious believers can say exactly the same thing. There are problematic interpretations of Christianity, for instance, that deserve our moral condemnation. Here too atheists should join forces with theists in trying to stop those ideas from spreading. The ideas that spawned the Inquisition in the Middle Ages, for instance, are not reasonable ideas, and so they obviously should not be considered when we are thinking about helping people become more virtuous.

Hence no religious believer should think that *all* forms of her religion, no matter how bizarre they might be, will lead to character improvement. Rather, as a Christian, for instance, she should support only those Christian outlooks that on biblical grounds celebrate education, health, charity, volunteering, and other widely accepted goods mentioned in the previous section. At the same time, she can join with other Christians in actively condemning extremist views and practices. The thought is, then, that the Inquisition, the Crusades, and the Salem Witch Trials have no place in this discussion. Same with the Westboro Baptist Church today. They are all antithetical to the very core of Christianity and its commitment to love your neighbor as yourself, where your "neighbor" is meant to encompass everyone.

One Final Idea about Character Improvement from Christianity

Many of the points raised about Christianity and character improvement carry over to other major world religions as well. In this final section, I want to briefly mention an idea that does not. It is the idea that God himself is at work in character development in the form of the Holy Spirit.

This idea turns character improvement upside down. Rather than people being left to their own devices in improving themselves, the thought is that God himself can intervene in an important way and actively contribute to the process. This is a bold idea that we have not seen before in this book.

First a bit of background on the Holy Spirit for readers who may not be familiar with this side of Christianity. In traditional Christian thought, the Holy Spirit is the third member of the Trinity, along with God the Father and God the Son. All three persons of the Trinity are said to be fully divine, equal in power, knowledge, and love, but also have different roles and responsibilities. The Father, for instance, is the ultimate Creator. The Son is the Redeemer, who became one of us in the form of Jesus Christ. He forgives sin and in the end will judge human beings.

The Holy Spirit's role is said to have become more pronounced after Jesus's death and resurrection. He was sent to be with Christian believers; as Jesus says:

> If you love me, keep my commands. And I will ask the Father, and he will give you another advocate to help you and be with you forever—the Spirit of truth. The world cannot accept him, because it neither sees him nor knows him. But you know him, for he lives with you and will be in you.[63]

More specifically, one of the central roles of the Holy Spirit in Christian thinking is carrying out the process of what is known as *sanctification*.

Roughly, sanctification has to do with the period of time after someone becomes a follower of Jesus. It describes the process whereby a believer is changed into a perfected version of herself.

The thought is that God initially designed human beings to be a certain way, and in particular a *virtuous* way. But we have all fallen far short of that standard, as the examples throughout this book illustrate. The process of sanctification is, then, the slow, gradual process of restoring in the Christian the person God designed her to be.

The key idea for our purposes is that sanctification, in the Christian conception, is not something left up to Christians to try to do all on their own. It is not a solitary process. It also involves more than the help of fellow believers in the church (important though that is). Rather as the philosopher William Alston writes, in sanctification, "It is recognized on all hands that God is at work within the believer to transform her into the kind of person God wants her to be, the kind of person capable of entering into an eternal loving communion with God."[64]

So now we come to the key idea. In the Christian conception, there are many things that a believer can do which effect character change. We have already talked about prayer and tithing, for instance. *In addition*, there are many things that God via the Holy Spirit is doing which bring about character change in a believer as well.[65]

These points can be neatly interwoven. One way the Holy Spirit can change a Christian's character is *through the very rituals and practices* that she is engaged in, such as prayer. Prayer becomes, then, an avenue for the Holy Spirit to do its work. In fact, the Holy Spirit might even have prompted the Christian to engage in prayer in the first place.

The emerging picture from a Christian perspective, then, is one of human and divine cooperation on the path to becoming people of good character.

How exactly does the Holy Spirit effect character change? That is a vexed question in Christian theology, one whose answer will likely be for the most part inscrutable to human beings in this life. Different models have been proposed that try to explain how it might work. For example, on one model God directly makes changes in the believer's psychology, as suggested by a passage in the Book of Philippians: "You must work out your own salvation in fear and trembling; for it is God who works in you, inspiring both the will and the deed, for his own chosen purpose."[66]

On another model, God only tries to influence the believer in a better direction, perhaps using divine callings and communications and exhortations, presentations of God as a role model, the making of his love more obvious, loving encouragements, and so forth. As the Book of John says, the Holy Spirit will "teach you everything, and will call to mind all that I have told you."[67]

In still another model, the one favored by Alston himself, sanctification involves being drawn into the divine life and participating in it to some limited extent.[68] Relevant here is the verse from Second Peter that through the indwelling of the Holy Spirit we "come to share in the very being of God."[69]

For our purposes, we do not need to try to determine *how* the Holy Spirit effects character change. The only point is that, according to long-standing Christian teaching, the Holy Spirit *does* have an effect.

Furthermore, the process is not meant to be a passive one. It is not as if the Christian can just sit back and expect God to make him a better person without any contribution of his own. Rather, as mentioned already, the picture is one of *joint activity*, where the Christian and the Holy Spirit both work together, in some way, in shaping his character.[70]

Finally, it is worth noting that there is never any suggestion that this process will be completed during this lifetime, or even come close to being completed. The Christian on his deathbed may still have a long way to go to acquire a virtuous character full of faith, hope, love, honesty, forgiveness, and all the other virtues. This leads to the natural thought that the process of sanctification can continue beyond this life and into the next.[71]

Conclusion

In this chapter I have briefly examined various resources provided by Christianity for bridging the character gap and becoming more virtuous people. As we said, many of these resources are available in other major world religions too. One of the resources, however, is uniquely Christian in the form of the internal workings of the Holy Spirit during the process of sanctification.

Hence, in the final three chapters of this book, we have seen a wide variety of different approaches to character improvement. Some of them seem to me to be more promising than others. But ultimately all of them deserve much further study. These are still early days in our thinking about character improvement, especially from the perspective of empirical research.

May the coming years shed new light on the darkest recesses of our hearts. May they inspire us to replace that darkness with a better character. And may they provide us with greater insight into how to go about doing so.

Notes

1. 2 Peter 1:5–7. All passages are quoted from the New International Version, unless indicated otherwise.
2. Colossians 3:12–14.
3. Philippians 4:8.
4. Romans 3:10.
5. Romans 7:19.
6. Romans 7: 21–23.
7. Matthew 26: 41.
8. I have explored this more in Miller 2016b. I readily acknowledge, though, that there are strands of thinking in the history of Christianity which paint a much bleaker picture of human character than the one I have developed in this book. So on those views, the character gap is even wider than I think the psychological research would lead us to believe.
9. Hebrews 4:8.
10. 1 Corinthians 3:10. Similarly in the Old Testament we find the following: "The heart is deceitful . . . Who can understand it? I the Lord search

the heart and examine the mind, to reward a man according to his conduct, according to what his deeds deserve" (Jeremiah 17:9–10).

11. There is a way in which it might not be purely egoistic to want to avoid guilt and shame at the final judgment. It may be that feeling guilt and shame would be a sign that I had done something wrong, and what I really care about is not doing wrong things in God's eyes. It's not that I am ultimately motivated by trying to stop my feelings of guilt and shame. It's that I don't want to be the kind of person whose wrong actions lead to guilt and shame. In that case, then, I think we would have a much more positive view of a Christian's motivation.

12. I want to stress that Jesus was a perfect person "from a Christian perspective." Some might challenge whether he was in fact a perfect person, say in light of overturning the tables of the money changers (Matthew 21:12). Christians have plenty to say about passages like these, but here is not the place to enter into this long discussion.

13. Romans 7:23.

14. Acts 9:3–9.

15. For a helpful discussion, see Lewis 1943: Book IV, chapter 10. As Lewis writes, "Christian Miss Bates may have an unkinder tongue than unbelieving Dick Firkin. That, by itself, does not tell us whether Christianity works. The question is what Miss Bates's tongue would be like if she were not a Christian and what Dick's would be like if he became one" (163).

16. Matthew 6:9–13, Anglican Book of Common Prayer 1662 Version.

17. There is much more to be said here. For instance, Christians also pray for God to eliminate the sin in their lives, and to make them into better people, which is all about character improvement. As we will see in the final section of the chapter, Christians see prayers like this as invitations for the Holy Spirit to enter into their lives and actively change them. So prayer is not just the human speaking to God, but also (and more importantly) God being closely involved as well (even if the Christian never realizes it).

18. To be fair, though, there are ways in which, from a Christian perspective, prayer and confession can be carried out in a distorted way that is harmful

to one's character. For instance, someone might think that he has the freedom to do something wrong whenever he wants to, so long as he will be forgiven by praying to God and confessing his sins.

Of course, there is much in the New Testament and the history of Christianity which makes it clear that this is *not* how God intends prayer and confession to work. Nevertheless, if that is *in fact* what many Christians are doing, then they may be damaging their characters as a result. Unfortunately, I don't know of any empirical evidence that would help shed light on the long-term effects for moral behavior and character development of prayer and confession specifically (apart from other Christian practices). Thanks to Walter Sinnott-Armstrong for raising these issues.

19. This paints a distorted picture in one way, in that it makes it seem like all the change is being brought about by the Christian's own hard work. But as we will see in the final section below, the Christian understanding of character change also involves God playing a central role too.

20. See, e.g., Acts 9:32, Philippians 1:1.

21. Many, but not all. Following footnotes 17 and 19, practices like prayer and confession do have some distinctive elements in the Christian understanding. In particular, just saying prayers, tithing, confessing, and the like will not be enough to become virtuous (or, in theological language, to become sanctified), as we are not capable of fixing ourselves on our own. Rather, God can play an active role as well through them, and Christian notions like transforming grace and the work of the Holy Spirit become central in this discussion. We will touch on the work of the Holy Spirit at the end of the chapter. I am grateful to Ryan West for discussion of these issues.

22. http://www.newadvent.org/cathen/13795a.htm. Accessed July 21, 2016.

23. http://www.newadvent.org/cathen/13795a.htm. Accessed July 21, 2016.

24. Proverbs 27:7 is often quoted in connection to this social role of character building: "As iron sharpens iron, so one person sharpens another."

25. Matthew 18: 15–17. See also 1 Corinthians 5:1–13.

26. Of course, the opposite is a possibility as well if being disciplined serves to alienate someone. He may fall prey to bitterness and resentment, and not want to have anything more to do with Christianity.

It is worth noting that a secular analog of Christian discipline might be an intervention where medical professionals, family members, and/or friends confront a person who is suffering from an addiction, for instance. The ultimate goal is recovery, and the intervention—no doubt an unpleasant experience for everyone involved—is designed to help the person acknowledge that there is a problem which requires help from others to treat.

27. Following the previous note, it would be interesting to consider what various secular analogs of these social dimensions might look like, and how effective they would be in developing good character. Such a project will have to wait for another occasion, but let me emphasize that I am not suggesting in this chapter that *only* religious approaches to character development will be successful if properly carried out.

28. The summary of empirical results that follows draws on Miller 2012.

29. Ellison and Anderson 2001. For similar results, see Fergusson et al. 1986 and Ellison et al. 1999.

30. Evans et al. 1995.

31. See, e.g., Lipford et al. 1993; Hull and Bold 1995; and Hull 2000.

32. Regnerus and Elder 2003.

33. Regnerus and Elder 2003: 644.

34. Regnerus and Elder 2003: 644, summarizing Muller and Ellison 2001.

35. See, e.g., Regnerus 2000 and Elder and Conger 2000.

36. Stack 1983 and Donahue 1995.

37. Gorsuch 1995 and National Center on Addiction and Substance Abuse 2001.

38. Schiller and Levin 1988 and Benjamins and Brown 2004.

39. Koenig et al. 1998 and Gillum 2005.

40. Clarke et al. 1990; Cochran 1993; Koenig et al. 1994; and Cochran et al. 1998.

41. Hill et al. 2007.

42. Larson et al. 1992 and Levin and Chatters 1998. For more on the positive link between religion and health, see Koenig et al. 2001.

43. Hummer et al. 1999 report US life expectancy estimates for a twenty-year-old as 55.3 more years, versus 62.9 more years, depending on attendance at

religious services. For African Americans it was 46.4 more years versus 60.1 more years!

44. Benjamins, Trinitapoli, and Ellison 2006.
45. Ellison 1991.
46. Witter et al. 1985.
47. Ellison et al. 1989.
48. Ellison and George 1994.
49. Hansen 1987 and Dudley and Koslinski 1990.
50. See Brooks 2006.
51. Brooks 2006: 39.
52. Regnerus et al. 1998. See also Hoge et al. 1996.
53. Smith and Faris 2002.
54. However, in a few studies the link between religiosity and some good outcome was not always found. For example, Brinkerhoff et al. 1992 did not find the same differences in rates of domestic violence using Canadian participants. And Fox et al. 1998 studied Los Angeles women and did not find significant differences in breast cancer screening.

    Also, most of these studies use Western (and specifically American) participants. Much more needs to be done looking at non-Americans and also at religions besides Judaism, Christianity, and Islam.
55. Brooks 2006.
56. Acts 20:35.
57. For related discussion of these issues, with a focus on Arthur Brooks's work on charity as well, see Sinnott-Armstrong 2009: 44–52.
58. Note that this is quite compatible with there being plenty of other sources of evidence for a positive effect. Throughout this book I have relied on empirical research, but I *don't* mean at all to downplay the contributions of people's own experiences, what they have seen happen in the lives of other religious believers, what history or literature can tell us, and so forth.
59. See Dikötter 2010.
60. See Conquest 2007.
61. See the United States Holocaust Memorial Museum's *Holocaust Encyclopedia*, https://www.ushmm.org/wlc/en/article.php?ModuleId=10008193. Accessed August 5, 2016.

62. See the Yale University Cambodian Genocide Program, http://gsp. yale.edu/case-studies/cambodian-genocide-program. Accessed August 5, 2016.

63. John 14: 15–17.

64. Alston 1988: 128.

65. For Christians, this is a teaching of the New Testament, which was subsequently affirmed by the early Christian church and has remained a widely held commitment of Christianity ever since.

66. Philippians 2:13. For discussion of this model, see Alston 1988: 128.

67. John 14:26. For discussion of this model, see Alston 1988: 132.

68. Alston 1988: 139.

69. 2 Peter 1:4. The notion of participation, as well as related notions of insight and illumination, could be (and have been) richly explored in Christian theology in relation to better understanding the role of the Holy Spirit in character building.

70. On the human side of the equation, mistakes will still be made all the time in a Christian's life. Yet according to Paul, "There is now no condemnation for those who are in Christ Jesus, because through Christ Jesus the law of the Spirit of life set me free from the law of sin and death" (Romans 8:1– 2). So the Christian can work toward character improvement, trusting that she is helped by the Holy Spirit, believing she is free of condemnation, and confident that if she slips up, she is forgiven by God. That can inspire the pursuit of holiness even more.

Finally, for the theologically inclined, I do not intend any of the above to bear on matters of salvation or justification, as opposed to matters of sanctification. Whether salvation involves human cooperation with God, or is accomplished by God's grace alone, is a highly contentious debate in Christian theology (sometimes labeled the debate between monergism versus synergism), but that's not on my radar screen here.

71. For interesting discussion of how that process might continue in the afterlife, see Barnard 2007.

WORKS CITED

Adams, Robert. (2006). *A Theory of Virtue: Excellence in Being for the Good*. Oxford: Clarendon Press.

Alfano, Mark. (2013). *Character as Moral Fiction*. Cambridge: Cambridge University Press.

Algoe, S. and J. Haidt. (2009). "Witnessing Excellence in Action: The 'Other-Praising' Emotions of Elevation, Gratitude, and Admiration." *Journal of Positive Psychology* 4: 105–127.

Alston, William. (1988). "The Indwelling of the Holy Spirit." In *Philosophy and the Christian Faith*. Ed. Thomas V. Morris. Notre Dame: University of Notre Dame Press, 121–150.

Anderson, C. (1987). "Temperature and Aggression: Effects on Quarterly, Yearly, and City Rates of Violent and Nonviolent Crime." *Journal of Personality and Social Psychology* 52: 1161–1173.

Anderson, C. and B. Bushman. (2002). "Human Aggression." *Annual Review of Psychology* 53: 27–51.

Apsler, R. (1975). "Effects of Embarrassment on Behavior Toward Others." *Journal of Personality and Social Psychology* 32: 145–153.

Aquino, K. and D. Freeman. (2009). "Moral Identity in Business Situations: A Social-Cognitive Framework for Understanding Moral Functioning." In *Personality, Identity, and Character: Explorations in Moral Psychology*. Darcia Narvaez and Daniel K. Lapsley. Cambridge: Cambridge University Press, 375–395.

Aquino, K., B. McFerran, and M. Laven. (2011). "Moral Identity and the Experience of Moral Elevation in Response to Acts of Uncommon Goodness." *Journal of Personality and Social Psychology* 100: 703–718.

Aristotle. (1985). *Nicomachean Ethics*. Trans. T. Irwin. Indianapolis: Hackett Publishing Company.

Baier, Annette. (1990). "Why Honesty Is a Hard Virtue." In *Identity, Character, and Morality: Essays in Moral Philosophy*. Ed. O. Flanagan and A. Rorty. Cambridge: MIT Press, 259–282.

Barnard, Justin. (2007). "Purgatory and the Dilemma of Sanctification." *Faith and Philosophy* 24: 311–330.

Baron, R. (1997). "The Sweet Smell of... Helping: Effects of Pleasant Ambient Fragrance on Prosocial Behavior in Shopping Malls." *Personality and Social Psychology Bulletin* 23: 498–503.

Baron, R. and D. Richardson. (1994). *Human Aggression*. Second Edition. New York: Plenum Press.

Batson, C. (2011). *Altruism in Humans*. New York: Oxford University Press.

Batson, C., J. Batson, C. Griffitt, S. Barrientos, J. Brandt, P. Sprengelmeyer, and M. Bayly. (1989). "Negative-State Relief and the Empathy-Altruism Hypothesis." *Journal of Personality and Social Psychology* 56: 922–933.

Beaman, A., P. Barnes, B. Klentz, and B. McQuirk. (1978). "Increasing Helping Rates through Information Dissemination: Teaching Pays." *Personality and Social Psychology Bulletin* 4: 406–411.

Benjamins, M. and C. Brown. (2004). "Religion and Preventative Health Care Utilization among the Elderly." *Social Science and Medicine* 58: 109–119.

Benjamins, M., J. Trinitapoli, and C. Ellison. (2006). "Religious Attendance, Health Maintenance Beliefs, and Mammography Utilization: Findings from a Nationwide Survey of Presbyterian Women." *Journal for the Scientific Study of Religion* 45: 597–607.

Berkowitz, L. (1965). "Some Aspects of Observed Aggression." *Journal of Personality and Social Psychology* 2: 359–369.

Berkowitz, L. and A. LePage. (1967). "Weapons as Aggression-Eliciting Stimuli." *Journal of Personality and Social Psychology* 7: 202–207.

Bettencourt, B., A. Talley, A. Benjamin, and J. Valentine. (2006). "Personality and Aggressive Behavior under Provoking and Neutral Conditions: A Meta-analytic Review." *Psychological Bulletin* 132: 751–777.

Bowers, K. (1973). "Situationism in Psychology: An Analysis and a Critique." *Psychological Review* 80: 307–336.

Brinkerhoff, M., E. Grandin, and E. Lupri. (1992). "Religious Involvement and Spousal Violence: The Canadian Case." *Journal for the Scientific Study of Religion* 31: 15–31.

Brooks, Arthur. (2006). *Who Really Cares.* New York: Basic Books.

Brown, R. (1986). *Social Psychology.* Second Edition. New York: Macmillan.

Bryan, J. and M. Test. (1967). "Models and Helping: Naturalistic Studies in Aiding Behavior." *Journal of Personality and Social Psychology* 6: 400–407.

Burger, J. (2009). "Replicating Milgram: Would People Still Obey Today?" *American Psychologist* 64: 1–11.

Buschor, C., R. T. Proyer, and W. Ruch. (2013). "Self- and Peer-Rated Character Strengths: How Do They Relate to Satisfaction with Life and Orientations to Happiness?" *Journal of Positive Psychology* 8: 116–127.

Bushman, B. and R. Baumeister. (1998). "Threatened Egotism, Narcissism, Self-Esteem, and Direct and Displaced Aggression: Does Self-Love or Self-Hate Lead to Violence?" *Journal of Personality and Social Psychology* 75: 219–229.

Cacioppo, J., R. Petty, and M. Losch. (1986). "Attributions of Responsibility for Helping and Doing Harm: Evidence for Confusion of Responsibility." *Journal of Personality and Social Psychology* 50: 100–105.

Cann, A. and J. Blackwelder. (1984). "Compliance and Mood: A Field Investigation of the Impact of Embarrassment." *Journal of Psychology* 117: 221–226.

Caprara, G. (1987). "The Disposition-Situation Debate and Research on Aggression." *European Journal of Personality* 1: 1–16.

Carson, Thomas. (2010). *Lying and Deception: Theory and Practice.* Oxford: Oxford University Press.

———. (2015). *Lincoln's Ethics.* Cambridge: Cambridge University Press.

Carver, C., R. Ganellen, W. Froming, and W. Chambers. (1983). "Modeling: An Analysis in Terms of Category Accessibility." *Journal of Experimental Social Psychology* 19: 403–421.

Chekroun, P. and M. Brauer. (2002). "The Bystander Effect and Social Control Behavior: The Effect of the Presence of Others on People's Reactions to Norm Violations." *European Journal of Social Psychology* 32: 853–867.

Clark, R. and L. Word. (1972). "Why Don't Bystanders Help? Because of Ambiguity?" *Journal of Personality and Social Psychology* 24: 392–400.

———. (1974). "Where Is the Apathetic Bystander? Situational Characteristics of the Emergency." *Journal of Personality and Social Psychology* 29: 279–287.

Clarke, L., L. Beeghley, and J. Cochran. (1990). "Religiosity, Social Class, and Alcohol Use: An Application of Reference Group Theory." *Sociological Perspectives* 33: 201–218.

Cochran, John. (1993). "The Variable Effects of Religiosity and Denomination on Adolescent Self-Reported Alcohol Use by Beverage Type." *Journal of Drug Issues* 23: 479–491.

Cochran, J., L. Beeghley, and W. Bock. (1998). "Religiosity and Alcohol Behavior: An Exploration of Reference Group Theory." *Sociological Forum* 3: 256–276.

Coles, R. (1986). *The Moral Life of Children.* New York: Atlantic Monthly Press.

Confucius. (1979). *The Analects.* Trans. D. C. Lau. London: Penguin.

Conquest, Robert. (2007). *The Great Terror: A Reassessment.* 40th Anniversary Edition. New York: Oxford University Press.

Cornelissen, G., S. Dewitte, L. Warlop, and V. Yzerbyt. (2007). "Whatever People Say I Am, That's What I Am: Social Labeling as a Social Marketing Tool." *International Journal of Research in Marketing* 24: 278–288.

Corwin, Miles. (1982). "Icy Killer's Life Steeped in Violence." *Los Angeles Times,* May 16.

Cunningham, M., J. Steinberg, and R. Grev. (1980). "Wanting to and Having to Help: Separate Motivations for Positive Mood and Guilt-Induced Helping." *Journal of Personality and Social Psychology* 38: 181–192.

Darley, J. and B. Latané. (1968). "Bystander Intervention in Emergencies: Diffusion of Responsibility." *Journal of Personality and Social Psychology* 8: 377–383.

DePaulo, B. (2004). "The Many Faces of Lies." In *The Social Psychology of Good and Evil.* Ed. A. Miller. New York: Guilford Press, 303–326.

DePaulo, B. and K. Bell. (1996). "Truth and Investment: Lies Are Told to Those Who Care." *Journal of Personality and Social Psychology* 71: 703–716.

DePaulo, B., D. Kashy, S. Kirkendol, M. Wyer, and J. Epstein. (1996). "Lying in Everyday Life." *Journal of Personality and Social Psychology* 70: 979–995.

DePaulo, B. and D. Kashy. (1998). "Everyday Lies in Close and Causal Relationships." *Journal of Personality and Social Psychology* 74: 63–79.

DePaulo, B., M. Ansfield, S. Kirkendol, and J. Boden. (2004). "Serious Lies." *Basic and Applied Social Psychology* 26: 147–167.

DeYoung, Rebecca. (2009). *Glittering Vices: A New Look at the Seven Deadly Sins and Their Remedies*. Grand Rapids: Brazos Press.

Diener, E. and M. Wallbom. (1976). "Effects of Self-Awareness on Antinormative Behavior." *Journal of Research in Personality* 10: 107–111.

Dikötter, Frank (2010). *Mao's Great Famine: The History of China's Most Devastating Catastrophe*. New York: Walker and Company.

Donahue, Michael. (1995). "Religion and the Well-Being of Adolescents." *Journal of Social Issues* 51: 145–160.

Donnerstein, E., M. Donnerstein, and G. Munger. (1975). "Helping Behavior as a Function of Pictorially Induced Moods." *Journal of Social Psychology* 97: 221–225.

Doris, John. (2002). *Lack of Character: Personality and Moral Behavior*. Cambridge: Cambridge University Press.

Dudley, M. and F. Kosinski. (1990). "Religiosity and Marital Satisfaction: A Research Note." *Review of Religious Research* 32: 78–86.

Edelmann, R., J. Childs, S. Harvey, I. Kellock, and C. Strain-Clark. (1984). "The Effect of Embarrassment on Helping." *Journal of Social Psychology* 124: 253–254.

Elder, G. and R. Conger. (2000). *Children of the Land: Adversity and Success in Rural America*. Chicago: University of Chicago Press.

Ellison, Christopher. (1991). "Religious Involvement and Subjective Well-Being." *Journal of Health and Social Behavior* 32: 80–99.

Ellison, C., D. Gay, and T. Glass. (1989). "Does Religious Commitment Contribute to Individual Life Satisfaction?" *Social Forces* 68: 100–123.

Ellison, C. and L. George. (1994). "Religious Involvement, Social Ties, and Social Support in a Southeastern Community." *Journal for the Scientific Study of Religion* 33: 46–61.

Ellison, C., J. Bartkowski, and K. Anderson. (1999). "Are There Religious Variations in Domestic Violence?" *Journal of Family Issues* 20: 87–113.

Ellison, C. and K. Anderson. (2001). "Religious Involvement and Domestic Violence Among U.S. Couples." *Journal for the Scientific Study of Religion* 40: 269–286.

Emmons, R. and M. McCullough. (2003). "Counting Blessings versus Burdens: An Experimental Investigation of Gratitude and Subjective Well-Being in Daily Life." *Journal of Personality and Social Psychology* 84: 377–389.

Epictetus. (1983). *The Handbook*. Trans. N. White. Indianapolis: Hackett.

Evans, T., F. Cullen, R. Dunaway, and V. Burton. (1995). "Religion and Crime Reexamined: The Impact of Religion, Secular Controls, and Social Ecology on Adult Criminality." *Criminology* 33: 195–217.

Faulkender, P., L. Range, M. Hamilton, M. Strehlow, S. Jackson, E. Blanchard, and P. Dean. (1994). "The Case of the Stolen Psychology Test: An Analysis of an Actual Cheating Incident." *Ethics and Behavior* 4: 209–217.

Fergusson, D., L. Horwood, K. Kershaw, and F. Shannon. (1986). "Factors Associated with Reports of Wife Assault in New Zealand." *Journal of Marriage and the Family* 48: 407–412.

Fleeson, W. (2001). "Toward a Structure- and Process-Integrated View of Personality: Traits as Density Distributions of States." *Journal of Personality and Social Psychology* 80: 1011–1027.

Foss, R. and N. Crenshaw. (1978). "Risk of Embarrassment and Helping." *Social Behavior and Personality* 6: 243–245.

Fox, S., K. Pitkin, C. Paul, S. Carson, and N. Duan. (1998). "Breast Cancer Screening Adherence: Does Church Attendance Matter?" *Health Education and Behavior* 25: 742–758.

Funder, D. (2008). "Persons, Situations, and Person-Situation Interactions." In *Handbook of Personality: Theory and Research*. Third Edition. Ed. O. John., R. Robins, and L. Pervin. New York: Guilford Press, 568–580.

Gallardo-Pujol, D., E. Orekhova, V. Benet-Martínez, and M. Slater. (2015). "Taking Evil into the Lab: Exploring the Frontiers of Morality and Individual Differences." In *Character: New Directions from Philosophy, Psychology, and*

Theology. Ed. Christian B. Miller, R. Michael Furr, Angela Knobel, and William Fleeson. New York: Oxford University Press, 652–670.

Geen, R. (2001). *Human Aggression*. Second Edition. Buckingham: Open University Press.

Gillath, O., A. Sesko, P. Shaver, and D. Chun. (2010). "Attachment, Authenticity, and Honesty: Dispositional and Experimentally Induced Security Can Reduce Self- and Other-Deception." *Journal of Personality and Social Psychology* 98: 841–855.

Gillum, R. (2005). "Frequency of Attendance at Religious Services and Cigarette Smoking in American Women and Men: The Third National Health and Nutrition Examination Survey." *Preventive Medicine* 41: 607–613.

Gino, F., S. Ayal, and D. Ariely. (2009). "Contagion and Differentiation in Unethical Behavior: The Effect of One Bad Apple on the Barrel." *Psychological Science* 20: 393–398.

Gino, F. and J. Margolis. (2011). "Bringing Ethics into Focus: How Regulatory Focus and Risk Preferences Influence (Un)ethical Behavior." *Organizational Behavior and Human Decision Processes* 115: 145–156.

Giumetti, G. and P. Markey. (2007). "Violent Video Games and Anger as Predictors of Aggression." *Journal of Research in Personality* 41: 1234–1243.

Gonzales, M., J. Pederson, D. Manning, and D. Wetter. (1990). "Pardon My Gaffe: Effects of Sex, Status, and Consequence Severity on Accounts." *Journal of Personality and Social Psychology* 58: 610–621.

Goodwin, Geoffrey, Jared Piazza, and Paul Rozin. (2015). "Understanding the Importance and Perceived Structure of Moral Character." In *Character: New Directions from Philosophy, Psychology, and Theology*. Ed. Christian Miller, R. Michael Furr, Angela Knobel, and William Fleeson. New York: Oxford University Press, 100–126.

Gordon, A. and A. Miller. (2000). "Perspective Differences in the Construal of Lies: Is Deception in the Eye of the Beholder?" *Personality and Social Psychology Bulletin* 26: 46–55.

Gorsuch, R. (1995). "Religious Aspects of Substance Abuse and Recovery." *Journal of Social Issues* 51: 65–83.

Gottlieb, J. and C. Carver. (1980). "Anticipation of Future Interaction and the Bystander Effect." *Journal of Experimental Social Psychology* 16: 253–260.

Grüne-Yanoff, Till. (2012). "Old Wine in New Casks: Libertarian Paternalism Still Violates Liberal Principles." *Social Choice and Welfare* 38: 635–645.

Grusec, J., L. Kuczynski, J. Rushton, and Z. Simutis. (1978). "Modeling, Direct Instruction, and Attributions: Effects on Altruism." *Developmental Psychology* 14: 51–57.

Grusec, J., P. Saas-Kortsaak, and Z. Simutis. (1978). "The Role of Example and Moral Exhortation in the Training of Altruism." *Child Development* 49: 920–923.

Grusec, J. and E. Redler. (1980). "Attribution, Reinforcement, and Altruism: A Developmental Analysis." *Developmental Psychology* 16: 525–534.

Haidt, Jonathan. (2000). "The Positive Emotion of Elevation." *Prevention and Treatment* 3: 1–5.

———. (2003). "Elevation and the Positive Psychology of Morality." In *Flourishing: Positive Psychology and the Life Well-Lived*. Ed. C. Keyes and J. Haidt. Washington: American Psychological Association, 275–289.

Haines, V., G. Diekhoff, E. LaBeff, and R. Clark. (1986). "College Cheating: Immaturity, Lack of Commitment, and the Neutralizing Attitude." *Research in Higher Education* 25: 342–354.

Hansen, G. (1987). "The Effect of Religiosity on Factors Predicting Marital Adjustment." *Social Psychology Quarterly* 50: 264–269.

Hansen, P. (2016). "The Definition of Nudge and Libertarian Paternalism: Does the Hand Fit the Glove?" *European Journal of Risk Regulation* 7: 155–174.

Hansen, P. and A. Jespersen. (2013). "Nudge and the Manipulation of Choice: A Framework for the Responsible Use of the Nudge Approach to Behaviour Change in Public Policy." *European Journal of Risk Regulation* 4: 3–28.

Hausman, Daniel and Brynn Welch. (2010). "To Nudge or Not to Nudge." *Journal of Political Philosophy* 18: 123–136.

Herndon, William and Jesse Weik. (1949). *Herndon's Life of Lincoln: The History and Personal Recollections of Abraham Lincoln as Originally Written by William H. Herndon and Jesse W. Weik.* Cleveland: World Publishing Company.

Higgins, S., C. Wong, G. Badger, D. Haug Ogden, and R. Dantona. (2000). "Contingent Reinforcement Increases Cocaine Abstinence during Outpatient Treatment and 1 Year of Follow-Up." *Journal of Consulting and Clinical Psychology* 68: 64–72.

Hill, T., C. Ellison, A. Burdette, and M. Musick. (2007). "Religious Involvement and Healthy Lifestyles: Evidence from the Survey of Texas Adults." *Annals of Behavioral Medicine* 34: 217–222.

Hoge, D., C. Zech, P. McNamara, and M. Donahue. (1996). *Money Matters: Personal Giving in American Churches.* Louisville: Westminster John Knox.

Hope, Sara. (2015). "Can Text Messages Make People Kinder?" In *Character: New Directions from Philosophy, Psychology, and Theology.* Ed. Christian B. Miller, R. Michael Furr, Angela Knobel, and William Fleeson. New York: Oxford University Press, 412–442.

Hull, B. (2000). "Religion Still Matters." *Journal of Economics* 26: 35–48.

Hull, B. and F. Bold. (1995). "Preaching Matters: Replication and Extension." *Journal of Economic Behavior and Organization* 27: 143–149.

Hummer, R., R. Rogers, C. Nam, and C. Ellison. (1999). "Religious Involvement and U.S. Adult Mortality." *Demography* 36: 273–285.

Hursthouse, Rosalind. (1999). *On Virtue Ethics.* Oxford: Oxford University Press.

Jensen, R. and S. Moore. (1977). "The Effect of Attribute Statements on Cooperativeness and Competitiveness in School-Age Boys." *Child Development* 48: 305–307.

Kallbekken, S. (2013). "'Nudging' Hotel Guests to Reduce Food Waste as a Win-Win Environmental Measure." *Economics Letters* 119: 325–327.

Kant, Immanuel. (1996). *Practical Philosophy.* Trans. Mary Gregor. Cambridge: Cambridge University Press.

Karakashian, L., M. Walter, A. Christopher et al. (2006). "Fear of Negative Evaluation Affects Helping Behavior: The Bystander Effect Revisited." *North American Journal of Psychology* 8: 13–32.

Kashy, D. and B. DePaulo. (1996). "Who Lies?" *Journal of Personality and Social Psychology* 70: 1037–1051.

Kidder, Tracy. (2009). *Mountains beyond Mountains: The Quest of Dr. Paul Farmer, a Man Who Would Cure the World.* New York: Random House.

Klein, H., N. Levenburg, M. McKendall, and W. Mothersell. (2007). "Cheating during the College Years: How Do Business Students Compare?" *Journal of Business Ethics* 72: 197–206.

Koenig, H., L. George, H. Cohen, et al. (1998). "The Relationship between Religious Activities and Cigarette Smoking in Older Adults." *Journal of Gerontology: Medical Sciences*. 53: M426–M434.

Koenig, H., L. George, K. Meador, D. Blazer, and S. Ford. (1994). "The Relationship between Religion and Alcoholism in a Sample of Community-Dwelling Adults." *Hospital and Community Psychiatry* 45: 225–231.

Koenig, H., M. McCullough, and D. Larson. (2001). *The Handbook of Religion and Health.* New York: Oxford University Press.

Konečni, V. (1972). "Some Effects of Guilt on Compliance: A Field Replication." *Journal of Personality and Social Psychology* 23: 30–32.

Krahé, B. (2001). *The Social Psychology of Aggression.* Philadelphia: Taylor and Francis.

Kraut, R. (1973). "Effects of Social Labeling on Giving to Charity." *Journal of Experimental Social Psychology* 9: 551–562.

Krebs, D. (1970). "Altruism: An Examination of the Concept and a Review of the Literature." *Psychological Bulletin* 73: 258–302.

Larson, D., K. Sherrill, J. Lyons, F. Craigie, S. Thielman, M. Greenwold, and S. Larson. (1992). "Associations between Dimensions of Religious Commitment and Mental Health Reported in the *American Journal of Psychiatry* and the *Archives of General Psychiatry*, 1978–1989." *American Journal of Psychiatry* 149: 557–559.

Latané, B. and J. Dabbs. (1977). "Social Inhibition of Helping Yourself: Bystander Response to a Cheeseburger." *Personality and Social Psychology Bulletin* 3: 575–578.

Latané, B. and J. Darley. (1968). "Group Inhibition of Bystander Intervention in Emergencies." *Journal of Personality and Social Psychology* 10: 215–221.

————. (1970). *The Unresponsive Bystander: Why Doesn't He Help?* New York: Appleton-Century-Crofts.

Latané, B. and J. Rodin. (1969). "A Lady in Distress: Inhibiting Effects of Friends and Strangers on Bystander Intervention." *Journal of Experimental Social Psychology* 5: 189–202.

Latané, B., K. Williams, and S. Harkins. (1979). "Many Hands Make Light Work: The Causes and Consequences of Social Loafing." *Journal of Personality and Social Psychology* 37: 822–832.

Latané, B., S. Nida, and D. Wilson. (1981). "The Effects of Group Size on Helping Behavior." In *Altruism and Helping Behavior: Social, Personality, and Developmental Perspectives.* Ed. J. Rushton and R. Sorrentino. Hillsdale, NJ: Lawrence Erlbaum, 287–313.

Latané, B. and S. Nida. (1981). "Ten Years of Research on Group Size and Helping." *Psychological Bulletin* 89: 308–324.

Levin, J. and L. Chatters. (1998). "Research on Religion and Mental Health: A Review of Empirical Findings and Theoretical Issues." In *Handbook of Religion and Mental Health.* Ed. H. Koenig. San Diego: Academic Press, 33–50.

Lewis, C. S. (1943). *Mere Christianity.* New York: Collier Books.

Lindsey, L. (2005). "Anticipated Guilt as Behavioral Motivation: An Examination of Appeals to Help Unknown Others through Bone Marrow Donation." *Human Communication Research* 31: 453–481.

Lipford, J., R. McCormick, and R. Tollison. (1993). "Preaching Matters." *Journal of Economic Behavior and Organization* 21: 235–250.

Lycan, William and George Schlesinger. (1989). "You Bet Your Life: Pascal's Wager Defended." In *Reason and Responsibility: Readings in Some Basic Problems of Philosophy* Seventh Edition. Ed. Joel Feinberg. Belmont, CA: Wadsworth, 82–90.

Marshall, Robert. (2013). *In the Sewers of Lvov: The Last Sanctuary from the Holocaust.* London: Bloomsbury Reader.

Mazar, N., O. Amir, and D. Ariely. (2008). "The Dishonesty of Honest People: A Theory of Self-Concept Maintenance." *Journal of Marketing Research* 45: 633–644.

McCabe, D., and L. Treviño. (1993). "Academic Dishonesty: Honor Codes and Other Contextual Influences." *Journal of Higher Education* 64: 522–538.

McCabe, D., L. Treviño, and K. Butterfield. (2001). "Cheating in Academic Institutions: A Decade of Research." *Ethics and Behavior* 11: 219–232.

McCabe, D., K. Butterfield, and L. Treviño. (2006). "Academic Dishonesty in Graduate Business Programs: Prevalence, Causes, and Proposed Action." *Academy of Management Learning and Education* 5: 294–305.

McClure, J. B. (ed.). (1879). *Anecdotes of Abraham Lincoln and Lincoln's Stories.* Chicago: Rhodes and McClure.

McCullough, M., R. Emmons, and J. Tsang. (2002). "The Grateful Disposition: A Conceptual and Empirical Topography." *Journal of Personality and Social Psychology* 82: 112–127.

Mead, N., R. Baumeister, F. Gino, M. Schweitzer, and D. Ariely. (2009). "Too Tired to Tell the Truth: Self-Control Resource Depletion and Dishonesty." *Journal of Experimental Social Psychology* 45: 594–597.

Meeus, W. and Q. Raaijmakers. (1986). "Administrative Obedience: Carrying Out Orders to Use Psychological-Administrative Violence." *European Journal of Social Psychology* 16: 311–324.

Mele, Alfred and Joshua Shepard. (2013). "Situationism and Agency." *Journal of Practical Ethics* 1: 62–83.

Merritt, Maria. (2000). "Virtue Ethics and Situationist Personality Psychology." *Ethical Theory and Moral Practice* 3: 365–383.

Merritt, Maria, John Doris, and Gilbert Harman. (2010). "Character." In *The Moral Psychology Handbook.* Ed. J. Doris and the Moral Psychology Research Group. Oxford: Oxford University Press, 355–401.

Milgram, S. (1963). "Behavioral Study of Obedience." *Journal of Abnormal and Social Psychology* 67: 371–378.

———. (1974). *Obedience to Authority.* New York: Harper & Row.

Millar, K. and A. Tesser. (1988). "Deceptive Behavior in Social Relationships: A Consequence of Violated Expectations." *Journal of Psychology* 122: 263–273.

Miller, Christian. (2012). "Atheism and the Benefits of Theistic Belief." In *Oxford Studies in Philosophy of Religion.* Ed. Jonathan Kvanvig. Volume 4. Oxford: Oxford University Press, 97–125.

———. (2013). *Moral Character: An Empirical Theory*. Oxford: Oxford University Press.

———. (2014). *Character and Moral Psychology*. Oxford: Oxford University Press.

———. (2016a). "Virtue Cultivation in Light of Situationism." In *Developing the Virtues: Integrating Perspectives*. Ed. Julia Annas, Darcia Narvaez, and Nancy Snow. New York: Oxford University Press, 157–183.

———. (2016b). "Should Christians Be Worried about Situationist Claims in Psychology and Philosophy?" *Faith and Philosophy* 33: 48–73.

Miller, D. and C. McFarland. (1991). "When Social Comparison Goes Awry: The Case of Pluralistic Ignorance." In *Social Comparison: Contemporary Theory and Research*. Ed. Jerry Suls and Thomas Ashby Wills. Hillsdale, NJ: Lawrence Erlbaum, 287–313.

Miller, R. (1996). *Embarrassment: Poise and Peril in Everyday Life*. New York: Guilford Press.

Miller, R., P. Brickman, and D. Bolen. (1975). "Attribution versus Persuasion as a Means for Modifying Behavior." *Journal of Personality and Social Psychology* 31: 430–441.

Mills, R. and J. Grusec. (1989). "Cognitive, Affective, and Behavioral Consequences of Praising Altruism." *Merrill-Palmer Quarterly* 35: 299–326.

Mischel, W. and H. Mischel. (1976). "A Cognitive Social-Learning Approach to Morality and Self-Regulation." In *Moral Development and Behavior: Theory, Research, and Social Issues*. Ed. T. Lickona. New York: Holt, Rinehart, and Winston, 84–107.

Muggeridge, Malcolm. (1971). *Something Beautiful for God: Mother Teresa of Calcutta*. London: Harper and Row.

Muller, C. and C. Ellison. (2001). "Religious Involvement, Social Capital, and Adolescents' Academic Process: Evidence from the National Longitudinal Study of 1988." *Sociological Focus* 34: 155–183.

Murdoch, Iris. (1971). *The Sovereignty of the Good*. New York: Schocken Books.

National Center on Addiction and Substance Abuse. (2001). *So Help Me God: Substance Abuse, Religion and Spirituality*. New York: Columbia University.

Park, N., C. Peterson, and M. Seligman. (2004). "Strengths of Character and Well-Being." *Journal of Social and Clinical Psychology* 23: 603–619.

Park, N., and C. Peterson. (2008). "Positive Psychology and Character Strengths: Application to Strengths-Based School Counseling." *Professional School Counseling* 12: 85–92.

Peterson, C., J. Stephens, N. Park, F. Lee, and M. Seligman. (2010). "Strengths of Character and Work." In *Oxford Handbook of Positive Psychology and Work*. Ed. P. Linley, S. Harrington, and N. Garcea. New York: Oxford University Press, 221–231.

Petty, R., K. Williams, S. Harkins, and B. Latané. (1977a). "Social Inhibition of Helping Yourself: Bystander Response to a Cheeseburger." *Personality and Social Psychology Bulletin* 3: 575–578.

Petty, R., S. Harkins, K. Williams, and B. Latané. (1977b). "The Effects of Group Size on Cognitive Effort and Evaluation." *Personality and Social Psychology Bulletin* 3: 579–582.

Plato. (1968). *The Republic of Plato*. Trans. Allan Bloom. New York: Basic Books.

Prentice, D. and D. Miller. (1996). "Pluralistic Ignorance and the Perpetuation of Social Norms by Unwitting Actors." In *Advances in Experimental Social Psychology*. Ed. M. Zanna. Volume 28. San Diego: Academic Press, 161–209.

Proyer, R. T., F. Gander, T. Wyss, and W. Ruch. (2011). "The Relation of Character Strengths to Past, Present, and Future Life Satisfaction among German-Speaking Women." *Applied Psychology: Health and Well-Being* 3: 370–384.

Regan, D., M. Williams, and S. Sparling. (1972). "Voluntary Expiation of Guilt: A Field Experiment." *Journal of Personality and Social Psychology* 24: 42–45.

Regnerus, Mark. (2000). "Shaping Schooling Success: Religious Socialization and Educational Outcomes in Urban Public Schools." *Journal for the Scientific Study of Religion* 39: 363–370.

Regnerus, M. and G. Elder. (2003). "Staying on Track in School: Religious Influences in High- and Low-Risk Settings." *Journal for the Scientific Study of Religion* 42: 633–649.

Regnerus, M., C. Smith, and D. Sikkink. (1998). "Who Gives to the Poor? The Influence of Religious Tradition and Political Location on the Personal Generosity of Americans Toward the Poor." *Journal for the Scientific Study of Religion* 37: 481–493.

Rick, S. and G. Loewenstein. (2008). "Commentaries and Rejoinder to 'The Dishonesty of Honest People.'" *Journal of Marketing Research* 45: 645–653.

Roberts, B. (2009). "Back to the Future: Personality and Assessment and Personality Development." *Journal of Research in Personality* 43: 137–145.

Rokovski, C. and E. Levy. (2007). "Academic Dishonesty: Perceptions of Business Students." *College Student Journal* 41: 466–481.

Rosenhan, D. and G. White. (1967). "Observation and Rehearsal as Determinants of Prosocial Behavior." *Journal of Personality and Social Psychology* 5: 424–431.

Ross, A. and J. Braband. (1973). "Effect of Increased Responsibility on Bystander Intervention: II. The Cue Value of a Blind Person." *Journal of Personality and Social Psychology* 25: 254–258.

Rota, Michael. (2016). *Taking Pascal's Wager: Faith, Evidence and the Abundant Life*. Downer's Grove: IVP Academic.

Rothschild, Alonzo. (1917). *"Honest Abe": A Study in Integrity Based on the Early Life of Abraham Lincoln*. Boston: Houghton Mifflin.

Rushton, J. and A. Campbell. (1977). "Modeling, Vicarious Reinforcement and Extraversion on Blood Donating in Adults: Immediate and Long-Term Effects." *European Journal of Social Psychology* 7: 297–306.

Samuels, Steven and William Casebeer. (2005). "A Social Psychological View of Morality: Why Knowledge of Situational Influences on Behaviour Can Improve Character Development Practices." *Journal of Moral Education* 34: 73–87.

Sarkissian, Hagop. (2010). "Minor Tweaks, Major Payoffs: The Problem and Promise of Situationism in Moral Philosophy." *Philosophers' Imprint* 10:1–15.

Schelling, Thomas. (1978). "Economics, or the Art of Self-Management." *American Economic Review* 68: 290–294.

Schiller, P. and J. Levin. (1988). "Is There a Religious Factor in Health Care Utilization? A Review." *Social Science and Medicine* 27: 1369–1379.

Schwartz, S. and A. Gottlieb. (1980). "Bystander Anonymity and Reactions to Emergencies." *Journal of Personality and Social Psychology* 39: 418–430.

Shimai, S., K. Otake, N. Park, C. Peterson, and M. Seligman. (2006). "Convergence of Character Strengths in American and Japanese Young Adults." *Journal of Happiness Studies* 7: 311–322.

Shu, L., F. Gino, and M. Bazerman. (2011). "Dishonest Deed, Clear Conscience: When Cheating Leads to Moral Disengagement and Motivated Forgetting." *Personality and Social Psychology Bulletin* 37: 330–349.

Sinnott-Armstrong, Walter. (2009). *Morality Without God?* New York: Oxford University Press.

Slingerland, Edward. (2011). "The Situationist Critique and Early Confucian Virtue Ethics." *Ethics* 121: 390–419.

Smith, C. and R. Faris. (2002). *Religion and American Adolescent Delinquency, Risk Behaviors and Constructive Social Activities*. Chapel Hill, NC: National Study of Youth and Religion.

Sorensen, Roy. (2007). "Bald-Faced Lies! Lying without the Intent to Deceive." *Pacific Philosophical Quarterly* 88: 251–264.

Sosik, J. J., W. Gentry, and J. Chun. (2012). "The Value of Virtue in the Upper Echelons: A Multisource Examination of Executive Character Strengths and Performance." *Leadership Quarterly* 23: 367–382.

Stack, S. (1983). "The Effect of the Decline in Institutionalized Religion on Suicide, 1954–1978." *Journal for the Scientific Study of Religion* 22: 239–252.

Stevens, Walter. (1998). *A Reporter's Lincoln*. Ed. Michael Burlingame. Lincoln: University of Nebraska Press.

Strenta, A. and W. DeJong. (1981). "The Effect of a Prosocial Label on Helping Behavior." *Social Psychology Quarterly* 44: 142–147.

Taylor, Gabriele. (2008). *Deadly Vices*. Oxford: Oxford University Press.

Thaler, Richard and Cass Sunstein. (2008). *Nudge: Improving Decisions about Health, Wealth, and Happiness*. New Haven: Yale University Press.

Thorkildsen, T., C. Golant, and L. Richesin. (2007). "Reaping What We Sow: Cheating as a Mechanism of Moral Engagement." In *Psychology of Academic Cheating*. Ed. E. Anderman and T. Murdock. Amsterdam: Elsevier Academic Press, 171–202.

Tice, D. and R. Baumeister. (1985). "Masculinity Inhibits Helping in Emergencies: Personality Does Predict the Bystander Effect." *Journal of Personality and Social Psychology* 49: 420–428.

Vitz, P. (1990). "The Use of Stories in Moral Development: New Psychological Reasons for an Old Education Model." *American Psychologist* 45: 709–720.

Vohs, K. and J. Schooler. (2008). "The Value of Believing in Free Will: Encouraging a Belief in Determinism Increases Cheating." *Psychological Science* 19: 49–54.

Wachtel, P. (1973). "Psychodynamics, Behavior Therapy, and the Implacable Experimenter: An Inquiry into the Consistency of Personality." *Journal of Abnormal Psychology* 82: 324–334.

Wagner, L. and W. Ruch. (2015). "Good Character at School: Positive Classroom Behavior Mediates the Link between Character Strengths and School Achievement." *Frontiers in Psychology*. doi: 10.3389/fpsyg.2015.00610.

Weyant, J. (1978). "Effects of Mood States, Costs, and Benefits on Helping." *Journal of Personality and Social Psychology* 36: 1169–1176.

White, G. (1972). "Immediate and Deferred Effects of Model Observation and Guided and Unguided Rehearsal on Donating and Stealing." *Journal of Personality and Social Psychology* 21: 139–148.

Willard, Dallas. (1998). *The Divine Conspiracy: Recovering Our Hidden Life in God*. San Francisco: Harper.

Wilson, J. and R. Petruska. (1984). "Motivation, Model Attributes, and Prosocial Behavior." *Journal of Personality and Social Psychology* 46: 458–468.

Witter, R., W. Stock, M. Okun, and M. Haring. (1985). "Religion and Subjective Well-Being in Adulthood: A Quantitative Synthesis." *Review of Religious Research* 26: 332–342.

Zhong, C., V. Bohns, and F. Gino. (2010). "Good Lamps Are the Best Police: Darkness Increases Dishonesty and Self-Interested Behavior." *Psychological Science* 21: 311–314.

Zimbardo, P. (2007). *The Lucifer Effect: Understanding How Good People Turn Evil*. New York: Random House.

INDEX